OUTWARD BOUND
BACKPACKER'S HANDBOOK

Third Edition

GLENN RANDALL

FALCONGUIDES

GUILFORD, CONNECTICUT
HELENA, MONTANA

AN IMPRINT OF GLOBE PEQUOT PRESS

Copyright © 1999, 2013 Glenn Randall
Published in 1994 as *The Modern Backpacker's Handbook* by Lyons and Burford.

ALL RIGHTS RESERVED. No part of this book may be reproduced or transmitted in any form by any means, electronic or mechanical, including photocopying and recording, or by any information storage and retrieval system, except as may be expressly permitted in writing from the publisher. Requests for permission should be addressed to Globe Pequot Press, Attn: Rights and Permissions Department, PO Box 480, Guilford, CT 06437.

FalconGuides is an imprint of Globe Pequot Press.
Falcon, FalconGuides, and Outfit Your Mind are registered trademarks of Morris Book Publishing, LLC.

Gore-Tex® and Windstopper® are registered trademarks of W. L. Gore & Associates. Teflon® is a registered trademark of the DuPont Company. Polarguard® is a registered trademark of Invista. Velcro is a registered trademark of Velcro Industries. Therm-a-Rest® is a registered trademark of Cascade Designs. Speedy Stitcher® is a registered trademark of Stewart Manufacturing Company. Thinsulate™ is a trademark of 3M Company. Keds® is a registered trademark of Collective Brands, Inc. eVent is a trademark of BHA Group, Inc. MICROspikes is a registered trademark of Kahtoola, Inc. PrimaLoft is a registered trademark of PrimaLoft, Inc. Climashield is a registered trademark of HarVest Consumer Insulation, Inc. Whisperlite and Pocket Rocket are trademarks of Cascade Designs, Inc. Jetboil is a trademark of Jetboil, Inc. Potable Aqua is a registered trademark of Wisconsin Pharmacal Company.

Illustrations by Jack Tom
Text design: Eileen Hine
Layout: Sue Murray
Project editor: Julie Marsh

The Library of Congress has cataloged a previous edition as follows:
Randall, Glenn, 1957–
The Outward Bound backpacker's handbook / Glenn Randall.
p. cm.
Rev. ed. of: The modern backpacker's handbook. c1994.
Includes index.
ISBN 1-55821-941-2
1. Backpacking. 2. Backpacking—Equipment and supplies.
I. Randall, Glenn, 1957– Modern backpacker's handbook.
II. Outward Bound, Inc. III. Title.
GV199.6.R36   2000
796.51—dc21   99-22236

ISBN 978-0-7627-7855-3

Printed in the United States of America
10 9 8 7 6 5 4 3 2 1

CONTENTS

ABOUT OUTWARD BOUND

Outward Bound, America's preeminent experiential education organization, has been a pioneer in the field of wilderness experiential learning since it was established in the United States in 1961 and has continued to deliver unparalleled outdoor educational programs ever since. Today Outward Bound provides adventure and learning for teens, adults, veterans, at-risk youth, and professionals, helping them achieve their full potential and inspiring them to serve others.

A Brief History

Outward Bound is based on the educational ideas of Kurt Hahn, an influential German-born educator. Hahn established the school at Schloss Salem in an attempt to combat what he perceived as the deterioration of values in post–World War I Germany. Salem's progressive curriculum focused on character development through physical fitness, skill attainment, self-discipline, and compassionate service. In 1933, thirteen years after establishing Salem, Hahn fled Nazi-ruled Germany to Britain. Soon after his arrival, he set about establishing the Gordonstoun School in Scotland to continue his work under the motto *Plus est en vous* ("There is more in you than you know").

In 1941, in a joint effort with British shipping magnate Sir Lawrence Holt, Hahn founded the first Outward Bound Sea School in Aberdovey, Wales. The name of the school was adopted from the nautical term used when ships leave the safety of the harbor for the open seas: They were said to be "outward bound" for unknown challenges and adventures. The school not only taught sailing skills but also integrated Hahn's core belief that character development was just as important as academic achievement. Hahn's goal was to teach self-reliance, fitness, craftsmanship, and compassion as a way to provide the youth of Great Britain with the benefits of life experience and prepare them to serve their nation in the struggle against Nazi Germany. The program revolved around a series of increasingly rugged challenges designed to develop the self-confidence, fortitude, and leadership skills required to survive harsh physical and mental challenges.

Josh Miner, an American who taught under Hahn at Gordonstoun, was inspired to bring Outward Bound to the United States. Working with a small group of committed supporters, Miner founded the Colorado Outward Bound School in 1961, bringing the principles of hands-on learning and compassionate service through outdoor adventure to America.

Outward Bound Today

Today Outward Bound has expanded to thirty-six countries throughout the world. In the United States the organization has close to one million alumni who stay connected and engaged through Outward Bound's alumni association (outwardboundalumni .org). Central to its mission are the values of inclusion and diversity, evidenced by its scholarship program designed to attract and benefit populations that are typically underserved. Approximately 25 percent of participants receive financial support, and they span ethnic, socioeconomic, and geographic diversity.

In the United States, to advance goals of transforming lives and developing compassionate, purposeful people, Outward Bound now offers its unique blend of adventure-based programs fitted to the needs of:

- Teens and young adults

- At-risk youth

- Adults

- Veterans

- Professionals

Although programs vary broadly in target population, location, and objective, they all contain the elements that Kurt Hahn espoused as central to the development of effective and compassionate citizens: adventure and challenge; learning through experience; integrity and excellence; inclusion and diversity; social and environmental responsibility; leadership and character development; and compassion and service. For participants in any of the varied programs, in any part of the world, these core values provide the foundation for their Outward Bound experience.

The Instructors

Outward Bound instructors are highly trained, qualified educators and outdoor skills specialists. Participant safety is a high priority—foundational to every program. Every course is accompanied by instructors who hold wilderness first-responder-level certifications at the minimum and who have received hundreds of hours of educational, safety, and student- and activity-management training. Staff members are proficient in—and passionate about—the specific wilderness skills of the activity they teach, whether rock climbing, sailing, mountaineering, sea kayaking, canoeing, or whitewater rafting. To help participants along their personal growth paths, instructors are trained in managing groups and individuals.

A vital component of every course is the instructors' ability to not only shepherd participants through individual course challenges but also to help them work as effective leaders and contributing members of the team.

Outward Bound's Lasting Impact

The impact of each expedition extends well beyond the course itself. This impact is different for each individual but can be seen in a variety of ways, including improved school performance, closer relationships with family and friends, and a new commitment to service. When Outward Bound participants return home, they bring with them a new sense of responsibility, an enhanced appreciation of the environment, and a strong service ethic that they share with friends and family. Most important, they bring a newfound belief that "There is more in you than you know" and an inspiration to act on that knowledge. In one participant's words, "What I was lacking I have found; now I have the tools to keep growing and to work hard to accomplish my dreams and to do anything I can to help others accomplish their dreams as well."

INTRODUCTION

> Another measureless mountain day in which we are dissolved
> and absorbed and sent pulsing onward we know not where.
> Life seems neither long nor short, and we take no more heed to
> save time or make haste than do the trees and stars. This is true
> freedom, a good practical sort of immortality.
>
> —*John Muir, 1838–1914*

Thirteen precious, fleeting backpacking seasons have flown by since I wrote the second edition of *Outward Bound Backpacker's Handbook*. How has backpacking changed? Backpacking clothing and gear have continued to shed weight, which is a good thing. Although I haven't added weight to my waistline, I have put another thirteen years of wear and tear on my knees. Backpacking food is now more nutritious and digestible, if not necessarily more palatable. Energy bars, pastes, chews, and drinks now come in a bewildering variety of consistencies and flavors. Though it's debatable if they actually taste better, I do find I can hike longer and stronger if I'm muscling down some of the new "products." (I hesitate to call some of these new items "food," since it now feels like I'm eating sour gummy bears for lunch.) Although marmots have inhabited the mountains far longer than backpackers, in the past decade they seem to have become the scourge of backpacking equipment, with an infuriating propensity to chew on anything that smells new or emits a chemical odor, such as the rubber-clad antenna on my brand-new, state-of-the-art GPS receiver. Convertible pants with zip-off pant legs, scorned in the 1990s as a fashion-challenged invention of the 1960s, are back—and for good reason. The electronic gadgets some backpackers love to carry have proliferated. You can now carry a smart phone with apps that log your trip, geotag your photos, help you locate constellations, and communicate with an emergency locator beacon that can send an SOS call via satellite virtually anywhere in the world. Tents, boots, packs, stoves, and sleeping bags have continued to evolve. All told, there are ample reasons for a third edition of this book.

The heart of backpacking, however, goes far beyond the acquisition and mastery of gadgets. As I enter late middle age, time seems to flow by at an ever-accelerating pace. Now more than ever, backpacking provides rich opportunities to slow down, to live in the present, and even to experience moments so beautiful that time seems to stop. For a timeless interval that cannot be measured in seconds or minutes, I'm no longer conscious of my aching feet or hungry belly or the mosquito buzzing around my ears. Instead, I am wholly absorbed in the sheer magnificence of our planet.

Even today backpacking remains an antidote to industrialized society, where the list of tasks that must be accomplished seems to multiply exponentially, yet the days never grow longer. Every day, newspapers recite an endless dirge of war, poverty, oppression, and environmental disaster. Backpacking provides an escape, temporarily, from life's complex and seemingly insolvable problems. In their stead, backpackers need only deal with a far more manageable set of concerns, each elemental in its simplicity: finding the easiest route, summoning the energy to walk that last mile, selecting a good campsite. Backpacking offers an abundance of life's most repeatable pleasures, the ones that never grow stale: resting when you're tired, eating when you're hungry, drinking when you're thirsty, and smashing a mosquito just before it bites.

To those basic pleasures I would add two more, less connected with survival of the body than with survival of the spirit. The first is the quest for adventure. From one perspective, struggling mightily to reach a pass or the summit of a lofty mountain is absurd, possibly even mildly deranged, and yet, as the bumper sticker says, "If I wasn't nuts, I'd go insane." Sol Roy Rosenthal, MD, has spent many years studying what he calls the "risk-exercise response," a powerful feeling of euphoria that follows participation in an adventurous sport. Rosenthal is quick to point out that he's not talking about life-threatening endeavors, but rather sports like skiing that contain an element of challenge, that cause participants to push themselves in some way, that provide some sense of venturing into the unknown. According to Rosenthal, the risk-exercise response goes beyond simply feeling good. Risk takers talk of living up to their potential, of feeling fulfilled and yet expecting more from their lives. For me, many of the hours I have spent hiking, climbing, and skiing in the wilderness stand out like lighthouse beacons in the night as I look back over the vast sea of undistinguished days that make up the bulk of my suburban existence.

When I was thirteen, my father and I hiked up Strawberry Peak, one of the smaller peaks in the ring of mountains that almost encircles Los Angeles. As we were coming down, we crossed a creek. We knew that the trail led away from the creek for a ways, avoiding the deep canyon into which the creek disappeared, then crossed the creek again a mile or so farther down as the canyon walls diminished in height. To my boyish mind the obvious proposition was irresistible: Why not follow the creek through its dark and mysterious gorge? My father agreed, and we plunged in. All too soon we discovered why the trail led around the canyon. The creek plunged over a 10-foot cliff, creating a lovely waterfall and a formidable obstacle to further progress. For a time we contemplated retracing our steps, but the day was old and our legs had lost their spring. I spied a line of footholds and handholds tracing a possible route around the falls and began inching down, no doubt worrying my father tremendously. When I succeeded, he had to follow—which probably worried him even more. Overjoyed at our success, but wondering if a larger, impassable waterfall lay just around the corner, we hurried around the next bend and discovered a marvelous limpid pool carved into the stone and filled to the brim by a bubbling cascade. I said to my father, "That's so perfect it looks man-made." He replied, in words that have stuck with me for more than forty years, "That's the kind of perfection man strives to imitate."

Though more than four decades have elapsed since that simple hike, the excitement of our little adventure and the small but stunning vision of beauty it offered are still the twin keys to my lifelong fascination with wilderness. There are no blank spots on the map anymore, no places marked "terra incognita," but there are still thousands of blank spots in my experience, thousands of peaks to climb and canyons to explore, thousands of wilderness vistas to feast upon with awestruck eyes. For me no painting, sculpture, or photograph; no city, monument, or building—nothing man-made—has ever compared to the beauty of nature at its grandest. Wilderness is so inspirational for me that in 1993 I began spending more and more time making wilderness landscape photographs, primarily in Colorado. Eventually I became a full-time wilderness landscape photographer. Ever since then I have been privileged to spend about fifty days a year, in all seasons, hiking and backpacking in the most remote and spectacular regions of one of the most beautiful states in the nation. Much of the advice in this book on recent advances in backpacking gear and technique has been gleaned from that ongoing experience.

Backpackers don't set the twenty-first century aside when they hoist their loads and head into the wilderness. Backpackers don't live off the land in any significant sense. If every backpacker cut his own bough bed, felled saplings to build a lean-to, and speared a porcupine for supper, the woods would become a wasteland in short order. In fact, far from spurning technology, backpackers frequently embrace it. The backpacking boom that began in the early 1970s was spurred on significantly by the application of sophisticated technology to the task of creating clothing, tents, stoves, and packs that could reasonably be carried on a bowed but unbroken human back. Necessarily, however, the use of technology is limited by backpacking's iron law: If you want it with you, you have to carry it (unless, of course, you can bribe your companion). Some backpackers—perhaps all of them at one time or another—become fascinated by the equipment game, minutely comparing the merits of one stove against another, one rain jacket against a second and third. Choosing gear that allows you to balance convenience, comfort, and utility with weight and bulk is an amusing sport but one that ultimately misses the point. The gear only exists to make it possible to explore the wilderness. It is this experience that ultimately gives backpacking its value.

Although much of this book will be devoted to discussing advances in equipment, the soul of this book remains unchanged: the effort to instill a reverence for the wilderness that will allow low-impact hiking and camping practices to become second nature. These techniques have changed little since the first edition, but the need to apply them thoughtfully and consistently grows more urgent every year. Living simply in the woods is good practice for living in civilization. If we can learn to see the wilderness for what it is—a precious, irreplaceable, fragile treasure—then perhaps we can learn to see the whole world in the same light, and so save ourselves from the threat of ecological catastrophe.

That man is richest whose pleasures are the cheapest.
—Henry David Thoreau, 1817–1862

If you walk into a specialty outdoor shop and start pricing top-of-the-line gear as your first step toward going backpacking, you'll probably faint dead away and never set foot off pavement. Fortunately, there's no need to empty your bank account before you can start to enjoy the wilderness. For short day trips in the summer, you've probably got almost all the gear you need lying around the house. Sneakers are fine for your first outing and for many more besides. Throw a wool sweater, a rain jacket, a water bottle, and some snacks into any old kind of book pack or day pack, and head out.

As you extend your range, you'll probably want some other items. More supportive, protective, and waterproof footwear will probably be one of your first purchases, and perhaps a more commodious and comfortable pack. You'll surely want a map of the area and a compass, if only so you can orient the map so it's facing north and so directions on the map correspond to directions on the ground.

When you really get rolling, you'll probably get the itch to start investing in some of that lightweight, high-tech gear whose prices initially made you gag. As you'll soon discover, it costs about $100 a pound to lighten your pack. Don't jump in headfirst, however, and end up buying gear that either doesn't work well or isn't exactly what you need. That's doubly expensive, because you'll probably keep hankering for the right gear until you finally cave in and buy it. You can learn about gear you're interested in by reading customer reviews on the websites of major outdoor-equipment retailers and by talking to more experienced backpackers.

Once you've put some trail miles behind you, it's time to start thinking about your first overnight trip. Some outdoor shops have rental programs that offer overnight-size packs, tents, sleeping bags, and stoves. More experienced friends may be willing to lend you some gear for your first outing or two. You shouldn't have to make a big investment to try the sport for the first time.

Going Light

The quickest way to ruin your first trip is to overload your pack with too much stuff, then pick some ambitious itinerary requiring you to hike 30 miles and gain 5,000 feet of elevation every day. Backpacking may sound similar to back-breaking, but it shouldn't be synonymous with it. It's one of Murphy's Laws that packs invariably grow heavier as the day progresses. Backpackers loudly lament this fact, of course, and issue increasingly inflated estimates of the weight of their load. The longer the day, the bigger the pack of lies.

The key to enjoying backpacking, therefore, is to pare the load as much as possible. In the beginning, aim for no more than 25 percent of your body weight including food and water; less is always better. Even highly fit, experienced backpackers on long trips should keep their starting load at less than 50 percent of their body weight. Ultralight backpackers can go out for two or three days carrying only 15 or 20 percent of their body weight. Get in the habit of weighing gear on a postage or bathroom scale and knowing approximately how much all your gadgets and gizmos weigh. Learn what different pack weights feel like and what you can reasonably carry in different types of terrain. A weight that can be carried easily on well-groomed trails can be as cantankerous as a cross-eyed mule if you're climbing, scrambling, bushwhacking, or on skis. "Take half of it and go for it" is the half-joking philosophy of mountaineering that is equally applicable to backpacking. With experience you'll probably find that you can do without many of the items you considered essential at first. Once you've learned to leave behind all unnecessary gizmos, you'll have graduated from pack rat to pack mule.

Eventually, if the sport really grabs you, you'll want to invest in your own gear instead of renting and borrowing. My philosophy on buying equipment was defined as a boy, when my dad told me to always buy good tools. "If you buy a lousy one," he said, "you'll curse it forever, but you'll never want to spend the money to buy a good one because you'll already have one that's barely adequate." I try to define my needs carefully, buy the best I can afford, then take care of it meticulously and make it last. The cost of good gear, per year of use, is probably no higher than the cost of buying cheap gear and throwing it away when it breaks or falls apart after a year or two of service. When you factor in the satisfaction of using top-quality equipment, the investment begins to seem like a bargain.

The best place to find high-quality backpacking gear is undoubtedly at a specialty shop. Not only will the shop carry a good selection of the best gear, but the salespeople are likely to be knowledgeable about its strengths and weaknesses. Most specialty shops hire people who actively participate in a wide range of outdoor sports. They can often provide valuable suggestions on what will work best for your intended purpose as well as good places to go to use it. If there is no specialty shop in your area, consider shopping online at one of the big outfits like REI, Eastern Mountain Sports, or Campmor, which stock all the major brands. If you can, avoid the camping-supply sections of the discount chains like Walmart and Target. The gear there may be cheap, but it will also be heavy, bulky, and probably ineffective.

Good gear, meaning lightweight, durable, effective gear, is undeniably expensive. Console yourself with the thought that once you've made the purchase, you can vacation at will while hardly spending more than you would if you stayed home and commuted to work every day.

> If any normal person under fifty cannot enjoy being in a storm in the wilds, he ought to reform at once.
>
> —*Enos Mills, 1870–1922*

In July many years ago, my wife, Cora, and I were hiking in the popular Indian Peaks Wilderness near Denver when a powerful thunderstorm rolled in over Arapaho Pass. A hard rain began, which quickly congealed into stinging hail. Cora and I dove into our packs and pulled on the full rain suits—pants and jacket—that we carry on all but the shortest hikes, even at the height of summer. Now comfortably shielded from the storm's fury, we continued our hike, enjoying the wild peals of thunder and the staccato lightning bolts glimpsed through the trees.

Suddenly a couple in their early thirties appeared around a bend, heading for the parking lot a mile away as fast as they could run in their flip-flops. Their cotton shorts and T-shirts were already soaked through by the 35°F rain and melting hail. The man carried a baby in a frontpack, shielding it as best he could with the only piece of protective clothing they'd brought, a nylon windbreaker that was certainly not waterproof. We knew they would probably come out all right so long as neither of them sprained an ankle on the slippery, muddy trail, but we both shook our heads at the unnecessary misery as we stood aside to let them pass.

While that incident was an extreme case, it was not the first time, nor the last, that I've seen poorly prepared summer hikers blown like chaff before the wrath of a Rocky Mountain thunderstorm. When you leave the city on an 80°F summer morning, it's easy to forget that in the mountains it may be hailing and near freezing by 3 p.m.

Summer Clothing

Here's a quick list of the clothing I normally carry for summer day hikes and backpacking in the Rockies:

- ❐ woven nylon short-sleeve shirt
- ❐ nylon pants with zip-off legs that can convert to shorts
- ❐ woven polyester/rayon long-sleeve shirt
- ❐ sun hat
- ❐ hooded polyester fleece jacket

❒ ultralight down sweater

❒ fleece hat

❒ light gloves

❒ rain jacket and pants

If I'll be shooting sunrise from the summit of a Fourteener (a passion of mine), I throw in a pair of long johns to wear under my convertible pants. In the warm, humid climate of the central and southern Appalachians in summer and in the desert Southwest from May through September, you certainly won't need this much clothing. In the northern Appalachians, the Rockies, the Pacific Northwest, and the Sierras, however, the amount I carry is probably about right for most people.

That lengthy clothing list leads immediately to another of Murphy's Laws of backpacking: In good weather the packs carried by well-prepared hikers will always seem ridiculously large and heavy because they are crammed with all the foul-weather gear that may be needed in a few short hours.

Let's take the first few items on that list and fill in some details.

Although I wear a lot of cotton in the city, the **short-sleeve shirt** I wear when backpacking is 100 percent nylon. Cotton provides the illusion of comfort on a hot day by soaking up sweat when you're working hard. As I explain in more detail below, however, that wet cotton will chill you thoroughly when you climb up above timberline into a stiff breeze. The only solution is to remove the wet cotton T-shirt, stuff it in your pack, and put on something dry. Pull that wet T-shirt back out of your pack hours or days later, and it'll still be soaking wet and uncomfortable, not to mention fragrant. A synthetic short-sleeve shirt, by contrast, dries fast, so I can wear it constantly; I don't need to remove it and store it wet in my pack when the weather gets chilly. I prefer tightly woven shirts over knitted ones because a good woven fabric is impenetrable by all but the most voracious mosquitoes. Woven shirts are usually offered in a buttoned style with a collar and pockets. Woven shirts are less breathable than knitted shirts, however, so you may prefer a knitted shirt on a bug-free desert trip.

Despite all my warnings about being prepared for the worst, **shorts** certainly have their place in the mountains. I'm sure I've worn shorts for at least 75 percent of the summer miles I've ever hiked. A dilemma arises, however, when the temperature drops and the wind begins to blow. You could carry a separate pair of long pants and change into those, but that requires you to take off your boots and find shelter from ogling eyes. You could pull off the shorts, pull on long johns, and put the shorts back on top, but this has the same disadvantages as carrying a separate pair of long pants, along with the further disadvantage that mosquitoes can easily bite through most long johns. You could wear skin-tight stretch shorts like those bike racers wear (minus the chamois in the crotch) and pull your long johns right over the top, but you still have to take off your boots. Stretch shorts have another drawback: Mosquitoes easily penetrate the tightly stretched fabric and, as I can testify from personal experience, putting repellent directly on the fabric can dissolve the elastic, ruining the shorts.

Convertible pants, on the other hand, solve the dilemma beautifully. The zip-off pant legs weigh only a few ounces and take up negligible room in your pack, yet they provide near-instant protection from bugs and chilly breezes. The best models have long separating side zippers in the pant legs in addition to the zippers that allow the legs to detach, so you can remove or attach your pant legs without dirtying the inside of the legs with your muddy boots. Although once deemed to be a fashion faux pas, convertible pants are now ubiquitous on the trail and are even finding their way into casual wear in the city. My current pair is made of a tough, lightweight, fast-drying woven nylon that is completely mosquito-proof and holds up well when I'm bushwhacking and scrambling.

Take care if you wear shorts with belt loops while carrying a heavy pack. The belt loops' bulky seams can chafe your hips and the small of your back. A leather belt can be an even worse offender. Wear a soft nylon webbing belt, or choose convertible pants that don't need a belt to prevent them from becoming ankle hobbles. I like to tuck my shirt inside my waistband to provide a little padding and protection against abrasion.

My **long-sleeve shirt** utilizes a button-down style with a couple of handy chest pockets, one secured with a hook-and-loop closure, the other with a zipper. It came from the factory impregnated with permethrin, a synthetic version of a natural insect repellent, to further discourage mosquitoes. Several companies now offer sun hats and pants that have received similar treatments.

Why carry both a short-sleeve and a long-sleeve shirt? Why not just wear the long-sleeve shirt and roll up the sleeves when it gets warm? The answer, for me, is that a short-sleeve shirt is significantly cooler than a long-sleeve shirt with the sleeves rolled up—enough cooler that I carry both.

The **sun hat** I like is a baseball cap with a skirt that hangs down to my collar. The skirt keeps both sun and mosquitoes off my neck. If you don't want to buy one, you can fashion one yourself with a baseball cap, an old handkerchief or bandanna, and some safety pins. When I'm feeling handsome and debonair, I think that wearing such a hat makes me look like a dashing member of the French Foreign Legion; when I'm in a mood to laugh at myself, I think it makes me look like the flying nun.

Fabrics for Backpacking Clothing

So far I've talked about garments designed as protection from stares, sun, and blood-sucking insects. Before I discuss the next items in my backcountry wardrobe, which are primarily designed to provide warmth, I need to digress for a moment and talk about insulation and backcountry fabrics.

Insulation in clothing is actually provided mostly by the air trapped in between the fibers of the garment, not by the fibers themselves. Air conducts heat far more slowly than clothing fibers, which differ little among themselves in terms of their heat conductivity. Air's low heat conductivity makes the preservation of tiny air pockets critically important in an insulating garment.

No matter how well your garment traps air, its ability to insulate will still deteriorate if it gets wet, whether from rain or from perspiration. To quote equipment innovator and in-the-buff nature enthusiast Jack Stephenson, "Nothing is warm when wet but a hot tub." Evaporation of water from your skin extracts an enormous amount of heat. In addition, wet skin is just plain uncomfortable. Manufacturers of insulating garments have responded to this problem by devoting a great deal of energy to creating (and hyping) fabrics that are supposed to wick moisture away from your skin, leaving it drier and more comfortable. At least in theory, wicking should also reduce the rate at which you become chilled from evaporative cooling because the water will evaporate from the surface of the garment, well away from your skin, instead of directly from your skin itself.

Cotton is the worst cold-weather material. By its nature, cotton is a highly absorbent fiber that loses all its resiliency and springiness when it gets wet. That lack of wet-weather backbone causes all the tiny air pockets that really provide your insulation to collapse and disappear. To make matters worse, water conducts heat about twenty times faster than dry air, ten times faster than dry cotton. If your cotton T-shirt or sweatshirt gets wet, you've got the worst of both worlds: no air pockets to provide insulation and a dense mat of saturated, highly conductive fibers clinging to your skin and conducting heat like crazy. Water evaporates directly off your skin, increasing your frigid misery. To add a final insult, cotton clings tenaciously to the water it absorbs, so it dries on a geologic time scale. Cotton does still have one last place in my summer clothing ensemble. I wear cotton briefs because I get much less itchy after three or four days in the backcountry wearing them than I do wearing synthetic briefs. Since I always carry rain pants, my briefs almost never get wet, and since briefs are very compact, I can carry a spare pair. And although it's not strictly clothing, I do carry a cotton bandana to dry my glasses after a rain.

Wool shares cotton's bad habit of sucking up water like a sponge, but it has one redeeming feature that made it the fiber of choice before synthetics: It retains its resiliency when wet. That means it retains its ability to trap tiny air pockets and won't collapse against your skin like cotton. The problem with wool is that it dries just as slowly as cotton. If the sheep from which it came happened to have a particularly dyspeptic disposition, it also makes my skin itch and even break out in a rash. On the plus side, if economy is your main criterion, you can probably pick up military surplus woollies for a song. Just be aware that you may be singing the blues if they get wet the first day, because they'll probably stay wet for the rest of the trip.

Synthetics offer three significant advantages compared to cotton: They retain their resiliency and insulating capacity when wet; they absorb very little water, so they dry fast; and they're more abrasion-resistant than cotton, so they last longer. Polypropylene was the first synthetic to be widely used in outdoor clothing, but it quickly came under fire for its rather harsh, plastic feel, its penchant for shrinking into doll clothes if thrown into the clothes dryer, and its tendency to lovingly embrace body odors and refuse to let them go, even under threat of repeated washings in paint thinner. Polyester seems to be the material of choice now for long underwear and for the large and varied assortment of thick, heavily napped fabrics loosely called pile or fleece. Polyester can be knitted into lightweight, wonderfully soft, and comfortable styles for long underwear and bulkier forms for sweaters and jackets. It doesn't cling to odors as much as polypropylene and bears up well under normal washing and drying procedures. Nylon, while ubiquitous as the shell fabric in rain gear and insulated parkas because of its great strength and abrasion resistance, is rarely used to provide the insulation itself.

Layering

Let's return now to my clothing list for backcountry adventures in summer and continue with the insulating garments. As you begin selecting these garments, think in terms of layers, a concept for which we are indebted to the late Benjamin Thompson, a.k.a. Count Rumford. Rumford, to quote one biographer, was an "unprincipled opportunist, a ruthless self-promoter, and overbearingly arrogant." He was also, history tells us, the discoverer in the 1780s that the insulating property of clothing comes primarily from trapped air. From this he concluded that several thin layers of clothing were warmer than one thick one because they trapped air in between the layers as well as within the layers themselves. Carrying several thin layers, rather than one thick layer, has an additional advantage: It gives you the flexibility to fine-tune the amount of clothing you're wearing to exactly match your heat output and the current temperature. If you bring just a heavy parka and a short-sleeve shirt, for example, you might have the same total amount of insulation available to you as if you brought a short-sleeve shirt, a midweight underwear top, a fleece sweater, and a wind shell, but in a very inconvenient form. With no ability to have just a medium amount of insulation, you'll probably be too hot wearing the parka or too cold wearing just the short-sleeve shirt.

The first fleece garment I put on top of my long-sleeve shirt always has a hood. The hood insulates my neck, which is well supplied with blood vessels that run near the surface. These vessels, with their cargo of warm blood, provide a large escape hatch for heat. In cold weather it pays to insulate them well. Hooded fleece garments weren't always available. For my second Alaskan expedition, in 1980, my climbing partners and I sewed thin fleece balaclavas onto long john tops, then added a neck zipper. I was so sold on the concept after that expedition that I tried to persuade Yvon Chouinard, founder of Patagonia, one of the most innovative outdoor clothing companies, to offer hooded fleece sweaters through his company. He responded, "Go buy a cotton sweatshirt at Kmart. Hooded fleece pieces won't sell."

Yvon eventually changed his mind. Patagonia, along with many other specialty outdoor companies, now produces excellent hooded garments. Year-round I never go into the backcountry without one. I also bring a warm fleece hat. That gives me three options for insulating my head and neck: the hood by itself, the hat by itself, or the hood and hat together. Simply by varying the amount of insulation on my head and neck, I can hike comfortably in a wide variety of temperatures and wind speeds without ever stopping to remove or replace an entire layer.

Fleece today comes in many varieties, including fabrics made largely from recycled soda bottles. Fortunately, the performance in terms of drying speed and resiliency when wet doesn't vary much. Warmth does vary with thickness. After deciding on what thickness you need, choose your fleece jacket based on fit and overall attractiveness. Look for a full-length front zipper that lets you ventilate easily. Hand-warmer pockets are welcome on cool mornings, and a zippered chest pocket or two are handy for keeping small valuables accessible while wearing a pack. If you're really cold-blooded, like Cora, you should consider adding fleece pants to your summer layering system. Look for a pair that has full-length zippers along the outside of the pant legs. Better yet, look for a pair with side zippers that separate at the top next to the waistband, so in the wintertime you can put them on without taking off your skis or snowshoes.

Insulated Sweaters and Jackets

The final insulating layer in my summer clothing ensemble used to be a second fleece jacket. Recently, however, a number of companies have begun producing ultralight down sweaters that provide as much insulation as a fleece jacket, yet weigh as much as a pound less and pack into a tiny stuff sack that would barely accommodate a fleece jacket's sleeves. Down sweaters are great for lounging around camp on cool mornings and evenings on a summer backpacking trip. Summer temperatures are warm enough that I never need to wear a down sweater while hiking. In winter I still carry a second fleece sweater because it's cold enough that I sometimes need to wear both sweaters while snowshoeing. The fleece sweater retains its insulating value under the compression of the pack straps and back panel, while the down sweater would collapse into two sheets of nylon.

Down is not the only filling available in ultralight insulated garments; some of these insulated sweaters use a synthetic filling. Since you'll face the same choice in an even more important context when you buy a sleeping bag, I'll hit the subject lightly here and go into more depth in the sleeping bag discussion in chapter 6.

For years chemists have sought a synthetic equivalent to down, the innermost plumage of ducks and geese. So far nothing they have produced can equal high-quality down on the basis of insulating capacity for a given weight. Good down is also more compressible than the best synthetics, which saves room in your pack. While down costs more than synthetics initially, it retains its loft longer, so the cost per year is usually less if you take good care of the shell fabric. On the negative side, down, like cotton, loses all its resiliency when it gets wet. A wet down jacket is as worthless as a pack of used bubble gum, and it's likely to remain worthless until you get a day of brilliant sunshine or drop a lot of quarters in the nearest Doozy Duds clothes dryer. Synthetic insulators retain their loft when wet and dry much faster.

My preference in parka insulation, summer or winter, has been honed by my experiences in the wintertime Rockies and in the high, glaciated mountains of the Alaska Range. For those climates, which are very cold and relatively dry, I prefer down, particularly if protected by a water-resistant shell. In the wetter climate of the Northwest and Northeast and in coastal Alaska and Canada, a synthetic-filled parka is probably a better bet.

Rain Gear

The outermost layer in your summer clothing arsenal should always be some solidly built rain gear. I am still dumbfounded at the number of times I've seen people with a cotton sweatshirt tied around their waist blithely heading upward above timberline as a vicious squall gathers strength and begins bearing down on its clueless victims.

The least expensive rain gear is a plastic poncho, a large square of vinyl with a hole in the middle capped with a hood. Unfortunately, ponchos are only useful in brief, gentle rains not accompanied by wind—a description that doesn't fit the typical high-mountain thunderstorm. In a real thunderstorm a poncho's loose, floppy fabric is guaranteed to billow up around your face with the first gust, leaving you blinded and stumbling while the wind-driven horizontal rain soaks everything below your shoulders. Don't waste your money on a glorified tablecloth, no matter how cheap it seems; you'll want something better almost immediately.

The next step above a poncho is a rain jacket made of nonbreathable, urethane-coated nylon. Such garments are waterproof if the seams are sealed and the coating hasn't worn away under the abrasion of your pack straps, but they allow sweat to escape only at the cuffs, neck, and waist, not through the fabric itself. If you wear such nonbreathable rain gear while you're inactive (fishing, swearing at fishing, swearing off fishing forever, etc.), then it performs adequately. If you're active, however (storming back to camp after snagging five flies on the same underwater log), it's difficult to prevent sweat from building up inside your rain gear and soaking your insulating layers. When hiking hard in nonbreathable rain gear, you face two ugly options: Get soaked by sweat, or remove your rain gear and get soaked by rain.

This eternal dilemma has spurred the development of dozens of fabrics that claim to be both waterproof and breathable. The first was Gore-Tex. By all reasonable standards, Gore-Tex is indeed impenetrable by liquid water; by most reasonable standards, in most situations Gore-Tex does indeed breathe, allowing moisture in the form of water vapor to escape from your sweaty body. This miracle is achieved by the construction of a two-layer composite. One layer is made of expanded polytetrafluoroethylene, PTFE for short, better known as Teflon. This material is laced with nine billion pores per square inch. These pores are larger than the water molecules found in water vapor, but smaller than a droplet of liquid water. First-generation Gore-Tex contained only this layer, but hikers soon found that if the fabric became contaminated by skin oils or mosquito repellent, water could begin wicking through the pores and the fabric could start to leak. Second-generation Gore-Tex solved the problem by coating the microporous layer with an oleophobic (oil-hating), nonporous polyurethane layer that absorbs water molecules on the warm, humid side of the material next to your body, and discharges those molecules on the drier, cooler side away from your body. The Gore-Tex membrane "breathes" when the temperature and humidity on the inside of the fabric next to your body are greater than the temperature and humidity on the outside of the fabric. In most situations where you want to be wearing rain gear and other shell clothing, such conditions prevail.

The current version of Gore-Tex certainly works well, but it's very expensive. Other manufacturers have tried to capitalize on the consumer demand for waterproof/breathable garments created by the Gore-Tex advertising avalanche by coming up with a wide variety of much cheaper alternatives. Some manufacturers have tried urethane coatings that have been allowed to "foam" so that tiny air bubbles form within the coating. In theory these air bubbles allow water vapor to escape while preventing liquid water from entering. Others have tried monolithic (nonporous), water-loving membranes that absorb water molecules on the inside and allow them to evaporate on the outside, driven by the typically higher water-vapor pressure on the inside of the garment. At the time of this writing, several manufacturers are using a particularly promising and relatively new fabric called eVent that, like Gore-Tex, uses an expanded PTFE membrane. Unlike Gore-Tex, however, eVent has been treated so the individual fibrils, as they are called, are oleophobic, which means they resist contamination by body oils and dirt. That, in turn, allows the fabric to remain waterproof even if contaminated by skin oils without the necessity of adding a second, nonporous layer that arguably reduces breathability. According to at least some tests, eVent fabric rivals or even beats Gore-Tex in breathability. Its durability, however, is less well established than that of Gore-Tex, which has been refined and improved over thirty years. The variations are endless, and new contenders seem to pop up every season.

Waterproof/breathable fabrics go a long way toward soothing the hiker's lament, but don't expect miracles. All waterproof/breathable fabrics have limitations. Sweat can only escape in vapor form. If it's extremely cold and your sweat condenses into liquid droplets before it reaches the inside of your jacket, the moisture will remain trapped inside your clothing. I've pulled off a Gore-Tex shell glove in 0°F temperatures and found the fleece liner glove inside covered with frost. My sweat was evaporating off my skin, migrating through the fleece, hitting the cold shell, and condensing. In those situations a waterproof/breathable fabric scarcely breathes at all. Sweat can also only escape if the temperature and humidity inside the garment are higher than the temperature and humidity outside. If you're working hard during a steamy Georgia thunderstorm, your rain gear probably won't seem very breathable.

For a time, manufacturers of waterproof/breathable fabrics seemed intent on waging an MVTR war, with legions of shock troops rolling out statistics on the Moisture Vapor Transport Rate of their fabrics. The MVTR is usually expressed in terms of the number of grams of moisture that can pass through a square meter of fabric in twenty-four hours under specified conditions of temperature and humidity. Things have gotten pretty quiet on that front lately, in part because every manufacturer has its own test, often chosen to show its own fabric in the most favorable possible light. The variety of tests in use makes it impossible to compare results among different manufacturers. The best use of MVTR numbers is to compare products within one manufacturer's line.

Suffice it to say, however, that even the most breathable fabrics can only pass a certain amount of moisture per hour. If I go running during a Colorado thunderstorm, I often find upon my return that the inside of my rain jacket is damp. The jacket feels like it leaked, but when I test the fabric with a device that forces water against the fabric under pressure, I find that the material is still waterproof. It simply can't breathe fast enough to dispel the amount of moisture I produce during very vigorous exercise.

You can enhance the breathability of your rain gear during rainstorms if you maintain the surface water repellency of the fabric. All waterproof/breathable fabrics have a durable water-repellent finish (DWR for short) on the exterior of the fabric. This finish is completely separate and distinct from the coating or membrane on the inside of the fabric that makes it waterproof. The function of the DWR finish is to cause water to bead up and roll off the surface of the fabric. Without this finish, water spreads out in a thin film covering the surface the fabric. That film of water chills the fabric by evaporation, which promotes condensation inside the jacket. The water film can also reduce breathability. Unfortunately, the "durable" in DWR is more marketing hype than reality. Dirt, body oils, and simple wear and tear will eventually degrade the DWR finish. When you see water spreading out over your jacket instead of beading up, try washing it in an ordinary washing machine, then giving it about fifteen minutes in a clothes dryer on medium heat. Specialty shops sell detergents specifically designed for waterproof/breathable rain gear. These detergents rinse out cleanly, unlike ordinary household detergents, which helps preserve your rain gear's breathability. Specialty shops also sell wash-in and spray-on DWR products that will renew the DWR finish for a time. As strange as it may sound, you can renew some types of water-repellent treatments on shell gear by careful ironing. Check the manufacturer's website or your jacket's garment tag or hang tag for specifics.

Like breathability, waterproofness is a relative term. Here the statistics are usually given in terms of pounds per square inch (psi) of water pressure that the fabric will withstand. REI, a major distributor and manufacturer of outdoor gear, considers any fabric that can withstand three psi to be waterproof and cites statistics showing that even hard, wind-driven rain only exerts about two psi. According to W. L. Gore & Associates, makers of Gore-Tex, a 165-pound man kneeling on wet ground is pushing water against the fabric of his rain pants with a force of about sixteen psi. When he's sitting, he's exerting a pressure of about three psi. Although the military has several standards for waterproofness depending on the application, the number most often used is twenty-five psi. Some manufacturers give the waterproofness of their fabric in terms of the height of a column of water that the fabric will withstand. ("Our fabric will withstand a column of water four meters high!") While these numbers may sound impressive, they're actually not. A water column four meters high, for example, exerts a pressure of less than six psi. Don't buy a jacket solely because of a high waterproofness rating; beyond a certain point, additional waterproofness adds no value.

Despite all these caveats, waterproof/breathable rain gear is still a major improvement over nonbreathable gear. In the past I insisted that all my rain gear be Gore-Tex. I even paid a premium price for three-season and winter sleeping bags with Gore-Tex shells. More recently, however, the breathtaking price of Gore-Tex (as much as four or five times the cost of competing products), coupled with the bulk, weight, and stiffness of the Gore-Tex fabrics often used in rain gear aimed at backpackers, have persuaded me to try several of the alternatives, which have proved to be surprisingly good. All rain gear adds a lot of warmth, and no rain gear breathes as well as you might like. The solution, for me, is to strip down to nylon shorts and a synthetic shirt when it starts to rain, then put on my rain jacket and pants. As long as I'm hiking hard with a load, I stay reasonably warm but don't overheat. If sweat does accumulate inside my rain gear, it can only dampen two thin, nonabsorbent layers of clothing. Once the rain stops or I reach camp and put up my tent, I shed the rain gear and pull on all the warm, dry, insulating clothing I've carefully stowed in my pack. My shirt and shorts soon dry, and I'm once again toasty warm. With that approach it doesn't seem to matter much whether my rain jacket is Gore-Tex or not.

I used to believe that only a rain jacket was really needed, and that rain pants were an unnecessary weight and expense. Then, like the people I now decry, I pushed for the summit of 14,259-foot Longs Peak one August day many years ago, foolishly disregarding the approaching thunderstorm. I yanked on my rain jacket, which kept my torso dry, but the wind-driven horizontal rain, hail, and snow immediately saturated my unprotected long johns. The evaporative cooling from my legs was so severe that no amount of dry insulation on my torso could keep me warm. A few years later, having inadequately learned my lesson, I asked Jeff Lowe, one of America's most experienced Himalayan mountaineers, if he was going to bring rain pants when we tried a climb on Longs's formidable east face. I assumed that a tough guy like Jeff, intent on going fast and light, would disdain such frivolities as rain pants. "I always bring them," he replied. I did so too and was glad—we were hammered by a severe thunderstorm only halfway up the peak and forced to retreat. I've brought rain pants on mountain ventures ever since, whether I'm off to do a difficult climb or just take a stroll up to some beautiful lake.

You could do worse than to select your rain jacket on the basis of how well you like the hood design. In general I prefer integral hoods that are sewn permanently to the jacket because they're easier to pull up over your head, particularly while wearing gloves in a high wind. The alternative is a detachable hood that usually stows in a pocket in the collar. Detachable hoods only stay on your head in the wind if you fasten two flaps across your chin with Velcro or snaps, a feat that can be awkward while wearing gloves. Stuffing the hood into the pocket on the collar usually turns the collar into a cervical brace—fine if you're planning on rolling your truck in a crash on the way to the trailhead; not so great for comfortable hiking.

In most situations you'll be wearing a pack over your rain jacket. Make sure, therefore, that your pack's shoulder straps and hip belt don't cover up the pocket openings. Be sure, too, that the contents of the pockets can't drop down beneath the hip belt, where they can chafe and jab.

Useful Accessories

A few clothing odds and ends can help make the trip more pleasant. To prevent snow and gravel from falling in the top of your boots, you can wear a pair of gaiters, fabric tubes that cover the upper portion of your boots and extend up your calves. A strap that goes under your arch prevents the gaiter from riding up. Most gaiters use a hook-and-loop closure or a zipper, sometimes combined with snaps, to make it easy to fasten the tube of fabric around your calf. Short gaiters reaching just above the anklebone are sufficient to keep gravel out of your shoes. They also keep out gritty trail dust, which keeps your socks cleaner and reduces that hot burning sensation you can get when your feet have been in boots too long. Keeping the inside of your boots clean also prolongs the life of the boots' liner. Short gaiters resemble the spats worn by such delightfully eccentric characters as Hercule Poirot, Scrooge McDuck, and Babar the Elephant. If you don't mind a few quizzical looks, try a pair of short gaiters on your next summer backpacking trip. You'll be surprised at how much more comfortable your feet will feel. Longer gaiters reaching to just below your knee are essential in deep snow to keep snow out of your boots and to keep your pant legs dry. A few people wear knee-high gaiters in desert areas to protect their calves from thorny plants. I wear some form of gaiters on every trip year-round.

In high mountain areas, light gloves are a must even in summer. Early mornings, particularly, can be quite chilly on the fingers when handling stoves, pots and pans, and camera gear. I like fleece gloves with a windproof and water-resistant Windstopper membrane sandwiched between the inner and outer layers of fleece.

The Windstopper membrane, made by W. L. Gore, gives these gloves the best combination of warmth and dexterity in any lightweight glove I've found.

Although it may horrify some city folks to think about it, backpackers rarely bring a fresh change of clothes for each day of the trip. Socks are one exception; a fresh pair of cotton or synthetic briefs is another. Cora brings an extra synthetic long underwear top, both for the pleasure of wearing a fresh-smelling garment partway into the trip and for the option it gives her to doff a sweat-soaked shirt and put on a dry one when the wind starts to blow.

Like street clothing, outdoor garb comes with care instructions printed on a tag that's sewn to the garment. Fortunately, caring for the latest generation of outdoor clothing is usually simple. Gore-Tex, for example, can be machine-washed in warm water and dried on warm in an ordinary home dryer. Most of the popular polyester fleeces and long underwear fabrics can also be gently machine-washed and dried. Down- and synthetic-filled parkas should be hand-washed or washed in a large-capacity front-loading washing machine. See chapter 6 for more details.

After reading nearly 6,000 words on the subject of backpacking attire, you could certainly be forgiven for agreeing with Henry David Thoreau's admonition to "beware of all enterprises that require new clothes." But take heart: If you're like me, you'll soon find that the new clothes you buy for backpacking are so practical, durable, and comfortable that they quickly become the old clothes you wear all the time, whether you're in the wilderness or not.

Gaiters keep snow, rocks, and dirt out of your boots.

Walk away quietly in any direction, and taste the freedom of the mountaineer. Camp out among the grasses and gentians of glacial meadows, in craggy garden nooks full of nature's darlings. Climb the mountains and get their good tidings. Nature's peace will flow into you as sunshine flows into trees. The winds will blow their own freshness into you and the storms their energy, while cares will drop off like autumn leaves. As age comes on, one source of enjoyment after another is closed, but nature's sources never fail.

—*John Muir, 1838–1914*

It was time to buy Cora her first pair of cross-country ski boots. I well remembered my own first pair: cheap, low-cut, and poorly insulated, which contributed to the frostnip I suffered on my little toes during one particularly stormy ski tour along the Continental Divide. The boots' injection-molded soles eventually broke in half in the middle of a 12-mile tour. I vowed not to repeat that mistake with Cora. Instead, we would buy her top-quality boots to start with, saving money in the long run because we wouldn't buy cheap boots, discard them after a year, then buy the good boots she would certainly want.

We bought her a beautiful pair of heavy-duty black telemark boots costing over $300 (in 1990 dollars!). The boots kept her feet warm, supported her ankles perfectly, and gave her the worst case of blisters I'd ever seen. She might as well have worn cheese graters on her heels. Now, it must be said that Cora develops blisters more rapidly than anyone I've ever met. She can get blisters in well-fitted, well-used running shoes. Still, we had committed a cardinal sin: We bought her too much boot.

My first pair of hiking boots, purchased forty years ago, performed the same atrocities on my heels. Constructed entirely of stout leather with massive, heavily lugged soles, those ancient millstones weighed as much as the modern plastic boots I've worn on the summit of 20,320-foot Mount McKinley when it was twenty below. An old army adage holds that a pound on your feet is equivalent to five pounds on your back in terms of the energy you must exert while walking. To add insult to injury and exhaustion, the boots were so stiff that they made me walk like a one-year-old with fused ankles. In reaction to those cement-block blister boxes, I then spent most of the next fifteen years scampering around the summertime mountains in various pairs of running shoes. True, sharp stones bruised the soles of my feet and rasped the skin off my anklebones, and the shoes got thoroughly soaked at the first crack of thunder and the first malevolent glance from a blade of wet grass. Nonetheless, they were light, comfortable, and never gave me blisters. If you aren't prone to spraining your ankles and you plan to hike on dry, summertime trails with a light day pack, there's not much wrong with running shoes, particularly since you may already own a pair. Just make sure they have enough tread left to prevent you from slipping excessively on the gravel.

Hiking Boot Construction

In the mid-1990s I spent five years writing equipment reviews for *Outside* magazine. One frequent topic was hiking boots. I began my research by lacing up a boot from one pair on my left foot and a boot from a different pair on my right so I could compare the two models in side-by-side use. Then I'd load up a pack with forty-five pounds and hike for an hour up and down a steep, rocky trail. After that I'd call the manufacturer for all the details of the construction and write the review. I hope that this detailed research actually helped readers choose the right pair of boots. In retrospect, however, I often felt that my article could have been boiled down to two sentences: "Buy the boot that provides the support you need for the weight you'll have on your back," and "Buy the boot that fits."

Okay, there's a bit more to choosing boots than that. Let's start by talking about boot construction.

The uppers on most light- to moderate-duty boots are pieced together from panels of lightweight leather and tough nylon fabric in the same way that the uppers of running shoes are built. The uppers are then glued rather than stitched to the midsole and outsole. Done right, this type of construction can produce lightweight, moderately priced boots that last reasonably well. Fabric/leather boots are a good choice for day hikers and for backpackers who primarily do shorter trips on well-maintained trails.

The weak point of all fabric/leather hiking boots is the seams. As veteran boot repairman Steve Komito puts it, "Every place where you've got a seam, you've got a place where the boot can come apart." Fabric/leather hiking boots usually have a lot of seams. Manufacturers are aware of the problem and often add a wide rubber rand around the toe area to protect the seams in that heavily abused area. In some models the rand continues around the full circumference of the boot just above the sole.

The most durable uppers are made mostly or entirely of leather with the fewest possible seams. The most abrasion- and water-resistant (and heaviest) boots use full-grain leather containing the outer surface of the hide. Slightly less durable (and lighter) boots use split leather, a layer of the hide not containing the tough outer surface. All-leather boots last much longer than fabric/leather boots because good leather is more abrasion-resistant than fabric. Every thread in a woven fabric comes to the surface. Break one thread and you've got a hole. Leather's densely matted fibers tolerate much more abuse. In addition, boot makers using leather can cut the upper from a single, seamless piece. A boot with a one-piece upper will outlast any boot that's pieced together, whether the pieces are leather or fabric. All-leather boots usually provide better ankle support when you're hiking with a heavy load and have a certain time-honored aesthetic appeal. Application of the same running-shoe technology that allowed the creation of lightweight fabric/leather boots has also stripped pounds off the weight of the new all-leather boots. On the downside, all-leather boots cost considerably more initially than fabric/leather boots. However, if you do enough hiking to wear out a pair of boots regularly, the cost per year of use may actually be the same or even lower.

Two of the most important components of a boot, the insole and midsole, are hidden from view but contribute greatly to the performance and longevity of your footwear.

To a boot maker the insole is the stiff, structural part of the sole that gives you support underfoot. It's not the soft, removable layer of foam that actually touches your sock, which is properly called the footbed or sockliner. Today's insoles are actually often made of two separate components, a shank that extends from the heel to the ball of your foot, and a plate, which often incorporates the heel cup and may extend only around the periphery of the boot sole. Most good boots today use molded nylon, polypropylene, or urethane shanks and plates, which retain their stiffness much longer than old-fashioned insoles of bonded wood fibers, giving you durable support. The use of molded shanks and plates also allows boot makers to provide natural flex at the ball of your foot while retaining some degree of torsional rigidity, useful when you're trying to edge the side of the boot into a steep slope.

Price also determines the quality of midsole you get. To a boot maker the midsole is the layer between the insole and outsole that provides cushioning and shock absorption. Inexpensive boots often use EVA, the same spongy material found in running-shoe midsoles. EVA absorbs shock well when new, but tends to compress permanently after a while, which is why you commonly read the recommendation that regular runners should replace their running shoes every three to six months. Better boots use polyurethane midsoles, which retain their ability to absorb shock much longer, but which are less cushy when new and also heavier.

Don't worry too much about the pattern of the lugs on the sole. Out of nearly a hundred patterns I've tested for magazine articles over the years, none stood out as exceptionally better or worse than the others. If you are planning to hike off-trail, do look for deep lugs and a heel brake, the raised portion of the sole under your heel. The heel brake helps prevent your feet from sliding out from under you when descending on steep, loose dirt or scree.

Keeping Your Feet Dry

A second weakness of fabric/leather hiking boots (in addition to their spider web of seams) is that they're scarcely more waterproof than a pair of running shoes and there's no practical way to waterproof them for very long. You can apply various waterproofing compounds to the leather, which will enhance its waterproofness for a time, but there's nothing that's comparably effective that you can do to the nylon.

Fortunately, fabric/leather boots that incorporate some kind of waterproof/ breathable lining now crowd retailer's shelves. In the past the best (and practically only) material available was Gore-Tex, which was incorporated into the uppers of many fabric/leather hiking boots in the form of a seam-sealed Gore-Tex bootie. In my experience Gore-Tex is an expensive but highly valuable addition to a fabric/ leather boot. In one test I conducted, I immersed several pairs of Gore-Tex boots in 3 inches of water for four hours. None of them admitted a drop. Then I tested a nearly new, all-leather hiking boot without a Gore-Tex liner. At the end of four hours, I poured half a cup of water out of the boot.

Fortunately for hikers, the main patent on Gore-Tex has expired, and a host of cheaper competitors have entered the fray. Today the great majority of fabric/ leather boots intended for backpacking incorporate some kind of waterproof/ breathable lining. Don't bet too much on the breathability part of the equation. Your feet are still going to sweat. If you're looking for durable waterproofness, however, some kind of waterproof/breathable lining is your ticket to happy feet.

Despite the discouraging result of my immersion test, all-leather hiking boots that rely strictly on the water-resistance of their leather to keep your feet dry are still an excellent choice in a heavy-duty boot designed for hauling a multiday load. Well-made models that use good leather, if given regular applications of a waterproofing compound, are certainly far more water-resistant than any fabric/ leather boot that lacks a waterproof/breathable lining. A few all-leather models back up their leather with a Gore-Tex liner, providing two barriers against the wet world outside.

If your boots don't have a waterproof/breathable lining, you can buy waterproof/breathable Gore-Tex over-socks, to be worn over your regular socks. When I obtained my first pair of Gore-Tex socks, I tested them by going running on some very wet, snowy, and muddy trails. I put a polypropylene liner sock on both feet, then donned a waterproof but nonbreathable vapor-barrier sock on one foot, a Gore-Tex sock on the other. During the run I didn't notice any difference in the temperature of my feet. The Gore-Tex didn't breathe enough to provide noticeable evaporative cooling. When I finished my run, however, I noticed that the Gore-Tex–clad foot was considerably drier than the foot encased in the nonbreathable, waterproof sock. The Gore-Tex sock had allowed some sweat to escape. I found the same pattern when I compared nonbreathable, waterproof gaiters to Gore-Tex gaiters while snowshoeing. One caution: The Gore-Tex socks I've used add significant bulk, making my boots feel somewhat tighter. You may need to wear a thinner sock combination to allow room for the Gore-Tex socks.

As you extend your mountain hiking season into spring and fall, you'll find that waterproof boots become more and more important. In the spring, in any mountain range that gets significant winter snowfall, the trails become mud-banked rivers filled with icy snowmelt. In the fall, early storms often dump just a few inches of snow that makes the footing cold and soggy. Waterproof footwear not only keeps your feet dry, but it also allows you to stay on the trail with impunity rather than walking around the wet spots, which widens the trail and promotes erosion. I'll have more to say on this in the Trail Etiquette section in chapter 10.

Light Hiking Shoes, Mid-Cut Boots, and Backpacking Boots

Now it's time to talk about the different categories of hiking footwear, starting with the lightest available. The first step up from a running shoe is a low-cut boot with uppers that terminate below the anklebone. They're often called light hiking shoes or trail shoes, and they've become increasingly popular over the last few years. Light hiking shoes look and perform like beefed-up running shoes. Like a running shoe, the uppers are usually constructed of panels of tough nylon fabric and thin, lightweight pieces of leather. Unlike a running shoe, most light hiking shoes employ a durable urethane shank to provide greater support underfoot. Fabric/leather hiking shoes weigh less than higher-cut models, yet they still provide enough support underfoot to prevent every sharp rock from bruising your foot. The greater ankle flexibility they offer gives them a nimble feel. Better still, they require almost no break-in time. They're perfect for day hikes with light loads, and some backpackers even use them for extended trips. On many trails it's hard to argue that a hefty boot is really necessary. Legendary Grandma Gatewood hiked the Appalachian Trail three times, starting at age sixty-seven, wearing Keds sneakers. For the sake of your leg muscles, buy the lightest boot you feel you can get away with.

Light hiking shoes do have disadvantages, however. They allow more rocks, trail grit, and mud to enter your shoes. Plan on carrying one fresh pair of socks for each day's travel. If you're hiking in the spring, before the last snowfields have melted, they admit snow. Gaiters can help, but gaiters work best on taller boots because there's more overlap between the boot and the gaiter. If you're hiking off-trail on scree and talus, they are too low cut to prevent stones from bruising and abrading your anklebones. The ankle freedom they offer feels great—until you get a little too much freedom and sprain your ankle.

As the terrain gets wetter and rougher and you begin carrying larger loads, you may find yourself wanting more protective footwear. Mid-cut boots reach just above the anklebone; backpacking boots are usually an inch or two taller. Both types are usually stiffer underfoot than a lightweight hiking shoe. That extra stiffness helps support the extra weight on your back. In my experience testing boots, your feet can actually be more comfortable after a long day with a heavy load in a stiffer boot, even though the lightweight, supple boot felt much better in the store. The extra height also reduces the risk of ankle sprains, although the best preventative there may actually be a pair of trekking poles.

In part the choice between light hiking shoes and taller, heavier boots comes down to which set of compromises you favor. Like all backpackers I'm concerned about saving weight. As a professional landscape photographer, however, I usually pile sixteen to twenty pounds of camera gear on top of my load, so my pack could never be described as "light." I frequently travel off-trail, and I like climbing Fourteeners, which may still have significant snowfields as late as mid-July. My solution? Own two pairs of boots. In the spring and early summer, when the high peaks and passes are still holding snow, I prefer lightweight, all-leather, above-the-ankle backpacking boots that are just supportive enough to accept some form of traction device. For icy trails I carry a set of MICROspikes, which are roughly equivalent to a lightweight set of spiked tire chains for your boots. The teeth on MICROspikes are ⅜ inch long—great for slick but low-angle terrain. For steep snowfields I carry a pair of flexible, strap-on crampons, the spiked steel frames that climbers attach to their boots to gain traction on snow and ice. Crampon teeth are typically 1½ inches long. Once the snow melts, I switch to lightweight trail shoes. If owning two pairs of hiking boots strikes your significant other as extravagant, remind him or her that if you wear out both pairs of boots before old age sends you to your rocking chair, the cost per year will actually be the same as owning just one pair and replacing it twice as often.

Mountaineering Boots

Backpackers who leave the valley-bottom trails in pursuit of high summits will sooner or later find themselves confronting a steep, hard-packed snowfield or ice-filled gully. Dealing with such terrain isn't hiking anymore: It's mountaineering, with all its inherent dangers. Gravity works with surprising speed, and a slip not checked immediately on a 45-degree snowfield quickly becomes as unstoppable as a free fall off a vertical cliff. Mountaineering places a whole new set of demands on judgment, skill, experience, and equipment. If you're interested in learning about mountaineering, seek expert instruction first, then begin upgrading your gear.

Among the new items you'll need are a pair of mountaineering boots that can be fitted with crampons. Many models of heavy-duty backpacking boots, such as the ones I favor, will accept flexible crampons that lash on with neoprene or nylon straps. This setup is adequate for steep, firm snow, but too flimsy to deal safely with "water ice." This odd term refers to the brittle ice that forms when liquid water freezes (as opposed to glacial ice, formed by snow that has undergone repeated melt-freeze cycles, which is much less brittle and much easier to climb). The rigid steel crampons designed for true ice climbing clamp on with a mechanism that's reminiscent of a much-simplified alpine ski binding. To accommodate the pressures

Crampons give mountaineers good traction on snow and ice.

23

generated by attaching crampons, mountaineering boots must have rigid soles and stout uppers. That makes them feel heavy and uncomfortable when used for ordinary hiking.

Today's leather mountaineering boots are all single boots, meaning they have no removable inner boot and very little insulation, making them suitable for summer use only. Plastic double boots, by contrast, are now the universal standard on cold, high peaks from Alaska to the Himalayas, as well as for winter mountaineering in the Lower 48. These boots have a molded plastic outer shell and a removable inner boot made of leather, vinyl, foam, or felt. The nonabsorbent plastic shell is a vast improvement over leather because it doesn't absorb moisture during the day, then freeze hard as iron at night. It can be almost impossible to shove your foot into a frozen leather boot.

At least one company now makes custom-fitted foam inner boots. A boot fitter at a specialty retailer heats the inner boots in an oven, then slides them into the outer shell. The customer quickly slips his feet into the boots, laces them down snugly, and waits ten minutes until the foam has cooled into the exact shape of his foot. Buying custom-fitted inner boots has given me the best fit I've ever had in a pair of plastic mountaineering boots.

Take extra care when fitting mountaineering boots. Leather models soften only grudgingly; the shells of plastic boots don't soften at all. With plastic boots your only hope is that the inner boots will pack down a bit with use, allowing the foam or felt to mold comfortably to your feet. Sometimes, however, the foam compresses to the point where you'll need to wear a thicker pair of socks to keep your feet from rattling around inside your boots. Heel lift is a common problem in boots this stiff, so try to find a pair that cups your heel snugly. Whether leather or plastic, mountaineering boots sell only in limited quantities, so the price is high.

Winter Boots

If your hiking takes you out when the temperatures are much below freezing, you'll want to consider two other categories of footwear: pac boots and what I call winter hiking boots.

Boot guru Steve Komito's shop once contained a sign that read, DOUBLE BOOTS ARE CHEAP—ONLY $20 PER TOE. Although today the price tag varies depending on what you buy, the message is still relevant to anyone who goes out in frigid weather: Insulated, waterproof footwear is worth the price—especially considering that the price of inadequate winter footgear may be frostbite. After all, he who dies with the most toes wins.

Pac boots have an all-leather or leather and fabric upper stitched to a molded rubber bottom. A removable liner, usually made of wool or polypropylene felt, provides insulation. Wool liners cost less; polypro liners dry faster. For equivalent thickness, the warmth is about the same. Pac boots are warmer than winter hiking boots—sometimes too warm—and totally waterproof up to the top of the molded rubber. They're water-resistant above that. Pac boots are instantly comfortable, requiring no break-in time, but the fit is usually rather amorphous because the insulation compresses under your foot and the boots are normally available only in full sizes. When fitting a pair, make sure the top edge of the molded rubber doesn't jab you under the anklebone while traversing a slope.

Pac boots are perfect for aurora watching and other inactive pursuits. For strenuous hiking or snowshoeing in rough terrain where you want a snugger fit and better ankle support, look for a pair of insulated, waterproof winter hiking boots. They'll lighten your wallet more than pac boots, but also lighten the load on your feet.

Many of these boots are marketed as hunting boots because they're targeted to the hook-and-bullet crowd, but don't let the name put you off. Hunters spend a lot of time walking off-trail in cold, snowy, or marshy terrain, and they need warm, waterproof footwear more than most backpackers. Cold-weather hiking boots have all-leather or fabric/leather uppers that are stitched, cemented, or attached via injection molding to a stout lugged sole. All three construction techniques, including injection molding, which has been much improved in recent years, produce a durable boot. All-leather uppers typically cost more, weigh more, and last longer. The insulation, which is stitched permanently into the boot lining, is usually Thinsulate, a microfiber batting that resists compression and provides a lot of warmth with minimum thickness. Some manufacturers use various closed-cell foams as insulation, which don't provide quite as much warmth as Thinsulate for equivalent thickness. As with summer hiking boots, the best insulated winter hiking boots back up their leather with a sewn-in Gore-Tex bootie.

Neither pac boots nor winter hunting boots are good for multiday trips in the winter because even the best leather eventually absorbs water during the day, then freezes at night into a misshapen caricature of itself just like a leather mountaineering boot. My solution, an admittedly expensive one, is to use my double plastic mountaineering boots with a custom-fitted inner boot for all my winter camping trips, even those that don't involve mountaineering. Although stiffer than necessary for snowshoeing, the boots are warm, dry, and relatively light because of the custom inner boots. When I'm shooting sunrise on a 0°F morning, plastic double boots let me forget about my toes and focus on capturing the forbidding beauty around me.

Boots for Wet Summer Hiking

There's one other category of footwear to consider: boots for warm, wet conditions, such as you find while hiking in the summer in those rare canyons in the Southwest that have permanently flowing streams. In many places these streams are the trails; the banks are so choked with brush (and sometimes poison ivy) or hemmed in so tightly by cliffs that the only way to make progress is to walk right in the streambed. As a general rule I dislike letting my feet remain wet for long periods. Waterlogged skin softens and blisters easily and is susceptible to fungal infections. On the other hand the thought of wearing knee-high rubber boots on a 100°F July day in southern Utah is equally repugnant. River runners usually wear some kind of heavy-duty sandals that strap on securely so they won't wash away in rapids. Some models even have soles made of the same sticky, high-friction rubber used on rock climbing boots. Sandals offer the advantage of letting your feet dry out quickly once you do get back on shore, but they provide no ankle support and no protection against bruising and scratching by hidden, underwater rocks and branches. The best solution, I think, is to wear lightweight fabric/leather hiking shoes or boots with thin, nonabsorbent, synthetic socks. Once you're done with stream-walking for the day, change into sandals or a lightweight pair of camp shoes. On a backpacking trip you'll want to bring several changes of socks.

Fitting Boots

The advent of supple, easily broken-in fabric/leather boots and lightweight all-leather boots has alleviated much of the anxiety that used to accompany boot shopping. In the past the prospective victim trembled and asked himself: *Will I ever be able to break these monsters in? Will I curse myself for years for purchasing an exorbitantly expensive pair of blister machines?* Fortunately for backpackers, those days of fear and loathing are mostly gone. Still, a few words on fitting boots may be in order.

For starters, buy the socks you intend to wear before selecting your boots. The particular sock combination you choose affects the fit of your boots a great deal. As a general rule I recommend wearing one pair of thin, synthetic or wool liner socks with a thicker pair of wool or wool-blend socks on top. The smooth, tight knit of the liner sock tends to reduce friction and hold blisters at bay; the thick wool sock provides insulation and cushioning and absorbs moisture. Cotton socks are very comfortable if your feet will stay dry. If they get wet, however, as they inevitably will from either sweat, rain, or wet ground, cotton socks will lose their resiliency, then collapse against your skin and cling there, making your feet cold and clammy. Cotton is highly absorbent, which means it takes forever to dry. Some people recommend wearing liner socks made of silk because they believe silk socks reduce blisters. Although they don't seem to help Cora, my blister-prone wife, they might help you. I rarely have problems with blisters, so I can't speak to that claim from personal experience.

Once you've purchased the socks you'll be wearing, start trying on boots. In the past, when the lightweight boot revolution first hit, the hiker's decision was simple: Which boot is lightest? Now that revolution has reached a plateau, and the hiker faces a different decision: What balance of weight versus support do I want? The ultralight boot that feels as comfortable as a running shoe in the store (because that's basically what it is) may leave your feet bruised and battered after 10 heavily laden miles.

Boots are made on a last, a metal form that defines the shape of the boot. Different manufacturers use different lasts—some narrow, some wide—depending on what they think will fit the greatest number of feet. A few manufacturers offer different widths in the same size and model of boot. Don't accept the first pair that feels vaguely right. Try different models and different manufacturers, and even different stores, which may carry styles the first did not. Unlace the boot completely and shove your foot as far forward as possible, until your toes touch the front of the boot. If you can fit one finger in between your heel and the back of the boot, the length is about right. Lace up the boot and walk. Does your heel shift up and down inside the boot? A small amount of movement may be acceptable, particularly in a stiff, new boot. If the movement is excessive, however, it will cause blisters. Look for enough room at the front of the boot to "play piano with your toes," especially if you're buying a cold-weather boot. Snug boots restrict circulation, which can lead to cold feet and even frostbite.

If you're planning to carry a substantial load, try the boots on while wearing a pack. Stand on a sharp edge to test the arch support. Squat down and see if the toe box folds into a sharp wrinkle that jabs your toes. Let your foot roll to the side and see if the boot provides adequate ankle support. Walk down an incline and see if your foot slides forward, jamming your toes into the toe of the boot. You may be surprised at how quickly a lightweight day-hiking boot begins to seem inadequate for serious backpacking. Unfortunately, the stiffer the boot, the harder it is to judge if it will be comfortable over the long haul. That's another reason to buy no heavier and stiffer a boot than you really need. You're looking for the balance point between light weight and support—a balance point that will vary depending on the load on your back. Fortunately, most good shops will let you return boots a few days after purchase if you've only worn them indoors.

Boot Care

Good boots are like puppies: Treat them well when they're young, and they won't bite you when they're old.

The first priority is keeping your boots clean. Dirt left clinging to boots will work its way into the leather, fabric, seams, and stitching, then grind away until the boots fall apart. Consider it a moral imperative, akin to washing behind your ears, to clean your boots with water and a stiff scrub brush after a muddy trip; a little mild soap will help.

Next, dry your boots slowly, well away from any heat source. Leather is just the skin of another mammal. Don't put your boots any closer to a heat source than your own hand can comfortably tolerate. To speed drying, unlace the boots completely and remove the insoles (and inner boots if you've got pac boots or double mountaineering boots). To speed drying further, try stuffing the boots with crumpled-up newspaper, then replacing the newspaper every hour or so.

Cowhide, like your skin, was naturally oily when it clothed the cow. Also like your skin, cowhide can dry out, become brittle, and crack if soaked repeatedly in water or exposed continually to hot, dry conditions. Brand-new leather boots are highly water-resistant, but be skeptical of claims that any leather is "waterproof for the life of the boot." In my experience even the best leather boots eventually begin to leak. To preserve the leather's suppleness and waterproofness, I periodically apply some kind of leather conditioner. Here controversy reigns, with each manufacturer of conditioner finding some reason to claim that rival products will rot the leather, degrade the stitching, and delaminate the soles as well as give you night sweats and premature baldness. The safest course is to use the conditioner recommended by the boot manufacturer (if the manufacturer recommends one), if for no other reason than to preserve your rights under the warranty. Mink oil and neat's-foot oil are intended to soften leather that has become hard and brittle; they should not be used as waterproofing agents. Boot repairmen caution that using Sno-Seal, a venerable product with a devoted following, on a modern dry-tanned leather boot will make it nearly impossible to resole because adhesives will no longer bond to the leather.

If the stitching holding your boots together is starting to fray, you can apply some kind of liquid sealant or boot-patching compound to the seams to make them more abrasion resistant. No brand I've tried seems to resist peeling for more than a month or two, so I'll leave you on your own to explore the boot shop's shelves for the latest and greatest. Although you can resole a fabric/leather boot, it's rarely worth the expense. By the time the sole needs replacing, the uppers are usually shot. More durable all-leather boots may well be worth resoling.

Unlike puppies, boots that won't be used for a long time should be stored in a cool, dry, dark place.

If adventure has a final and all-embracing motive, it is surely this: we go out because it is in our nature to go out to climb the mountains and to sail the seas, to fly to the planets and to plunge into the depths of the ocean. By doing these things we make touch with something outside or behind, which strangely seems to approve our doing them. We extend our horizon, we expand our being, revel in a mastery of ourselves which gives an impression, mainly illusory, that we are master of our world. In a word, we are men, and when man ceases to do these things, he is no longer man.

—Wilfrid Noyce, 1917–1962

The road to hell is paved with good packs used badly. I still wince at the thought of my own mistakes. There was the time I finished a five-day ascent of Yosemite's 3,000-vertical-foot El Capitan, then packed sixty pounds of steel and aluminum rock climbing hardware into a day pack designed for twenty-five-pound loads and hauled it 7 miles back down to my campsite. Or the time seven friends and I climbed Alaska's 16,237-foot Mount Sanford. At the beginning of the expedition, we made two trips, carrying half our gear each time, from the bush landing strip to the foot of the glacier. Coming out, however, we were too eager for showers, pizza, and rock 'n' roll to adopt such a sane approach, so we decided to make only one trip, carrying everything in one gigantic load. At the foot of the glacier, I filled my gargantuan internal-frame pack to the brim, loosened the pack lid's extension straps to their limit, crammed in some more, then lashed a fiberglass sled and heavy mountaineering skis on top. My pack must have weighed ninety pounds—about two-thirds as much as I did. I felt like an Olympic weightlifter doing the clean-and-jerk on a gold-medal weight each time I hoisted my pack. After two repetitions it became impossible to lift it without assistance, and I was forced to ask for help in getting it on after each rest stop for the remainder of the trail-less 9-mile hike out over the tundra. Fortunately, someone else agreed to carry the 12-gauge shotgun we'd brought as grizzly insurance.

A couple of years later, I carried a similar-size load of camera gear into the Grand Canyon to photograph a rafting expedition. I had packed the pack while it was sitting on the tailgate of my pickup so I could slip it on without actually lifting it off the ground. That meant, however, that all the way into the canyon I could never set the pack down without finding a tailgate-high, flat-topped rock to set it on.

People stopped me on the trail repeatedly and said things like, "That's the biggest pack I've ever seen." At first I was secretly proud. Then the pain got too great, and I would just smile through tight lips and keep walking.

In all seriousness, carrying too much weight can severely injure your spine. Several years ago, after three decades of carrying too much weight for too many miles, I developed a herniated disc in my lumbar spine that eventually required two surgeries to repair. I can still carry a fifty-pound pack, but I'll certainly never carry seventy pounds again. Don't make the mistakes I did. Keep the weight under control. You'll enjoy your trip much more, and your knees, ankles, shoulders, and spine will thank you for it, particularly when you blow past fifty years of age.

Fanny Packs and Day Packs

If you're interested mostly in carrying an extra sweater and a water bottle during an evening jaunt or half-day stroll, then all you really need is a fanny pack or its upscale cousin with the tony name, the lumbar pack. Fanny packs range in size from watch-pocket-on-a-shoestring to bread-basket-on-a-girdle. As your hiking range increases and the weather gets more severe, you'll find the gear you need overwhelming even the biggest lumbar pack. When your fanny pack starts to look like a thrift store's giveaway box, bulging at the seams and overflowing the top, it's time to move up to a day pack.

At first you may want to carry the book pack you once used to haul *War and Peace* to school without breaking your arm. You'll quickly find, however, that you've entered a race between your growing dissatisfaction with the book pack's capacity and comfort and its accelerating tendency to explode at its flimsy zippers. I'm rooting for the zipper explosion, because that will give you the perfect excuse to buy a day pack that will last you for a decade and make your hiking days a pleasure.

The day packs I like share several features. First, they pamper your shoulders with amply padded shoulder straps. Second, they protect your spine from steely-hearted, back-stabbing pieces of equipment with a foam-padded panel that covers the entire back of the pack. (Let's clarify a bit of nomenclature here: The back of your pack faces your back, while the front faces away, so you can think of yourself as a two-headed push-me-pull-you as you walk down the trail.) Larger-capacity day packs, which are designed for higher loads, may protect your back with both foam padding and a sheet of stiff plastic called a framesheet. The plastic sheet also helps transfer weight to your hips. A well-padded hip belt makes that weight transfer more comfortable, but beware: Few day packs let you adjust the height at which the pack rides relative to your waist. The wrong size day pack can leave you with a hip belt that puts the squeeze on your stomach—and that extra cheese Danish you gluttonously gobbled—not your hips, where it belongs.

I prefer day packs with simple drawstring closures at the top, referred to as top-loading packs. The alternative is a panel-loading pack with a long, U-shaped zipper arcing across the front panel. Panel-loading packs provide convenient access to all your gear, but have one serious Achilles' heel. Even the most stout zipper tends to break or wear out eventually, particularly if it's used in sandy regions. Sand and grit get into the zipper teeth, then wear out the slider from the inside. You'll start zipping your pack shut one day and find that the zipper is unzipping itself behind the slider just as fast as you zip it together in front. With many panel-loading day packs, a zipper failure leaves you with no good way to close your pack and retain the contents inside. A top-loading pack with a drawstring can't fail in this manner. Panel-loaders also have the disadvantage that they must be laid flat on their backs to access the contents—an unappealing prospect when the ground is a sea of mud, since any mud that clings to the back of the pack is immediately transferred to your clothing when you put the pack on.

Your day pack should have a few other features. Look for a large pocket in the pack lid, but be aware that it's one of Murphy's Laws that you'll never have enough room in that pocket for all the essential items that you want to be immediately accessible. Many designers include a flat pocket for maps underneath the lid, but I prefer instead to put the map in a zippered pouch hanging from my shoulder straps or in a separate map case worn over one shoulder, where it's more accessible, and use the "map pocket" solely for invaluable items like car keys and wallet. Once those items are safely stowed, I refrain from unzipping that pocket until I'm back at the car, to ensure my keys won't slip out unnoticed and disappear between two unmovable boulders.

Better day packs have compression straps along the sides of the pack. These straps, usually two or three to a side, allow you to compress the load and prevent the contents from swaying to and fro, which can upset your balance when you're boulder-hopping, log-balancing, skiing, or swinging through the jungle with Tarzan in hot pursuit. Compression straps also give you a convenient way to lash on extra clothing and equipment, like a fly rod, tripod, or skis. I like to slide my skis tail-first down through the compression straps, then lash the tips together with a short accessory strap. Lashing the tips helps keep the skis from pivoting back and forth and whacking you in the head when you walk. Be sure the tails don't drop down so low that they hook the back of your knees or catch on the ground when you're walking down a steep hill. To further simplify attaching skis, look for a day pack with a quick-release buckle on the top compression strap instead of a ladder buckle, which must be painstakingly rethreaded if you undo it completely.

Most day packs provide lash patches on either the front of the pack or the lid. Lash patches are small leather or synthetic swatches of material sewn to the pack with slots behind them to accommodate lash straps, short lengths of nylon webbing with buckles on the end, used for attaching gear that won't fit inside. Technical day packs (meaning packs designed for climbers) include an ice ax loop, a small loop of webbing at the bottom of the pack that makes attaching an ice ax convenient. Ice axes are not just for demented people who like to climb frozen waterfalls; many early-season peak-baggers carry them to stop a slip while crossing hard-frozen snowfields in the early morning. If your ambitions include such ascents, look for a day pack with an ice ax loop. Be aware, however, that an ice ax is useless unless you know how to use it. Novice mountaineers should seek competent instruction from a qualified mountaineering school or highly experienced friends.

A typical day pack.

The best way to carry skis is to slip them through your pack's compression straps, then lash the tips together with a short accessory strap.

Multiday Packs

Day packs have neither the capacity to accommodate the gear you'll need for an overnight trip, nor a suspension system adequate to carry the weight with reasonable comfort. As you begin shopping for a multiday pack, you face the pack world's metaphorical Continental Divide, with external-frame packs on one side and internal-frame packs on the other.

My first multiday pack was an external-frame Kelty with an olive-drab pack bag, purchased in the early 1970s when I was a young teen. It possessed all the virtues that external frames still have today and served me well on my first backpacking trips into the Sierras with my father. The frame itself was built of stout aluminum tubing in the form of an abbreviated ladder about two and a half feet high. The two vertical members on the sides were curved to fit the curve of my spine. Four horizontal cross-members provided rigidity and strength. The pack bag had one top-loading main compartment closed with a simple fabric flap and several zippered side pockets. Broad mesh bands across the back of the pack forced the pack bag to ride slightly away from my back, permitting a cooling breeze to dry my sweat. The rigid frame effectively transferred most of the weight to the padded hip belt, where it belonged—your hips can carry more weight, much longer, than your shoulders. The shoulder straps served primarily to prevent the pack from toppling over backward. The forward curve of the frame as it rose above my shoulders allowed me to lash heavy items high, with the weight centered almost directly over my hips, so I could walk with a comfortable, nearly upright stance.

The same rigid frame that made carrying my Kelty so comfortable on smooth trails, however, proved to be a liability when my father and I left the trail and scrambled up a long, boulder-choked couloir to the summit of Mount Agassiz, a 13,891-foot peak that provided a stunning view of the surreal turquoise blue lakes at the base of the Palisades in California. With the rigid frame strapped on tightly with the hip belt and shoulder straps, I felt like I was wearing a body cast that prevented the natural bending and twisting required to keep my balance on the steep talus slope. Carrying the weight high compounded the problem because it raised my center of gravity and made me top-heavy. The efficient way to travel on talus is to move rhythmically from rock to rock in a flowing, dynamic balance. That goal was thwarted, however, by the pack's rigidity and high center of gravity. Similar experiences in the late 1960s led Greg Lowe to create the first parallel-stave internal-frame packs. His pioneering design is now the basis of most of the internal-frame packs manufactured today.

Lowe's goal was the first winter ascent of the Grand Teton's north face. For that he needed a large-capacity pack with a suspension comfortable enough to handle significant weight that would also allow him to climb effectively. His solution was a pack with two internal aluminum staves set vertically and parallel to each other in the back of the pack bag. With no horizontal cross-members to stiffen the frame, the pack could flex enough to permit a long reach for a good hold or a graceful jump turn while skiing steep snow. The staves were bent to fit the natural curve of the back, so the weight rode very close to the body, reducing the top-heavy feeling of carrying an external frame and preventing the pack bag from swaying to and fro and throwing the climber or skier off balance. Other pack makers jumped on the bandwagon, and soon internal-frame packs were the standard for mountaineers, backcountry skiers, and an increasing number of backpackers as well. I bought my first internal-frame pack in 1978, shortly before my first expedition to Alaska, and I've been using them exclusively ever since.

Not all internal-frame packs have two parallel aluminum stays like Lowe's original design. Some slant the two stays inward like a V or even crossed like an X. Others use a single stay, reinforced with a polyethylene framesheet, sometimes reinforced still further with flexible plastic or carbon-fiber stays running vertically along the edges of the framesheet. In one recent twist, called a perimeter frame, a thin aluminum tube is bent into an upside-down U that follows the perimeter of the back panel. No one design has emerged as demonstrably superior; instead, comfort seems to depend on the care with which each basic design is implemented.

Internal frames do have disadvantages. The back of your shirt is guaranteed to be soaked with sweat after an hour or two of walking because no cooling breeze can force itself into the paper-thin gap between your pack and your back. The load typically rides lower than in an external frame, which is good for balance but more tiring because it enforces a vaguely simian forward-leaning posture. Internal frames are also less forgiving of packing errors such as stowing the heaviest items at the bottom, and it's harder to lash on a big, awkwardly shaped load, like a hefty tripod, that won't fit inside the pack bag. (I'll discuss pack packing in more detail later.) Internal frames are almost always more expensive as well.

If you plan to stick mostly to summer trails and want to save money, consider an external-frame pack. If winter snowshoe or ski trips or lots of off-trail scrambling are in your plans, then an internal frame is a better bet. External frames are usually targeted at budget-oriented consumers, which means manufacturers generally haven't put as much design effort into the comfort of the harness as the best internal-frame manufacturers. For that reason I prefer a top-quality internal frame when I'm carrying a heavy load.

The front of a typical external-frame pack.

The back of a typical external-frame pack.

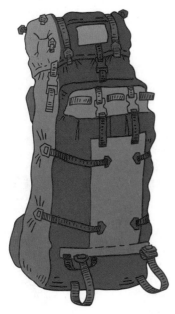

The front of a typical internal-frame pack.

The back of a typical internal-frame pack.

Selecting and Fitting a Multiday Pack

A well-built pack, treated with care, will last for years. My first day pack, a gift from my father, would probably still be going strong if I hadn't destroyed it hauling it up granite rock-climbs in Yosemite and Rocky Mountain National Parks. My second day pack suffered the same fate after a decade of hard use. Right now, after forty years of mountaineering and backpacking, I'm using my seventh multiday pack. None of the six previous packs ever really wore out (one, in fact, was stolen). I just decided that the grass would be greener if I jumped over the fence and bought that shiny new red pack with the come-hither gleam in its eye. The durability of a good pack makes it important to choose carefully. Take the time, and spend the money, to get a pack you'll be happy with for years.

Your first concern, when buying a new pack, is making sure it fits. Finding such a pack, however, is not quite as simple as it might seem.

In 1983 I guided an expedition on Mount McKinley. My assistant, Janet Gelman, was a former college ski racer who had once broken her back in a skiing accident. One week into the three-week expedition, her old injury began to hurt again. She was carrying a nearly new, top-quality internal-frame pack almost identical to the one I was carrying in relative comfort. (I say "relative" because carrying sixty pounds for eight hours will make your shoulders sore no matter what pack you're carrying.) Like most women, she had a much shorter torso than the average male. Like most "unisex" packs, hers had been designed for the average male torso. The result was a pack that always rode too low on her hips and put too much strain on her back, no matter how she adjusted it. Finally, in desperation, she took a stout sewing awl called a Speedy Stitcher and modified the suspension of her pack so it would ride higher on her back—a painstaking operation that took several numb-fingered hours at 14,300 feet.

The moral of this story may seem obvious: Make sure your pack fits before you buy it. As Janet found out, however, and as I've experienced myself with other packs, it can take a week or two of use, combined with constant fiddling, to get a pack's suspension tweaked to perfection. When buying a pack, look for a suspension that is as adjustable as possible. If you can, select a pack that seems to fit best when using the middle portion of the adjustment range, giving you the option of altering the fit in either direction. Women who find that men's packs don't fit should seek out a pack from one of the companies that now make packs specifically for women. Even these provide no guarantee of a perfect fit, however. The hip belt on Cora's first internal-frame pack, although designed specifically for women, had insufficient travel to cinch snugly about her small hips. We had to shorten the belt with a Speedy Stitcher to make it comfortable for her. The very best packs are made in several sizes each for both men and women. A knowledgeable salesperson can be invaluable in selecting the right size pack—another reason to visit a specialty shop.

Trying on an empty pack tells you nothing about the fit, so most good outdoor shops keep sandbags of varying weights in the pack department. Toss twenty-five or thirty pounds into the pack you're considering, then walk around the shop for a few minutes. You'll quickly gain a much better feel for the pack's load-carrying comfort.

Internal- and external-frame packs share similarities in the way they're fitted, even if the mechanism for making alterations is quite different. The first and most important adjustment is the distance between the hip belt and the point where the upper end of the shoulder straps attaches to the frame or pack bag. Let's call this the pack's torso-length adjustment. If this distance is too short, the pack's hip belt will ride too high, encircling your stomach instead of your hips when the shoulder straps are adjusted properly. If this distance is too long, the hip belt will ride too low even if you tighten the shoulder straps as far as they will go. A low-rider hip belt, chic though it may be, will constrict the muscles in your buttocks and the outside of your hips, causing discomfort and fatigue, and potentially causing back pain. This is the problem Janet experienced on McKinley. If the torso-length adjustment is set correctly, the hip belt will cradle the tops of your hip bones, and most of the pack's weight will ride comfortably on your hips. Normally, you'll only need to adjust the torso length once during the life of the pack. With the torso length correct, all the other adjustments should fall into place easily.

Sophisticated external-frame packs allow you to adjust the torso length by moving the attachment points of both the shoulder straps and the hip belt. On less expensive frame packs, the upper end of the shoulder straps attaches directly to a fixed horizontal frame member, so the height of the shoulder-strap attachment cannot be adjusted. Some of these inexpensive frame packs allow you to adjust the height of the hip belt's attachment to the frame; others provide different frame sizes to fit different torso lengths. The least expensive frame packs come in one size. Avoid these unless you're positive they fit perfectly and your primary concern is saving money.

To determine if the torso length you've selected for an external-frame pack is correct, first load the pack and slip it on. Adjust the shoulder straps to approximately the right fit, neither so tight that they squeeze your shoulders uncomfortably, nor so loose the pack seems to be dragging you over backward. Then fasten the hip belt and cinch it down firmly. It should snugly cup the high points of your pelvis. The pack's weight should feel like it's riding mostly on your hips. Now, if need be, tighten the shoulder straps slightly. For most external-frame packs, the shoulder straps should be horizontal where they attach to the pack frame. In other words the attachment point should be the same height as the top of your shoulders. If necessary, adjust the torso length until both hip belt and shoulder straps fit correctly. Once you've got the torso length correct, check a few other points. Are the shoulder straps acting like vampires, drawing blood from your neck because they're too close together? Are they acting like teens at a junior high mixer, so far apart that they weight the outermost parts of your shoulders uncomfortably? Good packs let you adjust the distance between the shoulder straps to fit your anatomy.

Internal-frame packs use a different method to adjust the torso length. With most internal frames, the upper end of the shoulder straps attaches to the shoulder yoke, which is positioned approximately between your shoulder blades. The height of this shoulder yoke can be adjusted up or down, usually via some arrangement of straps and buckles. Regardless of the method the goal is the same as with an external-frame pack: proper positioning of the shoulder straps in relation to the hip belt so that the pack's weight rides primarily on your hips, with the shoulder straps serving mostly to prevent the pack from swaying dramatically from side to side or falling over backward.

The advantage of attaching the shoulder straps to a shoulder yoke is that the straps wrap more comfortably around your shoulders than they do with many external-frame packs. The disadvantage of the shoulder-yoke design is the greater potential for the pack to sway. To prevent swaying, and to further reduce the pressure on your shoulders, internal-frame packs have shoulder-stabilizer straps, also known, rather misleadingly, as load-lifter straps. These straps attach to the shoulder straps at about your clavicle, then extend upward at a 30- to 45-degree angle to the pack's aluminum staves. Snug down your shoulder-stabilizer straps, then loosen the shoulder straps a bit, and the result is almost magical relief for your aching shoulders as the load shifts even more completely to your hip belt. When your hips start to complain, tighten the shoulder straps again, loosen the shoulder-stabilizers a little, and shift some weight back to your shoulders. These adjustments can be made on the trail, almost without breaking stride. Only the best external-frame packs offer shoulder-stabilizer straps.

Good internal frames can be fine-tuned even further. In an effort to allow your hips to move independently of your shoulders, the hip belt on most internal frames fastens to a lumbar pad that rides in the small of your back. By moving the attachment points of the hip belt relatively close to each other rather than positioning them at the outside corners of the pack bag, your hips can rock up and down like a teeter-totter when you walk, without pushing the pack bag up and down at the same time. That reduces fatigue and increases comfort, but introduces the possibility that your pack could roll side to side like a barrel on your back. To reduce that motion, pack designers introduced hip-stabilizer straps that run from the bottom corners of the pack bag to the hip belt. They should be loosened each time you remove your pack, then tightened again after you've put on your pack and snugged down your hip belt. Keep them lightly tensioned for greater comfort while trail walking; snug them down further for greater stability while skiing and off-trail scrambling.

The final adjustment, now almost universal on internal frames and increasingly common on external frames, involves the sternum strap, which connects the shoulder straps at the level of your sternum. This strap lets you fine-tune where the shoulder straps ride on your shoulders—close together for narrow-shouldered people, farther apart for broader-shouldered people. The point where the sternum strap attaches to the shoulder straps can usually be adjusted up or down so the sternum strap rides at a comfortable height across your chest.

By now you may feel that buying a modern pack means you'll spend half your vacation reading instructions and yanking on puzzling pieces of webbing rather than enjoying the wilderness. Perhaps pack makers are actually engaged in a diabolical plot to keep befuddled novices near the trailhead so they won't overcrowd the pack makers' favorite wilderness valleys. With a little perseverance, however, you can master your pack's intricacies, defeat this sinister scheme, and stride forth confidently into the wilds. Whatever you may read in the instructions, no matter whether you're carrying an external frame or an internal frame, your comfort is the final arbiter. Keep tweaking that suspension until it feels right, even if it means stopping in the middle of the hike to fiddle with it. Preventive maintenance on your pack's suspension will repay you many times over.

Like day packs, the pack bags that accompany both external- and internal-frame packs come in two basic styles: top-loading, in which you stuff everything in the top while holding the pack upright; and panel-loading, in which you lay the pack flat on its back and unzip a large panel on the pack's front. Simple top-loading internal frames close with a single drawstring. More complex internal frames have, in addition, a spindrift collar, essentially an extension of the main pack body that closes over the contents when the pack is full to keep blowing snow from sneaking into the pack. The pack lid on an internal frame with a spindrift collar often "floats." Adjustable straps allow the lid to be raised to cover an overstuffed pack or lowered to cover the pack's opening when the load is smaller. Floating lids and spindrift collars are particularly useful to winter campers, long-distance trekkers, and people who backpack with kids, all of whom need room for large volumes of clothing and food.

Most external-frame packs, whether top-loading or panel-loading, have a light aluminum framework called the hold-open bar at the top of the pack bag. On a top-loading pack the hold-open bar keeps the mouth of the bag open for easy loading. On a panel-loader it provides structure to the pack bag when the front panel is zipped open, again making loading easier. Large-capacity external frames often have a frame extension that rises above the hold-open bar. The extension provides additional lashing points when your gear begins multiplying like a family of love-starved guppies.

In general I prefer top-loading packs, whether internal frame or external frame, because they have no critical zippers to blow out and because you don't have to lay the suspension side flat in the mud to get at the contents. The disadvantage of a top-loader, particularly one with a single, undivided compartment, is that you have to think carefully about what goes in first, because everything else will go in on top, burying the first items on the bottom and making them inconvenient to get at when you're on the trail. The solution, of course, is to put items you won't need during the day, like your tent, sleeping bag, and stove, at the bottom. The problem of accessibility is manageable, but a few people still prefer panel-loaders because they provide easy access to all their gear at any time.

Most internal-frame packs these days come with some way of accommodating a hydration system, essentially just a soft, collapsible bladder with a drinking tube attached. Usually you stow the bladder in a pocket along the back panel, just inside the top of your pack bag, thread the drinking tube through a port in the pack bag, then clip the end of the tube, which has a bite valve, to a shoulder strap for easy access while hiking. Staying hydrated is certainly crucial, but I generally prefer carrying a pint bottle in a bottle holster on my hip belt. In my view hydration systems have a couple of disadvantages. I like sports drinks for long, hard days on the trail. It's much harder to clean a hydration system's bladder than a pint water bottle that you can scrub with a bottle brush (although the most recent versions of some hydration systems have wide mouths that make cleaning much easier). In well-watered country, which includes most of the Colorado Rockies, I prefer to carry only one pint of water at a time, stopping to filter water from a lake or stream whenever I need more. This solution saves weight compared to leaving the trailhead with a full day's supply, which may weigh four or five pounds. In desert country, of course, you may have no option other than to carry all the water you need for the entire day. In that situation a wide-mouth hydration system may be the perfect solution.

The capacity of the pack bag used to be expressed in cubic inches. These days it's more commonly expressed in liters. I've provided some conversion charts to help with comparison. If you choose an internal frame and plan to stick to summer trips, you'll need a pack with a capacity of fifty to sixty-five liters (about 3,000 to 4,000 cubic inches) for trips of two to three days. A capacity of sixty-five to eighty liters (about 4,000 to 5,000 cubic inches) should work well for four to seven days. Anything over eighty liters is for a full-blown Alaskan or Himalayan expedition. If you begin venturing out in the winter, you'll probably need a larger-capacity pack just to accommodate all the extra clothing and a larger sleeping bag. The capacity of an external frame's pack bag can be about twenty liters smaller because it's assumed you'll be lashing your sleeping bag and tent to the frame above and below the pack bag. A good way to add convenience and a little extra capacity to an internal-frame pack is to buy the accessory side pockets that many manufacturers offer. These usually attach to the compression straps on the sides of the pack. Side pockets do make you a bit more broad of beam, which is a disadvantage when canyoneering and bushwhacking.

Liters to Cubic Inches		Cubic Inches to Liters	
Liters	Cubic Inches	Cubic Inches	Liters
40	2,441	1,000	16.4
50	3,051	2,000	32.8
55	3,356	2,500	41.0
60	3,661	3,000	49.2
65	3,967	3,500	57.4
70	4,272	4,000	65.5
75	4,577	4,500	73.7
80	4,882	5,000	81.9
85	5,187	5,500	90.1
90	5,492	6,000	98.3

Traveling with Your Pack

Backpackers who travel frequently by air put additional demands on their packs. Airport baggage-handling systems have impeccable records when it comes to handling packs—they've never yet let one through unscarred. In fact, they usually treat packs with the loving care of a lion devouring prime rib. External frames sometimes get bent or broken; airport conveyor belts occasionally shear off a few of the straps and buckles that adorn internal frames. If you must send your pack on an airplane unprotected by a steel case, try to snug down all the straps and tuck the ends inside or tie them together to reduce the length and number of loose ends. A better solution is to wrap your pack, of either type, with a closed-cell foam sleeping pad, then throw the entire mummified affair into a giant duffel bag. Just don't use your Therm-a-Rest or, even worse, your $500 Gore-Tex down sleeping bag as padding. Some airlines now provide large, tough plastic bags, which do little to stop abrasion but do contain all the pack straps so that they cannot be caught in conveyor belts.

Another solution, which dispenses with the need to carry or store a duffel bag once you arrive, is to buy a specialized travel pack. Travel packs, all of which have internal frames, allow you to hide the suspension behind a fabric panel or to remove the suspension completely. At one end of the spectrum, travel packs can be glorified suitcases with uncomfortably skimpy shoulder straps. You wouldn't want to carry one on your back farther than the VIP slots of a small parking lot. At the spectrum's other end are full-featured packs suitable for weeklong treks. Despite pack makers' best efforts, however, even sophisticated travel packs tend to be a compromise between carrying comfort on the trail and durability while traveling. My preference is to protect my expedition-grade pack with a big duffel bag when I travel by air.

Be sure to take the following additional precautions before heading to the airport. First, go to the airline's website to get the latest on checked-bag fees and restrictions. At the time of this writing, most airlines are charging fees for all checked bags, but the fees skyrocket if the bag exceeds fifty pounds. Limits on small planes and overseas flights may be less, depending on the carrier. Some duffel bags and packs have double-pull zippers, with two adjacent sliders that let you unzip the bag from either end. Consider locking those two zipper pulls together to discourage casual theft. Be sure to use a TSA-approved lock, which can be opened by security officers using a master key. If you use an ordinary lock, it may be cut by security personnel so they can inspect the contents of your pack. Don't bring any backpacking fuel on board, whether in your stove, in your fuel bottle, or in the form of butane cartridges, whether attached to your stove or not. Carrying fuel on board is illegal because it creates an extreme fire hazard. After emptying your stove and fuel bottle, triple bag them to prevent fumes from contaminating clothing or food. One plastic bag won't necessarily stop all odors from penetrating your goodies. Bill Baker and I learned this the hard way during a nine-day, 150-mile sea-kayak journey in Kenai Fjords National Park. Bill had just purchased two brand-new fiberglass kayaks. Two days out we discovered that the pilot crackers we'd brought as a mainstay were absorbing fiberglass odors right through the heavy plastic bags in which we'd stored them. Not only did the crackers taste bad, they gave us rude, fiberglass-tainted burps that lasted for hours.

> How hard to realize that every camp of men or beast has this glorious starry firmament for a roof! In such places standing alone on the mountaintop it is easy to realize that whatever special nests we make—leaves and moss like the marmots and birds, or tents or piled stone—we all dwell in a house of one room—the world with the firmament for its roof—and are sailing the celestial spaces without leaving any track.
>
> —*John Muir, 1838–1914*

As a teenager venturing forth on my first backpacking trips, I was inspired by the example of John Muir, who roamed the High Sierra in the 1870s for days on end burdened only by a greatcoat, its pockets stuffed with biscuits. The ponderous sleeping bags and tents of his day were more suited to carting on the back of a mule than on the bowed shoulders of a human being, and Muir rightly preferred to ramble unencumbered. My attempts to emulate his example, however, soon showed me just how miserable such Spartan camping can be.

In August 1979 two friends and I set out to climb Mount Fay in the Canadian Rockies. We started up the approach in the evening, then bivouacked near the base of a steep, ice-floored gully with crumbling rock walls. Our plan was to rise before dawn and complete the ascent of the gully before the morning sun thawed the ice holding the shattered gully walls together, turning the gully into a bowling alley with fifty-pound limestone blocks as bowling balls and ourselves as human bowling pins. With no tent or sleeping bags, we would be traveling light and fast in the best tradition of John Muir.

The problem, as we quickly discovered, was that our bodies needed far more insulation to remain comfortable while sleeping than we expected. We donned every scrap of clothing we'd brought and curled ourselves into the tightest little balls we could, and still we were shivering and squirming. The idea of carrying an extra five or six pounds of sleeping gear, which we had scorned just hours before, suddenly seemed irresistible. "You have to spend at least part of each year living this way," said Joe Kaelin, rolling over for the twentieth time in a futile effort to rewarm those body parts that were nearing frostbite through contact with the cold ground. As I vowed never again to spend a night outdoors without at least a sleeping bag, I wondered if Joe had succumbed to the notion that self-denial would lead to mystic revelations, or if his ambitions extended only to enshrinement in the pantheon of climbing heroes. We rose long before dawn—no need for an alarm clock, as we were all wide awake—and climbed the gully as fast as our sleep-starved bodies would allow us. At midmorning we reached the high mountain hut that sat on the plateau above the gully and promptly took a long nap. After a much more comfortable night in the hut, we climbed Mount Fay the next day.

Muir may well have been much tougher than we were; he was certainly a mystic who verged on asceticism at times. However, he also availed himself freely, I suspect, of a luxury no longer available to the outdoor enthusiast of today: a crackling fire, perhaps built so its warmth would reflect off a granite boulder onto his backside. Fortunately, modern tents and sleeping bags make it easy to camp in comfort using only the gear you can readily carry on your back, since the burgeoning hordes of wilderness enthusiasts make fire building reprehensible in most situations. (I'll have more to say about campfires in chapter 11.)

Camping without a Tent

Today very few backpackers venture into the wilderness without a sleeping bag. A few still insist, however, that a full-fledged tent is an unnecessary burden, at least in some situations. In my young and impoverished days, I sometimes used a tube tent, a 10-foot-long, 5-foot-diameter tube of polyethylene. A string running through the tube and tied between two trees at waist height held the tube erect in the form of a poor man's pup tent. The intolerable flaws of a tube tent soon became apparent: Rainwater flowing along the ground quickly entered the high end of the wide-open tube, then obstinately pooled inside, while mosquitoes circulated in and out freely, each obtaining their pint of blood en route.

The other alternatives to a full-on tent are scarcely an improvement over the tube tent. Some backpackers still use a simple tarp, measuring about 9 by 12 feet in size, erected with the aid of guy lines and tree trunks. The same objections apply, however. In desert regions where rain is a rarity, a few hardy campers advocate the "Visqueen burrito." Spread your sleeping bag out on a plastic ground sheet (Visqueen is one trade name) and hope you won't be rudely awakened by fat raindrops exploding on your face. If you're unlucky, pretend you've just become a gooey mass of beans and cheese and roll yourself up in the ground sheet as if it were a tortilla. If the rainstorm is brief, the Visqueen burrito trick can work adequately and save you considerable weight. If you remain wrapped in your plastic tortilla all night, however, you'll be a very soggy burrito come morning. Condensation inside the impermeable plastic will have soaked your sleeping bag. The high-tech version of the Visqueen burrito is the bivouac sack, a waterproof/breathable bag a little bigger than a sleeping bag that is usually made of Gore-Tex or another waterproof/breathable fabric. Bivy sacks are the favored overnight shelter of alpinists intent on difficult multiday ascents of routes in moderate climates, but they're too small to do anything in them but sleep. If it's raining when it's time for dinner, you put on your rain gear, sit under a tree, and eat in the rain. The only backpackers who use them are extremely weight-conscious types on solo trips in regions where they're not faced with the possibility of waiting out a three-day blow. If you're traveling with a companion, it makes more sense to bring one small tent than two bivy sacks. The weight is about the same, and the comfort is much greater.

Enlightened by my early experiences with tube tents, I became forever skeptical of any wilderness shelter short of a full-fledged tent. The addition of a few extra pounds to the pack in the form of a tent makes the whole trip more enjoyable. The Southwestern deserts, I grant you, can be an exception, as they are bug- and rain-free in most seasons. Camping under the stars there can be a delight. But for all mountain trips, in any season, I bring a tent.

Basic Tent Designs

Once upon a time, in the days when all tent poles were as straight and rigid as a drill sergeant's spine, the A-frame or pup tent was the standard American backcountry tent. A-frames usually have two poles at each end in the form of an inverted V, plus a ridge pole forming the tent's backbone. While similar tents have been used for thousands of years, A-frames suffer from several inherent disadvantages. First, the

The advent of flexible aluminum tent poles made traditional A-frame tents like this one (shown without a fly) nearly obsolete.

broad, flat areas of unsupported fabric provide a perfect target for the wind, which sets the fabric to flapping loudly like a flag in a hurricane, robbing the beleaguered occupants of sleep. Second, the design uses materials inefficiently. Usable interior space is small in relation to the tent's weight, since the uniformly sloping walls restrict the occupants' ability to sit up anywhere but the middle of the tent. Finally, pitching an A-frame properly usually requires many stakes and guy lines, which are guaranteed to trip you up when you stagger groggily out of the tent at 2 a.m. to relieve yourself.

Like A-frames, pyramid tents reigned in the days when the only available tent poles were straight. As the name implies, pyramids resemble a miniaturized version of some pharaoh's monument to his ego, with a single central pole supporting the tent's peak. The same disadvantages that have relegated A-frames to the dust bin of tent design have forced retirement onto the pyramid, with one exception: A few pyramidal-shaped, floorless tarps supported by a single central pole can still be seen on occasion.

The invention of strong, flexible aluminum poles set tent designers loose on an orgy of innovation that still hasn't stopped. Dome tents, shaped like a half sphere,

Pyramid tent designs have largely been superseded by dome, tunnel, hybrid, and hub designs.

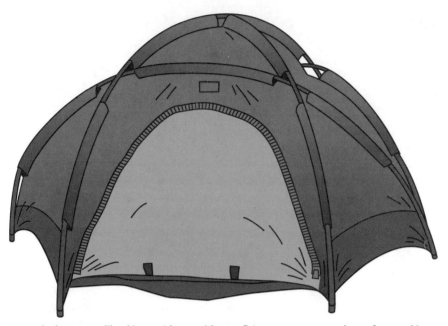

Four-pole dome tents like this one (shown without a fly) are very strong and are often used in the winter.

offer the greatest interior volume of any tent for a given surface area of tent fabric, which gives them a good volume-to-weight ratio. The tent walls are almost vertical near the ground, so occupants can sit up anywhere in the tent, greatly increasing the usable amount of floor space compared to an A-frame or pyramid. Geodesic domes, or geodomes, are supported by an interlocking structure of three or four poles that intersect to form triangles. This design means that only small areas of fabric are unsupported by poles. Dome tents easily shrug off high winds and resist the weight of accumulating snow. Most winter and expedition tents are geodomes. All domes are freestanding, which means they don't need to be staked in order to stand upright; however, all must be staked to prevent them from taking off like a kite when the breeze blows. When empty, freestanding tents can be picked up and moved without disassembling them, a convenient feature if the first site you pick proves to be an anthill.

Tunnel tents or hoop tents, shaped like a half cylinder, run a close second to dome tents in their volume-to-surface-area measurements. They often use fewer poles than domes, which gives them larger areas of unsupported fabric but saves weight. Designers have also experimented with nearly every other possible design

Tunnel tents are lighter but usually not as strong as dome tents (shown here without a fly).

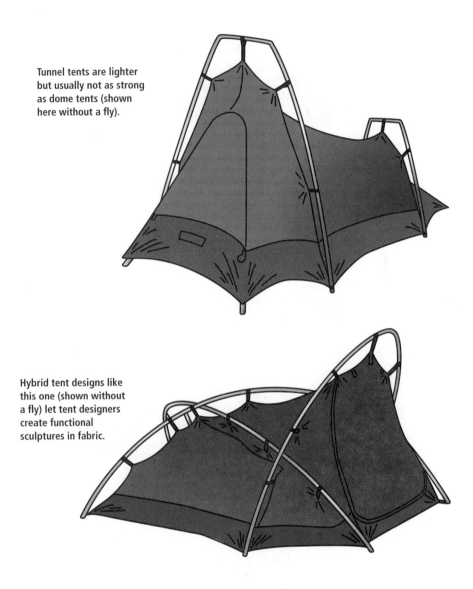

Hybrid tent designs like this one (shown without a fly) let tent designers create functional sculptures in fabric.

using continuous-arc poles, producing a wide variety of hybrids that fall somewhere between the basic dome and tunnel shapes. Many tents intended for summer use employ tunnel or hybrid designs.

In recent years yet another variation has debuted: hub tents, in which flexible poles radiate from one or more molded plastic or aluminum hubs located along the tent's spine. The pole structure gives some hub tents the look of sinister sci-fi insects; one designer named his creation the Preying Mantis. The principal

Hub tents can be a bit lighter than dome tents because not all poles must terminate at the ground; some can terminate at a hub, saving the weight of the extra length of pole. (This tent is shown with a fly.)

advantage claimed for hub designs is that the poles cannot move in relation to each other where they intersect, since they're connected via a rigid hub. This increases the tent's rigidity and therefore its ability to resist wind and shed snow. Hub designs can also be lighter, since not all poles have to reach to the ground; instead, they can terminate at a hub. In most hub designs the poles remain attached to the hub at one end with elastic shock cord. Theoretically at least, this can simplify pitching.

The Battle against Condensation

Condensation in tents has bedeviled designers ever since Julius Caesar set out to conquer Gaul. Condensation occurs when warm, moist air encounters a cooler surface and is cooled below the dew point, the temperature at which the air becomes saturated with moisture and dew begins to form. In a tent your breath is the most common (and unavoidable) source of warm, moist air. A person can exhale a pint of moisture per night. Evaporation of sweat and moisture from rain-soaked clothing further humidifies the air and increases the threat of condensation. Cooking inside a tent adds still more water vapor to the air, but that's by far the least of your worries. Running a stove in a poorly ventilated tent poses an extreme danger of poisoning by carbon monoxide. Cooking in any tent, even with the door and windows wide open, creates a serious fire hazard and should be avoided.

Most tents sold today fight condensation with a double-walled design that uses a waterproof rain fly over a non-waterproof tent body, called the canopy. In theory warm, moist air will rise through the uncoated canopy and condense on the fly. In temperatures above freezing it will then roll down the inside of the fly and drip onto the ground instead of the occupants. In temperatures below freezing the moisture will congeal into frost. If the wind shakes off the frost, it will land on the canopy and slide harmlessly down to the ground. The theory works, in most conditions, although you then have to deal with a wet or frosty rain fly in the morning. Be sure that any tent you're considering provides a good separation between the fly and canopy. If they touch, either when the tent is buffeted by the wind or when you brush up against the tent wall, condensation on the fly is sure to penetrate the canopy.

In severe cold, as well as in certain other conditions of cool temperatures and high humidity, the canopy's temperature can be below the dew point, so that moisture condenses on the canopy instead of passing through to the fly. I still remember waking up at 17,200 feet on Mount McKinley to find a veritable snowstorm raging inside the tent. Moisture from three deep-breathing bodies had condensed to a thick frost on the canopy. As the tent trembled under assault by the ever-present wind, the frost sifted down and covered everything. Opening our tightly closed sleeping bag hoods even a crack permitted a cascade of ice crystals to pour onto our faces. The only solution was to use the whisk broom we'd brought for just this purpose to dust off our sleeping bags and gear, then sweep the floor and shovel the piles of frost crystals out the door.

Tent makers also try to prevent condensation by providing ventilation in various ways. The problem is providing a way to let warm air escape without permitting rain to enter. Vents that penetrate the canopy but not the fly do little good. Opening the door can help if the fly extends as an awning over the door to prevent the entry of rain. Opening doors or windows on opposite sides of the tent (if the tent is so equipped) permits cross-ventilation, which works well if the night is graced by a breeze. The best venting systems combine roof-level and floor-level vents, so that warm, rising air can naturally flow out the top vent while cooler air flows in the bottom. Very few tents have a high/low venting system, however, because such vents are hard to seal against rain.

One group of tents that do have such a vent system is made by Stephenson Warmlite Equipment in Gilford, New Hampshire. Stephenson tents are unusual in another way: Both walls of his double-walled tents are made of waterproof material. The idea is to prevent condensation by keeping the inner wall warmer than the dew point. Stephenson tents try to achieve that by capitalizing on the "storm window effect," in which two panes of glass (or tent fabric) trap still air between them. That still air acts as an insulator, keeping the inner layer of fabric warm. To further increase the inner layer's temperature, Stephenson uses an aluminized fabric that acts as a radiant-heat barrier. I've used Stephenson tents on three expeditions to the Alaska Range and found that they keep condensation to a minimum. One final virtue: Stephenson tents use pre-bent, large-diameter poles that are some four times as strong as the typical flexible aluminum poles found in most other tents, yet are exceedingly light. The two-person Stephenson tent weighs under three pounds. On the negative side, the tents are expensive, and the lightweight waterproof coating on the ultralight fabric will wear through more quickly than heavier coatings, requiring more frequent touch-up with seam sealant.

Another approach to condensation is to build a single-wall tent from a waterproof/breathable fabric. Until 1986, W. L. Gore made a Gore-Tex tent fabric that several manufacturers used in a variety of tents. Unfortunately, those tents could not pass the rather arbitrary fire-retardancy tests that conventional tents could, and so could not be sold in a handful of states. Eventually Gore took the fabric off the market. Most tent manufacturers abandoned any attempt to make tents of waterproof/breathable material, but not Todd Bibler, a mountaineer turned paraglider pilot who found a way to produce his own version of Gore's tent fabric that he called Todd-Tex—essentially Gore-Tex by another name. Bibler tents, now manufactured by Black Diamond, are well made but quite expensive. I've used Bibler tents extensively in both winter and summer and found that the fabric breathes well and condensation is minimal. Today a number of other manufacturers make single-wall tents out of some kind of waterproof/breathable fabric, although not all the fabrics are as reliably waterproof and breathable as Todd-Tex.

The absolute lightest tents are single-wall tents made from an ultralight, nonbreathable fabric. The low weight is seductive, but beware: These tents will have the worst condensation problems. Choose one only if saving weight is more important than comfort in camp.

Choosing a Tent

Which tent design is best for you? It depends on when and where you want to camp, how much weight you're willing to carry, and how much you're willing to spend. Three-season tents, designed for spring, summer, and fall, typically try to save weight by using tunnel, hybrid, or hub designs that require only two or three poles. On the downside these lightweight tents start to whimper and whine when the wind cranks up, and knuckle under quickly when menaced by a bully of a snowstorm. Weights for good-quality three-season tents range from three to six pounds. Floor areas in the two-person models run from under 30 square feet, which is adequate but snug, up to a spacious 45 square feet. Larger tents, naturally, are more comfortable in camp, but the extra weight means longer and harder hours on the trail. Which size tent is right for you depends in part on your backpacking style. Do you like to hike a short distance, set up a base camp for a several-night stay, and day-hike from that camp each day? Or do you prefer to move camp every day and cover lots of miles between camps?

Many three-season tents have canopies made largely of mosquito netting. When the weather is fair, you can remove the fly and enjoy every cooling breeze while gloating over the frustration of the mosquitoes pressing their hungry little noses up against the netting. In winter, however, these tents are cold, and spindrift kicked up by the wind and blown up under the fly tends to sift down on the occupants—two more reasons that netting-canopy tents are only intended for three-season use. During windy periods in the desert, blowing dust and fine sand can also penetrate the mosquito netting, coating everything with a layer of grit. A vestibule—an extension of the rain fly over the ground in front of the door, like an awning on a porch—is particularly valuable in rainy weather, providing a relatively dry place to cook and store some gear.

Four-season tents, which are really designed primarily for one season—winter—are mostly domes that use four or even five interlocking poles that provide a great deal of strength and rigidity at the cost of greater weight, which varies from five to nine pounds. Floor areas for two-person models range from 45 to 55 square feet (including the vestibule) to provide extra room for bulky winter gear and to help prevent tent fever. Long, cold winter nights force winter campers to spend far more hours inside their tents than do summer campers. In winter the subtleties of tent design become more important. For example, you should be able to pitch a good winter tent without removing your gloves. Avoid tents with a flat spot at the apex of the roof, which will collect snow. Doors set into a sloping wall also tend to collect snow, which must be knocked off before the door is opened or else snow will fall into the tent. Doors set into vertical walls, particularly if the door opens from the top down, create fewer problems.

Don't assume that any backpacking tent you buy, whether rated four-season or not, will stand up to everything. Tents that will take the worst possible winds are more aptly described as buildings. The tent that famed British explorer Eric Shipton used while sledging across the Patagonian ice cap weighed fifty pounds. The Whillans Box that some expeditions laboriously hauled to their high camp on

Everest weighed thirty pounds. If a tent is light enough to be readily carried on your back, there is a gale out there, somewhere, that can destroy it.

Whether you're looking at a four-season or a three-season tent, virtually all high-quality tent poles today are made of aluminum. Fiberglass poles are generally weaker and heavier but less expensive. Other signs of quality include tight, even stitching with no fabric puckers that can concentrate stresses and create starting points for tears. The rain fly should generously overlap the coated portion of the canopy walls. If at all possible, pitch the tent you're considering at the store before buying it. A good tent should set up easily and be as tight as your belly after Thanksgiving dinner. Slack fabric will flap in the wind and drive you nuts. Climb inside with a friend and try to imagine living in the tent during a prolonged storm. If you start contemplating murder-by-tent-peg after five minutes, buy a bigger tent.

Caring for Your Tent

Good tents will give you many years of service if you take the time to care for them properly. Many of the better models now come with factory-sealed seams. If your tent did not, be sure to seal the seams with one of the products available in backpacking shops before using your tent for the first time. Reapply sealant as needed. Seam sealing is like paying taxes: It's surprising how quickly the time passes before duty calls again. Let the sealant dry thoroughly before packing away the tent. Uncured sealant is an effective glue.

Do your best to keep your tent clean. Don't wear your dirty, muddy boots inside; the grit will grind away at the coating. After each night's camp, shake all the loose sand and dirt out of the tent before stuffing it back into its stuff sack. Pay particular attention to keeping the zippers clean. Zippers are fragile under the best of circumstances, and dirty zippers wear out faster. The first item to fail on your tent is likely to be a zipper. Tent floors are more easily punctured than you might think. During the expedition to McKinley that I guided in 1983, my assistant kicked her heel on the tent floor trying to force her feet into her stiff, heavy mountaineering boots. She put her heel right through the floor. Sharp rocks and sticks can also cause tears if you pitch your tent atop them. A little ripstop repair tape, available at most backpacking shops, can patch small tears until you can get home and repair the tent permanently.

Avoid scraping the protective coating off the aluminum poles. The coating is important to prevent corrosion, which can lead to the sudden failure of the poles through a phenomenon called stress-corrosion cracking. Keep the pole joints clean so they don't jam together. When assembling a folded bundle of pole segments, don't hold on to the last segment and flip the bundle of segments forward, letting the pole assemble itself through the action of the elastic shock cord. This tactic is guaranteed to get dirt in the joints and allows the pole-segment ends to nick each other, causing the shock cord to fray. Instead, assemble the pole segments by hand, one by one, making sure each joint is clean. When you get home, pitch the tent in your backyard if the weather's dry, or in a spare bedroom or garage if it's raining. Gently sponge off any mud or dirt and let the tent dry thoroughly. Storing a tent while it's wet will cause the coating to mildew and peel like sunburned skin. Maintaining a tent is like nailing down the loose shingles on your roof: It reduces the chance that you'll wake up one night to the ominous drip, drip, drip that spells trouble.

> Life is either a daring adventure or nothing. Security does not
> exist in nature, nor do the children of men as a whole experience
> it. Avoiding danger is no safer in the long run than exposure.
>
> —*Helen Keller (1880–1968)*

In July 1978, when I embarked on my first expedition to the Alaska Range, nearly all mountaineers used sleeping bags filled with down, the fluffy underfeathers of ducks and geese. By comparison, sleeping bags filled with the synthetic alternatives of the day were quite heavy and bulky for the warmth they offered. Synthetics did offer one advantage, however, which became apparent soon after a bush pilot deposited our four-man team on the Ruth Glacier near Mount Huntington.

The day after we landed, the sun vanished and a weeklong onslaught of wet snow and rain began. Despite good rain gear and our best efforts, we gradually got wet. The inside of the tents became damp, then soggy, then positively swampy. Inevitably our sleeping bags became soaked. The three owners of down bags saw the loft of their bags shrink every day, until the bags became frigid sheets of nylon enclosing saturated feathers. I still have a photograph of Angus Thuermer wringing water out of his worthless down bag. Joe Kaelin's synthetic bag, on the other hand, retained its loft and, therefore, a bit more of its warmth. When the sun finally did return, Joe's bag dried much faster than our down ones. The moral, of course, is simple: If you let your down bag get wet, it will become just a watered-down version of its former self.

As this anecdote shows, the climate where you'll be backpacking helps determine whether a synthetic or down-filled bag is best for you. Despite the fiasco with the down bag I carried on Mount Huntington, I've brought a down bag on every subsequent trip to the Alaska Range. Why? Because all my other trips were to much higher and colder peaks, where rain never falls and where keeping a down bag dry was much easier than it was on Huntington.

In some ways, choosing a sleeping bag is more difficult than selecting a pack or tent, where every feature is exposed to view. With a sleeping bag, however, you can see only the shell and lining fabrics, leading to the crucial question: What is really inside this thing? Goose down? Chicken feathers? Recycled Kentucky Fried Chicken napkins? Your best defense is a good offense: Go to a well-established specialty outdoor shop that is staking its reputation on providing quality products. Discount store bags are for carrying on the backs of vehicles; they're too ponderous to tote on your back.

The Ups of Down

Your first task is choosing the filling. High-quality down still provides more warmth for its weight than any synthetic insulation yet devised, and it compresses into a smaller bundle. In addition, down is wonderfully soft, draping comfortably around your body in ways that the lower-grade synthetics can't begin to match. If you take good care of a down bag, it will retain its loft far longer than a synthetic one. However, if you find that you retire bags after three or four years because the shell has become stained or ripped, then spending the money on a long-lasting fill may be a waste.

Down's negatives are equally clear. As I found out in chilling fashion on Mount Huntington, a down bag collapses and loses all its loft when it gets soaked. A down bag also dries more slowly than a synthetic one and costs considerably more initially, although its cost per year, given good care, may actually be lower because of its longer life. Manufacturers are also beginning to experiment with ways to treat down to make it hydrophobic. That should mean it will resist absorbing water and dry faster than untreated down.

Down quality is measured by the volume that can be filled by one ounce of down. Very low-quality down may fill 450 cubic inches per ounce, a number so low that many places selling such gear won't even give the down a number. These days you're better off buying a synthetic bag than one filled with 450-cubic-inch down. Medium-quality down lofts about 550 cubic inches per ounce. Better down lofts 650 cubic inches per ounce. Some manufacturers are offering 800-fill down, and one even claims they have 850-fill down, the highest quality—and most expensive— down regularly available in sleeping bags. It's fun, of course, to own the best gear, but you should keep in mind what the weight difference between 550- and 800-fill down really amounts to. On a sleeping bag rated to be comfortable down to 20°F, (a typical summer-weight backpacking bag), using 800 down instead of 550 saves about ten ounces, or a little more than a cup of water. On a full-blown, keep-you-warm-when-hell's-freezing-over expedition bag rated to −40°F, it saves you about twenty-two ounces, or just under a pint and a half of water.

Your best assurance that the down you buy really will loft as advertised is the reputation of the manufacturer and the shop. There's no way that you, as a consumer, can independently test the manufacturer's claims. However, you can sometimes distinguish low-grade down from higher-grade down by the feel. A cheap down bag will often contain feathers as well as down. Feathers don't provide the same amount of loft that down does, and they break down much faster. A bag containing a significant amount of feathers will feel stiff, like it contains straw. Don't be seduced by labels like "prime, northern, gray, or white," which have no legal definition and aren't necessarily an indicator of quality. Goose down is normally considered superior to duck down because the down plumules from the larger bird are larger and therefore loftier, but good duck down is better than bad goose down. The stated fill power is your best indication of quality.

Alternatives to Down

New synthetic insulations debut regularly with great fanfare. Some stand the test of time; others quietly vanish. Many sleeping bag manufacturers now use their own proprietary names, which makes it hard to know what's really in their bags. Two broad categories of synthetic insulation have existed for many years, however, and so are worth discussing here.

All synthetic insulation used in backpacking sleeping bags is made of some form of very thin polyester fibers. Short-staple insulation uses short lengths of fibers. Continuous-filament insulation is a batting made of long, continuous strands of polyester, sometimes held together by a sprayed-on resin. The current king of short-staple insulators is PrimaLoft; Climashield is the current champ in the continuous-filament category. Continuous-filament insulation has a well-established reputation for durability, and the newer (and more expensive) versions are softer and more compressible than the old standbys like Polarguard. Short-staple insulation is softer and drapes better around your body than the continuous-filament contenders, but generally won't retain its loft as long. Both types of synthetic insulation have the virtues of drying fast and retaining more of their insulation value when wet than down. Neither provides as much warmth for a given weight as top-quality down nor do they compress as well as down. If you want a synthetic bag because you need to save money or you'll be camping in a very damp climate, go to a specialty shop and find out what insulation is currently the top dog in the synthetic sleeping bag wars.

Temperature Ratings

Nearly all manufacturers supply a temperature rating with their bags. In the past these ratings were based on the manufacturer's estimate of what the average person would need on an average night when the moon is full and Pisces is rising in the east. There was usually nothing too scientific in how they arrived at their guess, and even if there was, your own experience could easily differ. There were also lots of variables: Were you using a tent or sleeping under the stars? If you were in a tent, how many people in what size tent? How thick was your sleeping pad? How much clothing do you like to wear when you sleep? Do you sleep warm or cold? Are you a man or a woman? Recent testing has shown that the average woman needs a bit more insulation than the average man to be comfortable at a particular temperature.

These murky waters have cleared a good deal in the last few years as more and more manufacturers have adopted EN (European Norm) 13537 as a standardized testing procedure for three-season sleeping bags. (At this time winter bags, rated to 0°F or below, can't be tested accurately using available equipment.) In the EN 13537 procedure, which is conducted by independent, internationally certified labs, a mannequin dressed in one layer of long underwear and a hat is placed in the sleeping bag, which is set atop a sleeping pad in a climate-controlled chamber. The mannequin is heated, and sensors record the mannequin's skin temperature as well as the air temperature within the chamber. This data allows researchers to calculate the amount of insulation provided by the sleeping bag. The EN 13537 test produces three numbers. The first, called the comfort rating, is the lowest temperature at which the average woman can sleep comfortably. The second, called the lower limit, is the lowest temperature at which the average man can sleep comfortably. The third, called the extreme rating, is the lowest temperature at which the average woman could survive. We're not talking comfortable, mind you. This is a rating for a true emergency situation, not an enjoyable backpacking trip.

The adoption of a standardized testing protocol makes it possible for the first time to compare sleeping bags from different manufacturers on an apples-to-apples basis. So how warm a bag do you really need?

Most people can make an educated guess, based on comparisons with companions at home and during car-camping trips, whether they sleep warmer or cooler than average. Cora, for example, used to sleep comfortably beside me in a bag with nearly double the amount of insulation mine had. She used a bag rated to 0°F for summer backpacking even though the temperature almost never dipped below freezing, and she was rarely too warm. (More recently she has needed less insulation than I do—go figure). At the opposite extreme I've slept in a tent at 17,000 feet on McKinley in a sleeping bag rated to −15°F when the temperature outside the tent was −40°F. I got some sleep, but I can't say I was terribly comfortable, and I was wearing every scrap of clothing I'd brought, including four layers of long underwear and fleece on both my legs and torso, full shell clothing, and four fleece hats and hoods. Each person also varies in their need for insulation from time to time. If you go to bed wet, cold, exhausted, poorly fed, and dehydrated, you'll need a lot warmer bag to be comfortable than if you go to bed warm, dry, and full to the brim with a final cup of hot chocolate.

Gear junky and weight fanatic that I am, I have to admit that I actually own three sleeping bags. I have an ultralight, summer-only down bag rated to 30°F that weighs only one pound, seven ounces—an unheard-of weight for a sleeping bag when I wrote the second edition of this book. I have a "two-season" down bag I use in the fall and spring that's rated to 15°F. It weighs two pounds, thirteen ounces. And finally I have a luxurious, down-filled haven from winter's biting cold that's rated to −40°F. It tips the scales at four pounds, eleven ounces.

For most backpackers an Everest-rated sleeping bag is like a dental appointment: expensive and uncomfortable. Sleeping in a bag that's too warm can be surprisingly miserable. Opening just one side to ventilate is like trying to warm yourself at a fire: The side of you near the zipper freezes, while the side tucked into the bag sweats profusely. Excessively warm bags are also unnecessarily heavy and bulky. Your best bet is to buy a bag rated for the lowest temperature you'll encounter regularly. On extra-cold nights, wear more clothing. If your wallet allows it and your obsession with the sport demands it, you may eventually want to follow my lead and buy a bag for every season.

Vapor-Barrier and Radiant-Barrier Liners

Winter backpackers can add a lot of warmth to their sleeping bags by using a vapor-barrier (VB) liner: a 6-foot-long bag made of a waterproof, nonbreathable coated material. A VB liner stops the heat loss caused by evaporation of insensible perspiration, the water you constantly lose through your skin just because your skin is not watertight like a plastic bag. A VB liner also stops the evaporation of sensible perspiration, the kind you produce when you're overheating, so you will need to regulate your temperature carefully by shedding clothing if you start to sweat. Used properly, a VB liner can allow you to sleep comfortably in temperatures 10° or 15°F lower than you could without a liner. Used improperly, a VB liner will awaken you with the feeling you've encamped in tropical Borneo.

Vapor-barrier liners provide a crucial additional benefit: They help keep your sleeping bag dry. In severe cold, without a VB liner, the moisture that escapes from your body will condense inside your insulation, whether it's down or a synthetic, reducing its effectiveness. During my second expedition to Alaska, in 1980, the down bags used by my two companions collapsed completely as moisture built up during our thirteen-day epic ascent of the south face of Mount Hunter. Peter Metcalf said later that his bag became so useless he would simply have thrown it away if it hadn't cost so much. During Will Steger's dogsled expedition to the North Pole, the team's synthetic sleeping bags accumulated thirty-five pounds of ice through condensation because the team wasn't using VB liners. In 1982, when both Peter and I used VB liners inside our bags during our ascent of Reality Ridge on McKinley, both of our bags stayed dry and lofty, in large part because of the liners, but also because we took every possible opportunity to dry our bags.

For a time in the early 1980s, manufacturers experimented with a different kind of liner, one designed to block the loss of heat in the form of infrared radiation. Texolite was the most common brand name. The material did indeed prove its worth in the synthetic sleeping bags of the day, where adding the weight of the liner provided more additional warmth than adding an equivalent weight of insulation. The same was not true of good down bags, however, where a user needing additional warmth was better off adding more down than adding Texolite.

Texolite's problem, at least in the minds of summer users, was that the material was also a pretty effective vapor barrier. People complained that Texolite bags had too limited a comfort range: They found themselves overheating too easily. Partisans of vapor barriers like equipment designer Jack Stephenson would argue that all these complainers wanted was the license to sweat and soak their insulation, and that the better solution would have been for overheated users to take off some clothing. Despite such cogent arguments, however, the consumer rules in our society, and Texolite and its competitors have gone the way of the dodo bird, at least for now. I mention it here because radiant-heat barriers are like bell-bottom pants: They resurface periodically just like funky fashions in blue jeans.

Size, Shape, and Fit

Your sleeping bag's shape and fit greatly influence its warmth. Form-fitting bags contoured to fit a human body are called mummies because, like your mother when you were a kid, they hug you close and keep you warm (actually, they were named for the preserved bodies of dead Egyptians, which they resemble in shape, but I'd rather fall asleep thinking about my definition than the real one). More expansive bags, for those of substantial girth or those who like more wiggle room, are known variously as wide mummies or barrels (I can see my mother frowning); even more capacious bags are known as semi-rectangular bags. Fully rectangular bags (named, of course, for really square moms) are for slumber parties and warm-weather car-camping. They're too bulky and heavy for backpacking.

Snug-fitting bags are generally warmer than loose-fitting ones, in part because there is less cold air and icy sleeping bag surrounding you when you first climb in, so the bags warm up faster. More important, a snug-fitting bag, combined with an effective hood, helps prevent your movements from pumping warm air out of the mouth of the bag, then drawing cold air in. A bag that's too snug, however, will give you claustrophobia, so be sure to slip inside the bag at the shop before buying. Most good shops will let you try on a bag if you take off your shoes and look civilized. In recent years more and more manufacturers have begun making sleeping bags specifically for women. These bags are a bit narrower at the shoulder, wider at the hips, and shorter overall to accommodate a woman's shape. Women will find that the extra comfort and weight efficiency make these bags well worth seeking out.

Many winter campers like to buy an extra-long bag to provide room at the foot for items that should be kept from freezing, such as water bottles. Like most winter campers and high-altitude mountaineers, I always wear my foam inner boots to bed, which helps keep my feet warm and also helps the inner boots dry out. Wearing liners also requires extra foot room.

Several more details are worth considering. A hood is an integral part of all good mummy bags. It's designed so that tightening a drawstring cinches down the bag's mouth until only your face is exposed. In addition to a hood, good winter bags often have a draft collar, an insulation-filled collar that closes down over your shoulders and around your neck to further reduce the escape of warm air. Most bags are supplied with full-length zippers to make it easier to get in and out of them. That zipper can be another avenue of heat loss unless it's protected by a draft tube, a long, insulation-filled tube on the inside of the bag that covers the zipper. Cold feet seem to be a perennial problem on chilly nights. Better bags often have extra insulation in the foot area. Don't worry unduly about the other details of construction, such as which particular baffle system is used in a down bag, or whether a synthetic bag is described as having shingle or double-overlapping quilt construction. All the methods used by reputable manufacturers work just fine.

Most sleeping bags have an outer shell of porous nylon that makes no claim to be waterproof. Even as a novice I knew that sleeping unprotected in the rain would guarantee a soaking wet bag. But what about in winter? Shouldn't it be possible to sleep in the open, since it would be so cold that snow wouldn't melt on the bag? Such a tactic, if successful, would save the weight of a tent during winter climbs.

In 1977 Joe Kaelin and I set out to test that theory on our first effort to climb a major route in Rocky Mountain National Park in the wintertime. Already impressed with the cold, we bivouacked at the base of the face under a boulder, then started up the climb at first light. Darkness caught us only halfway up the route, and we searched futilely for some kind of sheltered bivouac site. At last we gave up, scooped out two body-size ledges in the midst of an unprotected gully, and crawled into our bags.

At midnight I awoke feeling that my sleeping bag had grown tremendously heavy. Spindrift pouring down the narrow slot above us had completely buried our bags. I pushed away the snow as I best I could from inside the bag and tried to go back to sleep, but in vain. Two hours later, with sleep impossible and our bags rapidly becoming drenched, we began soloing up the face by headlamp. We reached the summit a few hours after sunrise.

As we had so convincingly demonstrated, enough body heat escapes through your sleeping bag to melt snow or frost lying on the shell fabric. You don't need to do anything as foolish as exposing your bag to a nonstop spindrift cascade to get your bag damp in the winter. Frost sifts down from tent walls, while spindrift blows in each time the door is opened. Water drips from snow cave roofs while wind carries snow into the entrance. Even in summer, condensation dripping from tent walls can gradually dampen your bag. A sleeping bag with a waterproof/breathable or water-resistant shell will help keep your bag dry. Such bags are also a bit warmer because the shell is windproof, but I wouldn't buy such a bag just for that reason.

If you and your mate are like otters, who like to sleep half on top of each other, you may be interested in buying sleeping bags that can zip together into one giant love nest. One bag must have a right-hand zipper, the other a left. In addition, the zippers must be the same size. Most sleeping bag manufacturers offer bags that will zip together. Another option for highly compatible couples is to buy a semi-rectangular bag that can be unzipped completely so it lies flat like a comforter. The unfolded bag is then zipped to a simple cotton or nylon sheet with a zipper along its perimeter. The result is, again, a giant love nest, but this time one that has insulation only

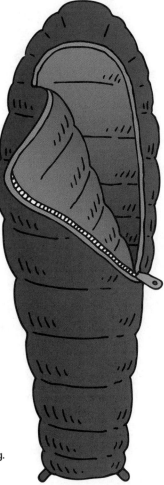

A mummy-style sleeping bag.

on top. The sheets that make this transformation possible are known variously as doublers, couplers, or couplets. The advantage of a doubler is that it lets you carry sleeping gear for two that weighs just a pound more than sleeping gear for one. Cora and I find that doublers work well down to about 40°F or so. Below that we sleep cold because it's impossible to cinch down the mouth of the bag to prevent the escape of warm air.

Sleeping Pads

Regardless of the sleeping bag you choose, the insulation will always smash flat beneath you. To prevent a close encounter with the cold, stony ground, you need a sleeping pad, which fortunately will set you back far less than your sleeping bag did.

As a kid you may have slept in your backyard on a slab of open-cell foam or a 3-inch-thick air mattress that made you dizzy as a top from the effort of inflating it. If either of these two items is still lingering in your closet, let it linger. Open-cell foam—the kind that crushes under body weight to about one-quarter of its original thickness—is generally too heavy, water-absorbing, and bulky for backpacking. Normal air mattresses, while comfortable in warm weather, are chilly when the ground is cold because air circulates freely inside them, drawing heat from your body through convection.

For years all I ever used as a sleeping pad while backpacking in the summer was a sheet of ½-inch-thick closed-cell foam. Closed-cell foam is lightweight and cheap, doesn't absorb water, and is highly durable. It's also rather uncomfortable to sleep on if you, like me, have spent years being spoiled rotten on an acre-wide Sealy Pamperpedic that hogs three-quarters of the bedroom floor. In the backcountry I always secretly envied my friends the luxury afforded by their Therm-a-Rests—essentially air mattresses filled with open-cell foam—even as I derided them as heavy, leak prone, even a touch bourgeois. My friends just smiled, indulging me in my tirades. Finally my inflated ego collapsed under the complaints of my bruised hips, and Cora and I bought a pair of Therm-a-Rests.

What luxury! Sure, they weighed two pounds five ounces each rather than ten ounces like my old closed-cell foam pad, but the comfort was worth it (or maybe I was just so much more tired after lugging the extra weight up the trail that I could sleep on porcupine hide). The open-cell foam prevents convection, so the pads are warm, while the waterproof, airtight shell keeps the foam dry. After our first seductive taste of backwoods luxury, Cora and I plunged farther into decadence and bought Therm-a-Rest chairs, ten-ounce fabric and webbing devices that convert a Therm-a-Rest into a legless chair that sits directly on the ground. No more aching backs while cooking dinner or lazing about watching the sunset! In the years since our original purchase, Therm-a-Rest has come out with lighter and lighter models. The very latest three-quarter-length pad now weighs a minuscule eight ounces. The fabric is so thin it's actually translucent. Like all ultralight gear it requires meticulous care to keep it intact. Therm-a-Rest is no longer the only brand of foam-filled air mattress available, but they do have a proven track record. A leaky or inferior brand could prove to be a letdown.

Therm-a-Rests now come in a variety of thicknesses. The thinner ones are great for summer but don't provide quite enough insulation for winter. My solution is to take my three-quarter-length luxury Therm-a-Rest, which is about 2 inches thick, and pair it with an old-fashioned, full-length closed-cell foam pad. It's a bulky and rather heavy arrangement (about two and a half pounds), but it ensures a comfortable night's sleep, even on a 0°F night.

I find a pillow even more essential for comfortable sleep in the woods than I do at home. For years my nightly backcountry ritual included meticulous construction of a pillow from extra clothing. I would neatly fold up my rain jacket and pants, place them inside a stuff sack, then place the stuff sack inside a fleece sweater with the arms folded just so. The fleece sweater provided additional padding and was much more comfortable against my face than a cold, slick nylon stuff sack. True, the slider on my rain jacket's zipper always seemed to end up against my cheekbone, which, like the proverbial pea under the princess's mattress, made it impossible to sleep. Then one day I discovered a tiny inflatable pillow weighing just two and a half ounces in an outdoor shop, and my days of struggling to sleep on a lumpy, makeshift pillow came to an end.

Sleeping Bag Care

Caring for your sleeping bag starts with proper storage. Never store your bag by stuffing it into its stuff sack and tossing it in the closet. The sustained compression of the insulation, whether down or a synthetic, will cause the bag to lose its loft. Instead, store your bag by hanging it in a closet, stashing it under your bed (laid out flat, not stuffed), or by placing it in the extra-large cotton storage sack sold by most sleeping bag manufacturers. Heat and compression combined are worse than compression alone. Don't store your stuffed bag in the trunk of your car during the summer, as you might be tempted to do if you are alternating backpacking pilgrimages with visits to city fleshpots during a two-week vacation.

You can also prolong your bag's life by keeping it clean. That means always sleeping in a tent or on a ground sheet, not directly on dirt, and wearing clothing when you go to bed. It's a lot easier to wash long underwear than it is to wash a sleeping bag. Alternatively, buy a sleeping bag liner made of cotton or polyester. Spot-clean stained areas as soon as possible after they get dirty rather than washing the entire bag. Airing your bag in the sun for a few hours after each trip will help kill any musty odors that develop.

When and if your entire bag finally does need washing, usually after years of hard use, the safest bet is to wash it by hand in your bathtub. Use one of the special down soaps available in specialty shops. These soaps dissolve easily and rinse out well, so they don't cause the insulation to clump. Do not use bleach. Fill the tub with warm water and immerse the bag gently. Knead the soapy water into the bag, then drain and rinse repeatedly until no more soap bubbles percolate through the shell. Press—don't wring—the water from the bag and gently lift it from the tub. Wet down is heavy, and the weight of it can rip the baffles loose from their moorings if the bag is manhandled. Air drying is safest. If that's not feasible, dry the bag in a tumble dryer on low or no heat, which can take several hours. Monitor the temperature of your bag carefully. Too high a heat can actually melt the nylon. Be sure the bag is thoroughly dry before storing it. With a down bag you may need to fluff the bag vigorously to break up clumps of down and restore the full loft.

Alternatively, take your bag to a commercial Laundromat with a large-capacity, front-loading washing machine. Do not use a top-loading, agitator-type machine, which can easily ruin your bag through rough handling. Front-loading machines tumble your bag and put much less stress on batts of synthetic insulation and the fragile baffles that hold your down in place. As before, use a special down soap. Your goal is not only to get soap into the bag to get it clean, but also to get all the soap back out. Soap residues in any bag can cause loss of loft.

Dry cleaning is not advisable. Some experts argue that dry cleaning strips oil from down and makes it brittle. Others argue that few dry cleaners take the care to make sure that all the dissolved dirt is rinsed out of the bag with clean solvent. In any case the fumes from solvent residues can give you headaches or worse.

Think of proper care of your sleeping bag as an exercise in feathering your own nest.

To those who have struggled with them, the mountains reveal beauties that they will not disclose to those who make no effort. That is the reward the mountains give to effort. And it is because they have so much to give and give it so lavishly to those who will wrestle with them that men love the mountains and go back to them again and again. The mountains reserve their choice gifts for those who stand upon their summits.

—Sir Francis Younghusband,
1863–1942

As someone who used to review equipment regularly for *Outside* magazine, I've had the privilege of experimenting with a wide variety of recently introduced equipment, including, on several particularly thrilling occasions, new stoves. The incident that provoked the most burning excitement occurred when I was reviewing a new multi-fuel stove from a company that shall remain nameless, since they fixed the problem with remarkable haste. This stove, ostensibly, was capable of burning both white gas and kerosene. Naturally I wasn't about to rely on this unproven contrivance to actually cook my dinner when I was in dire straits 10 miles from the nearest McDonald's, so I filled it with white gas while it was sitting in the middle of my concrete driveway, well away from important flammable structures like my garage, and fired it up. No problem. I shut it down, drained the remaining white gas back into its one-gallon steel storage container, and, like a flaming idiot, left the lid off the container.

For equally inexplicable reasons, I now moved the scene of operations to my front porch—I was still operating on concrete, mind you, but now was only about 3 feet from another important flammable structure, namely, my front door. I filled the innocent-looking stove with kerosene, pumped it up as directed, opened the valve, and flicked my Bic. A wispy flame sprang to life. I pumped again, and suddenly liquid kerosene flooded the burner. A miniature fireball erupted, with flames shooting 3 feet high. I grabbed the stove by its base, knowing it would only remain cool to the touch for another few seconds, and heaved the stove into the middle of my concrete driveway. Sandy Koufax couldn't have made the pitch to home more accurately—the flaming stove landed within inches of the wide-open, nearly full can of explosively volatile white gas. I sprinted down the steps of my front porch, snatched away the can of white gas, and stood there shaking as the broken and battered stove gradually sputtered out.

I called the company and immediately launched into an apology for breaking this marvelous example of American craftsmanship that they had entrusted me with, but only managed to utter a sentence before I was interrupted by the spokeswoman's profuse apology. They had just discovered, somewhat belatedly, that the stove's design was defective.

The moral, of course, is that the only difference between men and boys is the flammability of their toys. Seriously, though, all backpacking stoves can be dangerous if used by careless or ignorant people. Learn your stove's idiosyncrasies thoroughly by practicing with it in a safe place where nothing nearby can be damaged if the stove leaks and catches fire. Given my track record I should do my stove testing at the Nevada Test Site.

Once upon a time, when backpacking stoves (and backpackers) were scarce and firewood was plentiful, everyone cooked over an open flame. As I'll explain further in my discussion on clean camping in chapter 11, those days are gone forever in nearly all parts of the country. In many prime backpacking locations, campfires are illegal, immoral, and maybe even fattening. Good backpacking stoves today are moderately priced, readily available, and essential to preserving the wilderness feel of what little wild land still exists.

Liquid-Fuel versus Canister Stoves

Before selecting a particular model of stove, you must first decide which category of stove you prefer. North American backpackers have two main choices: liquid-fuel stoves and canister stoves. In the interest of journalistic objectivity, I'll start by describing the advantages and drawbacks of each. In truth I actually have a strong preference for one type, which I'll reveal at the end of this section.

The most common liquid backpacking fuel in North America is white gas, which is more accurately known as naphtha. White gas is not the same thing as automotive gasoline, either leaded or unleaded. Burning automotive gas in a white-gas-only stove will rapidly clog the burner orifice where the vaporized fuel emerges and ignites.

The main advantage claimed for liquid-fuel stoves is high heat output in all conditions, even in severe cold. A minor advantage is the lower cost of the fuel compared to fuel cartridges, but few people spend enough time backpacking for the cost to make much difference. The disadvantages of liquid-fuel stoves are the inconvenience of lighting them, the racket they produce when they're burning, and the greater amount of maintenance they require. White gas is extremely volatile, which means that spills evaporate readily without leaving an oily residue like kerosene does; it also means that accidentally igniting a spilled pool of white gas would cause a disastrous fireball that would make my little epic seem like a candle-lighting ceremony.

A modern liquid-fuel stove consists of a tank to hold the fuel, a pump to create pressure in the tank so the fuel will flow through the fuel line, a valve to control fuel flow, and a burner assembly where the gas mixes with air and burns.

To burn efficiently, white gas must first be vaporized by heat. Once the stove is running, vaporization takes place in the fuel line as the line passes directly through the flames emitted by the burner. The vaporized fuel then burns, the heat released vaporizes more fuel, and the cycle continues. The trick is getting the cycle going. To do that, most white-gas stoves must be primed, which is tech talk for preheating the fuel line by releasing a teaspoon of fuel into a small depression at the base of the burner, then igniting it. The easiest way to get the priming fuel in place is to give the pump a dozen strokes, then open the valve a crack, which lets a small amount of liquid fuel escape through the orifice and dribble down to the priming cup. Priming with white gas is a potentially dangerous maneuver that must be executed with great care well away from anything flammable. If you use too much priming fuel, the stove will flare up. If you use way too much priming fuel, the Russians will think we've launched an ICBM. (A few white-gas stoves don't need to be primed.) An alternative to priming with white gas is carrying a small squeeze bottle of stove alcohol or a tube of priming paste. Neither alcohol nor priming paste will flare up like an excessive amount of white gas will.

You may occasionally run across old white-gas stoves that lack a pump. Do not be tempted to buy one. These ancient geezers are supposedly "self-pressurizing," meaning that the heat of the flame is supposed to keep the tank hot enough to maintain sufficient pressure inside the tank for the stove to continue operating. Set the stove on cold ground, however, and you can gradually lose pressure and heat output. The pump found on all modern white-gas stoves makes the whole operation a lot less finicky because you can reliably add pressure to the tank whenever you need it.

Adventurous backpackers planning to trek through Nepal, Patagonia, or Outer Mongolia should look for a multi-fuel stove, which will burn kerosene as well as white gas and possibly other liquid fuels. International travelers will find that white gas is generally unavailable outside the United States. Kerosene is universally available, but the quality varies widely and it must be filtered carefully. Airline regulations prohibit carrying fuel of any type on board, so you'll have to plan on obtaining it once you arrive.

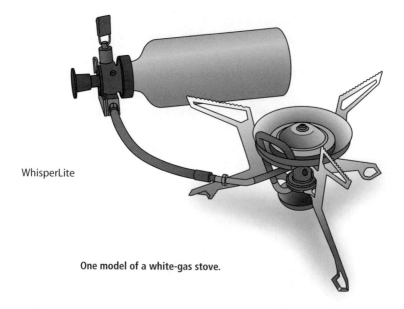

WhisperLite

One model of a white-gas stove.

The major advantage of canister stoves is simplicity. Essentially they contain three parts: a canister of compressed gas, a valve, and a burner. To light a canister stove, you open the valve and flick your lighter. Canister stoves weigh less and are cheaper than white-gas stoves, and they're mercifully quiet. There's no priming to worry about, no liquid fuel to spill, and essentially no maintenance to do. Canister stoves are not idiot-proof, but the average terminally confused backpacker has a hard time making them malfunction.

The main disadvantage of canister stoves is poor heat output in cold weather, particularly as the amount of fuel in the canister diminishes. Canister stoves only work if the cartridge is warm enough for the fuel inside to vaporize into energetic little gas molecules that are eager to flow out the nozzle and burn. In the past the only cartridges available contained ordinary butane, which condenses to a liquid at 31°F. Stoves burning ordinary butane produce practically no heat below that temperature because very little butane gas flows out through the burner when the valve is opened. Fortunately, cartridges containing nothing but butane are now history. Some modern cartridges contain a mixture of propane and butane. Propane liquefies at −44°F, so the combined fuel works better than normal butane in severe cold. Still better cartridges contain a blend of propane and isobutane, a variety of butane that liquefies at 11°F. Stoves running off these cartridges perform much better in the cold than stoves running off pure butane cartridges and somewhat better than those using a propane/butane mix. High altitude, with its lower air pressure, further increases the output of canister stoves compared to their performance at sea level. Just as water boils (vaporizes) at a lower temperature as you go higher, so too do butane, isobutane, and propane. A lower boiling point means more gas flows out at a given temperature. You'll get much better performance at 14,300 feet on McKinley at 0°F, for example, than you will during a January cold snap in Arches National Park at 5,200 feet.

The latest designs of canister stoves address some of these shortcomings. Several manufacturers are now making "integrated stove systems," which combine a canister stove with an effective windscreen, heat exchanger, and cooking pot. These integrated systems boil water faster, use less fuel, and are much more resistant to wind than conventional canister stoves. They are a bit heavier, bulkier, and costlier than simple canister stoves (what, you were expecting a free lunch?). In another innovation some manufacturers are now building "remote canister stoves," in which the canister is connected to the burner assembly with a flexible fuel line rather than screwed directly to the burner. This design lets you turn the canister upside-down, which increases performance both when it's cold and when the canister is nearly empty.

All right, so much for journalistic objectivity. Now it's time to confess my prejudices.

I hate liquid-fuel stoves.

There, I've said it. I feel so much better now.

Every white-gas stove that I've used, and I've used a lot, eventually malfunctioned in one way or another. Some of them clogged repeatedly. Others stopped burning cleanly, despite repeated efforts to repair them, which means they deposited soot on my pots. Handling the pots invariably left me looking like the grimy chimney sweep in *Mary Poppins*. I once spent an hour battling with a white-gas stove that was a little too warm to emit liquid fuel for priming and a little too cold to actually vaporize enough fuel to run properly. Almost every backpacker can tell you a story about a white-gas stove that became cantankerous.

I know, I know, there are undoubtedly legions of liquid-fuel fans out there who will write to me with stories of how their white-gas stove has performed flawlessly for twenty years. I don't doubt those stories. Maybe white-gas stoves have just had it in for me ever since I broke that beautiful new liquid-fuel stove by throwing it 20 feet onto my driveway. (Hey, the stove started it!)

I've used canister stoves almost exclusively since 1982, year-round, with virtually no problems. About the only problem I've had occurred recently, in the junction between a heavily used burner assembly and the canister. Somehow the needle that plunges through the canister's seal to release the gas had not penetrated fully. Simply rotating the canister in relation to the burner assembly allowed the needle

Pocket Rocket

JetBoil

On the right is a typical canister stove. On the left is an integrated stove system that includes the canister, burner assembly, windscreen, and pot.

to finish penetrating the seal. The gas then flowed normally, and the problem was solved. For me the simplicity and ease of use of a canister stove, particularly now that isobutane/propane cartridges are available, makes it the stove of choice. However, I grant you that using a canister stove successfully in the wintertime at normal altitudes, even with the new fuels, can be a tedious process. Conventional wisdom dictates that if you plan to do a lot of cold-weather backpacking, buy a liquid-fuel stove.

Stove Maintenance

Canister stoves require no routine maintenance. On expeditions I've always carried an orifice-cleaning tool (a stiff, tiny wire attached to a handle) to clean the orifice where the gas emerges, but I've only needed to use it on a handful of occasions.

The orifices on white-gas and multi-fuel stoves, on the other hand, do need periodic cleaning, particularly if you're burning kerosene. The second most common failure point for liquid-fuel stoves is the pump cup, which needs oiling periodically with two or three drops of a lightweight oil. In addition, liquid-fuel stoves have a variety of rubber seals and gaskets that need replacing on occasion. Good manufacturers sell spare parts for their stoves, which should be considered as essential as the stove itself. One final tip: Don't store fuel in the stove's tank. It can become gummy if the stove sits around unused for several months. Instead, light the stove and burn off the remaining fuel before storing the stove at the end of the season. Don't pour unused fuel down the drain or into the gutter, where it will become a highly toxic pollutant.

Selecting the rest of your kitchen kit is easy if you backpack in the style that Cora and I do. We like to spend our time hiking, searching for subjects to photograph, and watching the marmots pout and the pikas scold, rather than slaving over a stove in camp trying to prepare a gourmet meal. We bring just one four-cup pot. In addition, we each carry a metal spoon, a plastic mug with a lid, and a plastic bowl, which in its former incarnation was a food storage container. In winter, when I often eat inside my cluttered tent, I usually bring the lid for the container so I can set my half-eaten bowl of cereal down without worrying about spilling it. A pair of sturdy pot grips, available in backpacking shops, is another essential if your cooking pots don't come with one built in.

Some canister stoves come with piezo ignition switches, which generate a spark to light your stove. Even if your stove has such a feature, however, you'll need either a cigarette lighter or matches as a backup. Cora and I carry both because lighters, although convenient, have a disconcerting habit of failing if the lighter gets wet or the operator's hands are damp. Matches provide an excellent backup if they're carefully secured inside a plastic bag without holes. For even greater security you can find waterproof, strike-anywhere matches in backpacking stores. It's a good idea to throw an extra cigarette lighter into the repair kit or some other secure place, just in case.

Not everyone favors the simple kitchen setup Cora and I carry. Some backpackers choose to make the preparation and consumption of delicacies the central point of their trip. They bring a Teflon frying pan for the trout they hope to catch and a griddle to bake their pancakes. They buy a lightweight, collapsible oven that uses a backpacking stove as the heat source and turn out miniature pizzas and brownies alongside the shores of high-country lakes. We choose to burden ourselves with extra lenses instead of pots and pans, but that's the beauty of backpacking: There's room out there for fanatics of every persuasion. Room, too, for those sane souls who can shrug off their city obsessions and just enjoy the wilderness for what it is.

I used to envy the father of our race, dwelling as he did in the new-made plants and flowers of Eden. But I do so no longer. For I have discovered that I too live in creation's dawn. The morning stars still sing together and the earth, not yet half-made, grows more beautiful every day.

—*John Muir, 1838–1914*

Three friends—Lisa Cotter, Jenny Ball, and Cindy Carey—were planning an expedition to Mount McKinley, a peak that is infamous for the arctic gales that beset its slopes. Accordingly, they wanted to get some experience camping in high winds. They decided, a bit naively, that the ideal location for a training trip was the Boulderfield on Longs Peak in Rocky Mountain National Park. The Boulderfield is a bleak, rocky plain, far above timberline, that is raked by hurricane-force winds in the wintertime. One stormy February weekend a few months before the expedition, they invited me to join them, and we headed up. Winter days go fast, and the last pink glow of sunset was abandoning the peaks to the north when we finally got the tents erect in the stiff wind and crawled inside. Jenny and I, together in one tent, cooked dinner by the light of our headlamps. I noticed that the battery powering my headlamp was growing weak. No worries, I thought; we're only here one night, I'll only need my headlamp for another few minutes, and besides, I have a spare battery.

Soon after the last sip of hot chocolate, we doused the headlamps and plunged the tent into darkness. The wind began to grow stronger. The tent strained against the gusts as the taut fabric crackled noisily. I had been dozing restlessly for no more than half an hour when a loud snap, like a breaking tree limb, jarred me awake. The wind had broken one of the tent poles. An instant later the second one, now unsupported, fractured as well, and the tent began flapping and billowing like a giant jellyfish gone mad. I lunged for my headlamp and flicked it on to survey the damage. The beam faintly illuminated a gaping rip in the fabric. Afraid the tent would be destroyed completely and all our extra gear would blow away, Jenny and I began packing frantically. Suddenly my headlamp winked out, its battery shot. Fumbling in the dark, I plugged in my spare battery, confident that our lack of light was merely a temporary annoyance. Then I discovered that it too had somehow become drained. A minute later Jenny's headlamp failed as well. Fortunately, she also had a spare battery. Unfortunately, it too was dead. Embarrassed now as well as desperate, we borrowed a headlamp from Cindy and Lisa, finished stowing our gear, and packed up the tattered remnants of the tent. Cindy and Lisa's tent had also suffered a broken pole; a second pole was badly bent, but the tent, although lopsided, was still standing. The four of us squeezed inside and waited for dawn. When morning finally arrived, we abandoned our plans to climb Longs Peak and scurried for home.

Headlamps

Our experience illustrates the first law of nighttime disaster control: No headlamp is reliable unless you check the batteries—and the spares—in advance. Electronics stores usually sell inexpensive battery testers that work with all sizes of batteries. I bought mine (belatedly) at Radio Shack.

If we hadn't been able to borrow a headlamp from Lisa and Cindy, Jenny and I would have been in much worse trouble. The odds would have been good that some valuable piece of equipment would have blown away in the dark as we struggled to pack all our gear. It just goes to show that when darkness reigns, a headlamp is de-light. If you're a typical summer backpacker, you'll never need to worry about your tent exploding around your ears, but you're quite likely to need a reliable headlamp or flashlight, if only to investigate those mysterious midnight gnawing sounds that prove to be a porcupine chewing into your pack.

The concept of a headlamp is simple: Think of it as a flashlight you can wear on your head. Headlamps let you use both hands to pitch your tent, cook, or pack, which is why Cora and I prefer them over flashlights. For trail walking, however, you'll often find that carrying the headlamp in your hands makes it easier to pick out obstacles in the trail. The reason? Moving the light away from your eyes gives better definition to the scene by casting longer and more pronounced shadows.

Headlamps have come a long ways since I wrote the second edition. Today virtually all headlamps use LEDs (light-emitting diodes) rather than conventional lightbulbs. LEDs produce light far more efficiently than conventional bulbs, so your batteries last much longer. The housing containing the LEDs and a reflector is mounted on an elastic headband. With the lightest (but also the least bright) models, the batteries fit into the LED housing. In others the battery case is attached to the headband in back. Brighter and therefore heavier models usually have a strap that crosses the top of your head in addition to the one that encircles your head just above your ears. With a few models the battery case rides in your pocket, where the batteries stay warmer and therefore last longer. The disadvantage of that system, of course, is that you then have a wire running from a pocket to your head, which not only makes you look like an android, but also gives malicious tree branches the perfect handle to rip your headlamp from your head.

When traveling solo, I carry a full-size headlamp with spare batteries, plus a one-ounce backup headlamp with spare battery so I can change batteries in the main headlamp in the dark. I do a lot of nighttime hiking on my way to sunrise photo ops, so I prefer brighter headlamps even if they weigh more. If you usually only need a headlamp for brief nighttime excursions to water a bush, you can get away with something lighter.

The best batteries for the environment and for your pocketbook over the long run are rechargeable lithium-ion or nickel metal hydride (NiMH). They cost more initially, and you have to buy a battery charger as well, but they have a useful life of hundreds of charges, which makes them far more economical over time. One apparent disadvantage is that even fully charged, never-used rechargeables will gradually go dead over a period of two or three months and have to be recharged. I turn that "flaw" on its head by charging my batteries every time before I go out, so I know I'm always starting the trip with fully charged batteries. Be aware that virtually all AAA and AA battery chargers charge batteries in pairs. If you want to use rechargeable batteries, be sure your headlamp takes either two or four batteries. The best batteries for severe cold are the nonrechargeable lithiums, which will power a headlamp reliably at temperatures below zero. Lithium batteries are super light and have a very long shelf life, so they make a great backup set of batteries, but they are quite expensive.

Using a headlamp keeps your hands free for cooking or pitching a tent.

Other Essentials

A checklist of backpacking gear inevitably contains a host of other small but essential items. Some I'll discuss in later chapters. Right now I'd like to talk about a grab bag of miscellaneous gear. For example, Cora and I both carry a Swiss Army knife. The model we like has two knife blades, a can opener, scissors, tweezers, and a corkscrew. Carrying a knife lets you spread your peanut butter on a bagel, open a can of tuna, trim frayed fabric that keeps jamming in a zipper, pull a splinter, and pop the cork on a bottle of wine, should your party contain a strong-backed soul willing to carry it. Some knives even contain nail files, presumably so survivalists can sharpen their fingernails into claws.

If your boots are heavy or uncomfortable, you might want a pair of lightweight slippers or sandals to change into once you reach camp. If your feet are chronically cold in your sleeping bag at night, you may enjoy a pair of down booties.

Summer backpackers in wooded regions rarely need sunglasses. However, if you're hiking above timberline across early summer's lingering snowfields, sunglasses can prevent a lot of uncomfortable squinting or worse. Snow blindness—essentially a sunburn of the cornea of the eye—can cause severe pain for several days. Don't count on pain to warn you of the danger, however; the pain begins several hours after the damage is done. If you find yourself squinting heavily, you should put on your sunglasses. Time is the only cure for snow blindness, although victims normally get some relief by remaining in a darkened room or otherwise shielding their eyes from light. Desert hikers frequently find sunglasses a pleasure, and winter backpackers in snow country should routinely carry both sunglasses and goggles. People whose eyesight is so poor they would have trouble hiking out if their glasses were broken should bring a spare pair.

Large plastic garbage bags have many uses. You can slip one over your pack with the mouth pointing down to keep your pack dry if it rains during the night. If you're moving camp on a rainy day, you can slip your sleeping bag (in its stuff sack) and stuff sack of extra clothes into the garbage bag before stowing it in the bottom of your pack. Packs and stuff sacks are water-resistant, but certainly not waterproof, and hard rain will eventually penetrate both. If you choose to hang your pack at night to protect it from rodents, you can keep the contents dry by lining your pack with a garbage bag before loading in the extra gear you don't want cluttering up your tent. If the ground is muddy or sandy, you can keep small bags of food clean as you unpack them from your food bag by placing them on a garbage bag spread out flat on the ground. You can use a bit of duct tape from your repair kit to patch minor rips in your garbage bag and extend the bag's useful life.

Buying an Ice Ax

As I emphasized in the section on mountaineering boots in chapter 3, mountaineering is a sport that demands respect, proper training, and the right equipment. Among the items you'll need if you venture onto steep snowfields is an ice ax, a tool that actually bears little resemblance to its wood-chopping cousin. As you can see in the illustration, an ice ax has four parts: the shaft, normally made of extruded aluminum tubing; the pick, which the climber drives into the ice or hard snow with the force of his swing; the adze, used to chop out ledges to stand on while resting or belaying; and the spike, which helps the shaft penetrate hard snow and prevents the ax from slipping when it's used as a walking stick. If you will primarily be climbing snow, you want an ice ax that's long enough to reach comfortably from your hand to the ground so you can lean on it effectively. An ice ax designed for climbing frozen waterfalls, on the other hand, will have a shorter shaft and a differently shaped pick that is designed to hook into rotten or multilayered ice. Ice-climbing tools are a poor bet for snow climbing because the shaft isn't long enough to serve effectively as a cane.

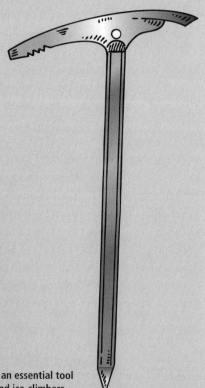

On a gentle snowfield a snow climber's ice ax is used mostly as a walking stick. As the slope steepens, climbers plunge the shaft in as far as it will go and grasp the head of the ice ax to steady themselves while they kick steps. As the snow hardens and turns to ice, climbers grasp the shaft of the ax near the spike and drive the pick into the snow with a stout swing. If the climber slips, he or she grabs the head of the ax with one hand and the shaft with the other, then presses the pick into the snow to brake and eventually stop a fall, a technique called self-arrest.

Mastering the use of an ice ax cannot be learned through reading. Seek competent instruction from experienced guides or very competent friends before attempting to climb steep snow.

An ice ax is an essential tool for snow- and ice-climbers.

After Cora had $4,000 worth of dental work done a number of years ago, we became remarkably conscientious about bringing toothbrushes, toothpaste, and floss on all our backpacking trips, even short ones. Our personal hygiene kit also contains (at Cora's insistence) hand sanitizer and a hairbrush. Even I insist on bringing toilet paper. A trowel is valuable for burying wastes (more on this subject later).

Embarrassed as I may be to admit my addiction to a quintessentially citified piece of gear, I find a watch to be an important item of wilderness equipment. Primarily I use it to keep track of our pace and timing. Will we make the campsite by dark? Will we make the top of the pass in time to shoot the sunrise? A watch also lets you time the cooking of your pasta and rice.

I discovered when my knees hit forty years of age that they apparently didn't come with a lifetime warranty. In an effort to extend their life as long as possible, I began hiking with a pair of trekking poles, the modern version of old-fashioned wooden walking sticks. You can buy fancy trekking poles that are adjustable in length for hikers of different heights, then telescope to half their normal length to lash onto your pack when the scrambling gets steep and poles are more a hindrance than a help. Or you can do what I've done for fifteen years and just buy used ski poles at a used sporting goods shop, thrift store, or flea market. Trekking poles not only spare your knees but also are a great aid when rock-hopping across small streams or fording bigger ones. They make it much easier to stay upright when crossing early-summer snowfields, trails covered with 6 inches of snow after the first big fall storm, and other kinds of slippery terrain. And finally, they also help you hike more efficiently by allowing you to use the muscles of your arms, chest, and back to supplement the efforts of your hardworking legs. Try them—you may find that you, like me, enjoy returning to your evolutionary roots as a quadruped. I should forewarn you, however, that hiking with ski poles in the summer will prompt knucklehead comedians to exclaim, "You forgot your skis!" To which I always reply, "That's true, but you forgot the snow, so it's really all your fault!"

A simple repair kit can save you a lot of grief even on a short trip. A basic kit might include:

- Spare parts for the stove and water filter.

- A little duct tape or ripstop repair tape to patch a hole in a tent, rain jacket, insulated parka, or sleeping bag.

- Extra clevis pins and split rings (if you're carrying an external frame pack that uses those devices to attach the pack bag to the frame).

- Spare bootlaces, which can also be used for lashing this to that.

- Spare 1- and 2-inch quick-release buckles to replace a broken buckle on your pack.

A more elaborate repair kit for a trip lasting a week or longer might also contain:

- Wire for lashing together a broken stove or snowshoe.

- Small needle-nose pliers with wire cutters to force the aforementioned wire into place.

- Heavy-duty sewing awl (Speedy Stitcher is my favorite brand), stout thread, and a scrap of heavy fabric.

- A 5-inch length of copper pipe with an inside diameter just larger than the diameter of your tent poles, to patch a broken pole.

If you've been clutching your wallet ever more tightly as you read chapter after chapter on what to buy, it's time to relax. With the exception of first-aid kits and water-purification devices, we're done with discussing what you need to own. Now, with the buying spree behind us, we can move on to everyone's favorite topic: What's for dinner?

An army marches on its stomach.

—Napoléon (attributed), 1769–1821

My early wilderness adventures were noted for their culinary disasters. I did my first backpacking trips with my father in the days when backpacking food was simply dried. Not freeze-dried, mind you; just dried, dehydrated, in reality, fossilized. Resurrecting the dried food of that era into something palatable was about as likely as raising *Tyrannosaurus rex* from the dead. I still remember boiling little chunks of dried carrot for hours and finally consuming them with a frustrating crunch. Then there was the time we set out to make an omelet and mixed up half a packet of dried eggs—but mistakenly used a full quotient of water, thus creating a nightmare version of egg drop soup.

Even more memorable, because it was actually planned and therefore inexcusable, was the horse fodder Joe Kaelin and I brought along for breakfast on an insanely windy Thanksgiving trip into Rocky Mountain National Park. (It's the only time I've ever been blown over flat while *kneeling.*) Joe, an impoverished college student with some misguided aspirations to healthy eating habits, thought he would relish oatmeal—raw oatmeal, briefly soaked in watery powdered milk instead of actually cooking it. To no one's surprise but our own, we ended up carrying half our oatmeal back out again. That we ate any at all is a tribute to the victory of tyrannical stomachs over rebellious taste buds.

With such lessons under our belt, so to speak, my comrades-in-arms and I gradually learned what we could carry, what we could actually cook, and most important, what we would actually eat while far away from refrigerators, microwave ovens, and telephone hotlines to Domino's Pizza.

One of the first things we learned is that beginners' eyes are much bigger than their stomachs. There is, quite naturally, a real fear of running out of food when the nearest supermarket is not minutes away but rather many hours, possibly even days. The almost irresistible temptation is to bring far more food than even William "The Fridge" Perry could consume. Hiking out at the end of a trip with half your food supply still burdening your pack will quickly teach you how much food you actually need for a few days in the wilds.

The errors encouraged by the eyeball method of packing provisions are compounded by the difference between city foods and backpacking foods. In the city much of our food already has water in it: fruit, vegetables, meat, soups, stews, milk, all canned foods, etc. In the backcountry, on the other hand, almost everything is brought in dry, and water from a lake or stream is added during preparation or cooking. Dry food, besides being lighter, is usually far more compact than hydrated food. A bag scarcely larger than a football can easily contain enough dry food for one person for three days, yet it looks like it contains only enough for a three-course dinner.

Weekend Trips

Worrying about weight and bulk is largely unnecessary if your trip will last only two days. Since you'll probably eat breakfast before you start and dinner after you get out, you only need to plan four meals. Over that space of time, almost anything goes. In fact, on a weekend trip there's really no need to cook at all if you don't feel like it. Dinner can just be a continuation of lunch, perhaps with a different filling between the slices of bread. With a little experience the eyeball method of assessing quantities will work just fine for a two-day trip. Sure, you'll probably have a pound or two of food left over, but on a trip that short, who cares? Although you can be a bit lackadaisical about quantities, do make an effort to cook only what you can eat. Leftover food should be packed out, not strewn around or buried, where it will corrupt the eating habits of jays and squirrels. Worse yet, burying scraps will also encourage bears to raid your camp.

Although it would be easy to turn our weekend trips into gourmet extravaganzas, Cora and I still prefer to keep our food packing simple. We eat breakfast the first day at home. For lunch we usually bring cold-cut sandwiches, corn chips, and a few granola bars for snacks. We keep the sandwiches fresh by packing them into our cooking pot with a frozen juice box or two, then wrapping the pot in an extra sweater. Dinner is a quick-cooking pasta or rice dish fortified with a can of tuna, chicken, or turkey. Most grocery stores sell packaged pasta and rice dishes that contain their own dried "sauce," or you can take plain pasta or quick-cooking rice and add a package of dried soup mix. We fill in the chinks with a bagel. For dessert we drink hot chocolate and sometimes split a candy bar (okay, I admit it, it's a big candy bar). Breakfast the second day (our first one in the field) is cold cereal with powdered milk for me, sports nutrition bars for Cora. Lunch the second day is usually bagels with peanut butter or a can of chicken or ham spread, and we're home or on the road for dinner. Backpackers who walk to eat, rather than eat to walk, can find legions of backcountry cookbooks to help them plan more exciting fare.

Three- and Four-Day Trips

As your adventures grow longer, you must pay increasing attention to exactly how much food you bring. The eyeball method leads to considerable errors when the trip is three or four days or more. Measuring out foods by volume can work if you know how many cups you typically eat for each individual item you want to bring. An easier way to bring exactly the right amount, however, is to weigh out your food on a postage scale. I know that five ounces of cereal, of any type, and one ounce of powdered milk is a satisfying breakfast for me. I have no idea how many cups of my six favorite cereals equal five ounces.

Foods differ greatly in their calorie content per ounce. As a general rule, carbohydrates and protein yield about 110 calories per ounce. Fats yield much more, about 250 calories per ounce. Since weight and bulk are a problem while backpacking, it's tempting to load up your pack with fats. Unfortunately, the best food for strenuous exercise consists of carbohydrates, which are relatively heavy for their caloric content. The best backpacking menu, therefore, is a compromise. Think of your food as firewood. Carbohydrates are the kindling, useful for getting the fire going fast and reenergizing a tired hiker quickly. Slow-burning fats and protein are like logs, good for fueling a steadily burning fire and stoking the inner furnaces during a long, cold winter night. Don't worry too much about obtaining sufficient amounts of vitamins and minerals while backpacking. It's impossible to become seriously deficient in any particular nutrient during a week or two of hiking.

You can often get away with bringing some perishable food for the first few days. In the summer in the Rockies, fresh bagels will keep for about three days without refrigeration. After that they become possible sources for exciting new antibiotics. To avoid becoming guinea pigs on the fourth day, we often substitute crackers for the bagel. Sugary foods are easy to bring backpacking, since they're compact and keep well, but Cora and I find that the sweetness becomes sickening if we bring too much. Salty foods that crunch are often in high demand in the backcountry, which is why we usually bring crackers. Eventually, of course, these brittle snack items crumble into bird food, but they're still quite palatable if you change your attitude. Simply decide that what you really wanted all along is croutons, and sprinkle them on your pasta or rice. These snacks are bulky but not heavy in comparison to their caloric content, and they have a side benefit: They make your pack look enormous, which encourages impressionable tourists to make laudatory comments on the trail. (Of course, you have to ignore the scorn of modern-day John Muirs who are out for a week with a pack no bigger than a baguette.)

Logan Bread

3 cups flour (any mixture of whole wheat and rye)

¾ cup wheat germ

¼ cup brown sugar

½ cup powdered milk

1 cup oil

½ cup honey

¼ cup molasses

¼ sorghum syrup or maple syrup (any combination of these four sweeteners totaling 1 cup works fine)

½ cup shelled walnuts or pecans

1 cup dried fruit (raisins, dates, apricots, peaches, etc.)

6 eggs

Beat all the ingredients together in a large bowl. Divide into two greased 5 × 9-inch loaf pans. The dough will be very stiff, so press it firmly into the pans. Bake at 275°F for 2 hours or until a tester comes out clean. The bread will be heavy and dense. Each loaf weighs 24 ounces.

When I was guiding expeditions on Mount McKinley, I found that most people quickly decided that hot cereal was about as appealing as snail slime. Perhaps the texture began to seem a little too glutinous to stomachs already unsettled by the altitude and enormous exertion; at any rate I remember cooking gallons of oatmeal and cream of wheat and seeing a few tablespoons disappear reluctantly into people's mouths. Cold cereal can always be made hot, if so desired, but the opposite is not true. People also quickly rejected excessively fatty food, such as salami, because it upset their stomachs when they began laboring uphill again after lunch. The candy bars everyone lapped up eagerly during the first few days also became tiresome quickly. One climber commented to me after a week on the glacier, "I don't want to see another Milky Way bar as long as I live." The foods that did retain their appeal were what I call "real food." Cold cereal always tasted good for breakfast. Mildly sweet logan bread for lunch never palled (see the recipe above). A bagel, carefully thawed then buttered, always went down well, as did a dinner glop richly reinforced with cheese and butter. Of course, we did have an advantage in planning palatable meals that summer backpackers in the Lower 48 do not: The weather was always cold, so we could bring perishable foods like bagels, cheese, and butter and be confident they would remain frozen and wholesome until we were ready to eat them.

So far I've only mentioned foods that are readily available in any well-stocked grocery store. One alternative is to buy freeze-dried food from a backpacking shop or online retailer. Freeze-drying is a high-tech method of preserving food that creates a product that can be rehydrated much more satisfactorily than ordinary dehydrated food. I gave freeze-dried foods a lot of flack in the second edition, but I must admit that the quality and variety have improved significantly since then, and the convenience is unbeatable. With most freeze-dried food, you simply add boiling water to the foil pouch and let it sit for ten minutes (twenty minutes if you're above 10,000 feet). There's no need to stir the glop to keep it from burning and no pot to clean, and you can be heating the water for your cup of cocoa while you eat your dinner—or, as we always did in Alaska, you can be melting more snow, an interminable task during high-altitude arctic trips. If the trip schedule allows me to be in camp at lunchtime, I'll frequently prepare freeze-dried scrambled eggs, which taste more like real food to me than sports nutrition bars.

Supermarket foods are generally much less expensive than freeze-dried food, and they can be just as tasty. The real key to enjoying backpacking food is variety, not expense. When I was helping guide an expedition on 22,834-foot Aconcagua, the highest peak in the Western Hemisphere, we brought a large number of Alpine Aire freeze-dried dinners because everyone had eaten so many Mountain House dinners on previous trips that they were heartily sick of them. Given a choice at the beginning of the trip, everyone immediately grabbed for the Alpine Aire dinners. After a couple of weeks of Alpine Aire, however, everyone suddenly decided that a Mountain House dinner would be a delectable feast.

For the past ten years or so, I've been carrying a high-end sports drink in a bottle tucked into a holster on my hip belt. Like the hydration systems described on page 41 on backpacks, my system lets me drink on the fly, so I stay better hydrated than if I have to remove my pack to get a drink. By using a sports drink rather than water, I provide an even flow of calories and electrolytes to hardworking muscles. Staying well hydrated and fueled certainly seems to increase my stamina during a long day with a big load. Altitude tends to dull the sensation of thirst, so I keep an eye on my watch and take a swig of sports drink every twenty minutes.

When I'm hiking, I abandon the city prejudice against between-meal snacks. Instead, I eat every two hours or less. On a strenuous hike, however, I often find that solid food becomes less and less palatable as the day wears on, particularly when I'm at high altitude. Lately I've become a fan of "electrolyte chews," as the company calls them, which remain digestible even when I'm hauling a thirty-pound load of camera gear to the summit of a 14,000-foot peak. The brand I currently favor has the consistency of a gummy bear. I carry a three- or four-hour supply in a small zippered pouch that's attached to my shoulder straps so I don't have to stop and remove my pack to eat. When on the trail I pop two chews into my mouth every twenty minutes, followed by a swig of sports drink. Rather than down the chews immediately, I tuck one into each cheek, which makes me resemble an educated alpine chipmunk, then let the chews dissolve slowly. If eating gummy bears for lunch isn't your thing, you can try powering down one of the various brands of energy gels that are now readily available. My new approach keeps my stomach happy and enables me to eat on the move, which is helpful when the weather is bad or when I need to make miles.

Most people need twenty-eight to thirty-two ounces of dry food per person per day. Cora, who's smaller than I am, needs a bit less than I do. Here's a prototype menu that I use for multiday trips. The quantities listed are merely suggestions to get you in the right ballpark. Granted, my taste in backpacking food is rather spartan. You'll undoubtedly want to substitute your own favorite foods for the ones listed here.

Food for One Person for One Day		
Item	Weight in ounces	Comments
Cold cereal	5	
Powdered milk	1	
Five packages electrolyte chews OR four packages electrolyte chews, one package freeze-dried eggs	11	
Two granola bars or energy bars	3	
Freeze-dried dinner	5	Weight varies, depending on the dinner, from four to six ounces
Chocolate bar	2	
Sports drink	3	Enough to make one and a half quarts per day
Bagged or instant coffee plus creamer (one cup of high-octane in the morning, one cup of unleaded in the evening)	1.5	About three-quarters of an ounce of creamer per day, two rounded teaspoons per cup
Total	**31.5**	

Long-Haul Backpacking

All the issues I've discussed earlier become critical if you're planning a trip lasting a week or longer. For most people, seven to ten days is about as long as they can go before they need to resupply. Even if you could find a pack big enough to carry more days of food, you probably couldn't pick it up without assistance once you filled it, and your shoulders, hips, knees, and feet would declare a sit-down strike after the first mile. Even if the trip lasts only a week, bulk can be a major problem. You may find yourself tying cumbersome items of clothing to the outside of your pack at the beginning of the trip. I like to lash my rain gear outside because it's usually the item of clothing I need in the biggest hurry. To prevent overhanging branches from tearing my rain gear, I usually put it in a stuff sack before lashing it on.

To help cut down on bulk, shed excess packaging. You'll find that much food as it comes from the grocery store is swaddled in unnecessary amounts of cardboard, foil, and paper. You can reduce the amount of bulk tremendously by repackaging these items. For example, several companies sell dried soups in individual serving packets. Rip open the packets and put three days' worth in a small plastic bag. You'll be amazed at how compact the bag is compared to the three foil-lined packets. One caveat: Be sure to save the cooking directions! Where possible, avoid items packaged as individual servings altogether. Instead, buy the same item in one large, undivided package, then measure it out yourself as needed during the trip. This saves room in the landfill as well as your pack. Cora and I do occasionally carry crackers in their cardboard boxes, since they resist crumbling much longer if carried that way. In most areas the cardboard can be recycled when you get home.

People hiking the full length of the Appalachian Trail, Continental Divide Trail, or the Pacific Crest Trail usually recruit a friend to serve as their "ground-control" person, whose job is to ship a box of food at weekly intervals to the towns closest to the hikers' route. Naturally, the hikers should pack each box in advance. Boxes should be left unsealed until the last minute so the ground-control person, perhaps better known as the baggage handler, can add a few fresh items just before sending the box on its way, addressed to "Hungry Hiker, General Delivery, Hottubandbeerville, Wildstate USA." Boxes should also contain a few other items, like a fresh book, more toilet paper, more sunscreen and lip sunblock, extra batteries for headlamps and cameras, etc. Long-distance hikers often find that they want to shed some items along the way, such as unnecessary items of clothing, maps whose usefulness is past, and guidebooks that led to three wrong turns in 3 miles. Each box should include tape and padded envelopes and perhaps a cardboard box, broken down flat, so that returning these items is easy. Before the trip, hikers should also gather together some items that may be needed in the event of unforeseen calamities.

These items might include spare tent poles, extra first-aid supplies, or extra spare parts for the stove. If required, the ground-control person can include the necessary items in the next shipment.

Food for backpacking will never quite equal the delights you can produce in your own kitchen or the delicacies you can pay restaurant chefs to produce in theirs. To remain blissfully content in the backcountry, you need to learn the truth of Lucius Annaeus Seneca's words, written in the time of Christ: "A great step towards independence is a good-humored stomach, one that is willing to endure rough treatment."

> Until one is committed there is hesitancy, the chance to draw back, always ineffectiveness. Concerning all acts of initiative (and creation), there is one elementary truth, the ignorance of which kills countless ideas and splendid plans: that the moment one definitely commits oneself, then Providence moves too.
>
> —*William H. Murray, 1913–1996*

It didn't seem like an ambitious undertaking when my dad and I decided to hike up Mount Baldy, a 10,000-foot peak in the mountain range ringing Los Angeles. After all, the trailhead was quite high, so we wouldn't need to gain much elevation to reach the summit. As we studied the map, we did notice that the trail led over several unnamed subsidiary peaks between the parking lot and the summit, but we dismissed these peaklets as pimples on the elephant's back, too insignificant to slow down an eager teenager and his unsuspecting father.

Ten hours later, with the sun already below the western horizon, the last pimple between our tired bodies and the car had been transformed into a peak of Himalayan proportions. Never again would we neglect to add up all the elevation gain along our proposed hike instead of just computing the difference between the starting point and the summit. Each of those subsidiary peaks had added some 500 feet of elevation gain to both the outbound and the return trips, turning what we had thought would be a romp into a late-evening ordeal. By the time we were able to call home and tell my mother we were fine, she was almost ready to alert the search-and-rescue squad.

Planning a Hike

The first step in planning a hiking trip, whether it will take a day or a month, is obtaining topographic maps of the area where you plan to hike. Like most maps a topo map shows mountains, lakes, and streams, as well as roads, trails, and other man-made objects.

Unlike other maps, however, a topographic map also shows the elevation and shape of the land's peaks and valleys by means of contour lines. These are lines drawn on the map that represent lines of equal elevation on the ground. For an example, take a look at figure A, which shows Mount Conehead, a mythical cone-shaped peak with contour lines drawn on its surface. Compare figure A to figure B, which shows how the same peak would be represented on a topographic map.

Topographic Maps

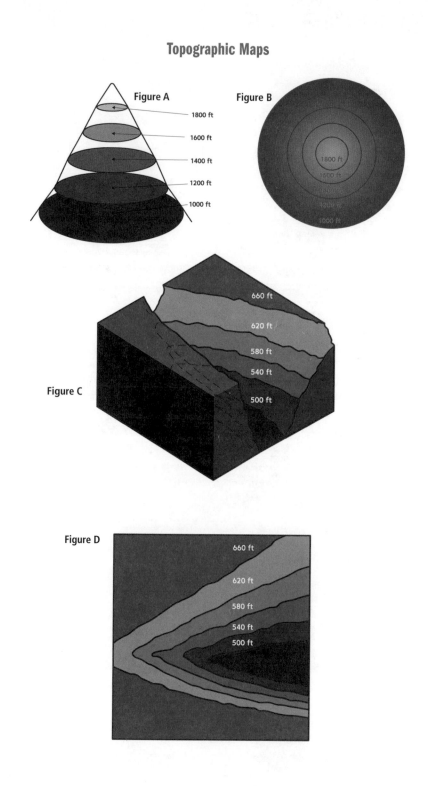

Figure C shows an oblique, cutaway view of deep, V-shaped Vildernest Valley as it cuts through a level plain. Figure D shows how Vildernest Valley would be represented on a topo map.

Figure E shows Bigbeak Peak, a misbegotten mountain with a pronounced ridge jutting out from its summit. Figure F shows how Bigbeak Peak would be represented on a topo map. Note how the soft Vs formed by the contour lines representing a valley in figure D point toward higher elevations, while the Vs formed by the contour lines representing a ridge in figure F point to lower elevations.

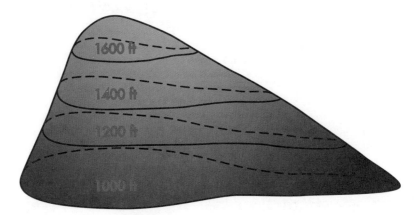

Figure E

Figure F

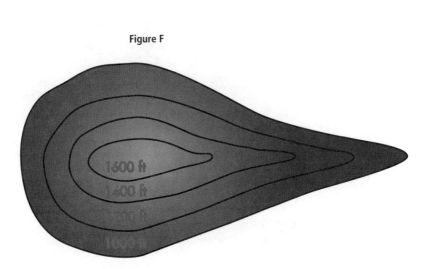

Use this fact to help you distinguish between valleys and ridges on confusing topo maps. The interval between light contour lines, called intermediate contours, is normally 40 or 80 feet in mountainous terrain or canyon country. Every fifth contour line, called an index contour, is darker. It normally represents an elevation change of 200 or 400 feet. The contour interval is always stated on the margin of the map.

The U.S. Geological Survey publishes detailed topographic maps covering practically every area in the United States where you might want to hike. The 15 minute series maps use a scale of 1 inch to the mile: 1 inch on the map equals 1 mile on the ground. Each map covers roughly 240 square miles. These maps have now been mostly replaced by the newer and much more useful 7.5 minute series maps, which use a scale of 1 inch to 2,000 feet, which equals 2⅝ inches to the mile. These maps are formally known as quadrangles, or quads for short. Each map covers roughly 60 square miles. You can obtain USGS maps from many outdoor shops and also by ordering online. To order online, you need to know the name of the map you want and its series. You can search the USGS website, or you can write to the USGS at the address in the appendix and request an index for the state you're interested in. The index is actually a large map of the state showing the name and location of each USGS map covering some part of the state.

In the wilderness, paper maps like those from the USGS live a life that's nasty, brutish, and short. A slightly more expensive but much more durable alternative is to buy maps printed on tough, flexible plastic sheets from Trails Illustrated, which is now owned by National Geographic. Another advantage of the Trails Illustrated topos is that they are updated more frequently than the USGS maps. One disadvantage: The scale is usually 1 inch or 1½ inches to the mile, which makes it harder to decipher fine detail. For really nitty-gritty route-finding off-trail, nothing can beat a USGS 7.5 minute quad. I always carry both types of maps.

No map is completely accurate. National map accuracy standards state that at least 90 percent of the points marked on a 7.5 minute map will be accurate within 40 feet horizontally and 20 feet vertically for well-defined features. Geographic features like summits, passes, lakes, and streams are generally marked quite accurately.

There are exceptions, however, as I discovered last September while looking for fresh locations to shoot photographs of fall foliage. As I was studying maps of the area near Owl Creek Pass, in the San Juans, I noticed a small lake I'd never visited. Coyote Lake, as it was called, was only about 3 miles from the road. I envisioned a great shot of yellow aspen and dramatic peaks reflected in clear blue water. On a beautiful fall day, I packed up for a sunset shoot and headed in.

A mile into the hike, the trail vanished completely. I recorded a waypoint with my GPS receiver so I could relocate the trail as I hiked back out in the dark, measured a compass course on the map, and pressed on through the trackless aspen grove. Soon I ran into another trail, which seemed to be heading in the right direction. Another mile, and I reached a trail junction. A sign pointed right toward the Coyote Lake Trail. Pulse quickening, I hurried on, keeping a close eye on my GPS receiver since the trail did not lead directly to the lake. At last the GPS unit told me the lake was just a hundred yards away up a steep embankment. Soon I crested the embankment, did a double-take, and stopped.

There was a small problem with my grand plan. Cows were grazing in the middle of Coyote Lake. No, these cows had not learned to walk on water. Coyote Lake was a meadow.

I checked the publication date on my map. It hadn't been field-checked in nearly fifty years. Coyote Lake had long ago filled up with silt. The sight was so absurd I simply had to laugh. Then I turned around and hiked back out, pausing along the way to shoot the sunset at a little knoll alongside the trail. At least I'd never shot from that vantage point before.

While geographic features are usually marked accurately, trails can be off significantly. That can happen because the trail was mapped inaccurately in the first place, perhaps because it wasn't clearly visible in the aerial photograph from which the map was made, or because the trail was rerouted after the map was published. USGS maps are frequently out of date by ten years or more. Check the map legend for the date when the map was most recently revised. Don't blindly trust any map, even a Trails Illustrated topo that supposedly was updated more recently than the USGS version from which it was derived. I've seen plenty of errors on USGS quads simply repeated on Trails Illustrated maps.

The best way to learn to read a topo map is to refer to it regularly whenever you're hiking. Practice relating the features on the map to the features on the ground. Although reading topo maps quickly and accurately takes a little practice, it's a crucial skill when estimating how long a hike will take.

With a topo map in front of you, you can estimate the length of your proposed adventure. A crude but simple method is to position one end of a piece of string at the start of your hike, then trace out the trail with the string, being careful to follow all the trail's windings as best you can. When you reach your destination, mark that position on the string with a thumbnail. Now bring the string to the mileage scale on the map's margin. The scale shows how many inches equals a mile. Measure the string with the mileage scale, counting in miles instead of inches, and you'll have a rough estimate of the length of your intended route.

Folding Maps

Paper maps are rather fragile things, so I like to carry them inside a one-gallon Ziploc bag. Unfortunately, folding a USGS 7.5 minute quad into quarters produces a folded map that's slightly too big to fit a one-gallon Ziploc. A slightly more sophisticated method is necessary. Whatever method you choose, use it consistently. Nothing destroys a map faster than repeatedly folding it in different ways.

To use the method I like, start with the map face-up with north at the top—the same position you'd use if you just wanted to read it.

(1) Bring the top edge down to the bottom edge with the printed side inside, as shown in the diagram, and crease the fold.

(2) Bring the top edge back up to the middle crease, this time with the printed side out. Bring the bottom edge up to the middle crease in the same way, again with the printed side facing out.

(3) With the north end of the map once again on the top, bring the left edge to the right edge.

(4) Bring the left edge back to the middle. Do the same with the right edge. The folded map will have the name visible in the upper right corner and will fit easily into a one-gallon Ziploc. I store my folded maps upright in a shoebox in alphabetical order with cardboard dividers indicating groups of letters (A–D, E–G, H–L, etc.).

An alternative is the accordion fold. Start as before, with the map's printed side facing up, with the map in "landscape" orientation (wider than it is tall). The north end of the map should be on the left.

(1) Bring the right edge to the left edge (printed side inside), make a sharp crease, then unfold the map flat again. Now bring the right edge to the center, making a quarter fold. Do the same with the left edge, bringing it to the center and making another quarter fold, as shown in the illustration.

(2) Fold the right edge back to the right-hand outermost edge of the folded map, making an eighth fold. In a similar way, fold the left edge of the map to the left-hand outermost edge of the folded map, making another eighth fold. Use these folds as a guide to make two more folds until you have eight accordion-like "facets."

(3) The map will actually have seven distinct creases dividing the map into eight sections.

(4) Fold the map in Z-like thirds, as shown. With this technique, you can look at any part of the map without unfolding the entire sheet.

1

2

3

4

A second, more accurate way to measure the length of a route is to buy a map measuring tool, which consists of a toothed wheel you roll along the map, following your proposed route, and a dial that reads out the number of miles you've traversed. Modern electronic map measuring tools let you input different map scales, so you can measure miles on both USGS 7.5 minute maps and Trails Illustrated maps, which often use nonstandard scales.

The high-tech way to plan your hike is to buy a set of topo maps on CD. Such collections are now available from at least two companies. Load the right map into your computer, and you can trace your route with the mouse. Instantly the computer

Training for Backpacking

We've all met body Nazis: people who ruthlessly punish their bodies with heinous workouts, then brag insufferably about their accomplishments as they sip Perrier at the party. Fortunately, there's no need to goose-step up the trail with military precision. You will enjoy backpacking more, however, if you make some effort to get in shape before the season begins, then continue a regular exercise program in between trips.

Aerobic fitness, the kind most important for backpacking, is defined as the ability to take in, transport, and utilize oxygen. One of the best measures of aerobic fitness, then, is the maximum amount of oxygen you can take in and use per minute. Since heavier people use more oxygen, maximum oxygen uptake is usually expressed in milliliters of oxygen consumed per kilogram of body weight per minute, or ml/kg/min. To estimate your maximum oxygen uptake, run as far as possible in fifteen minutes. Record the distance run in meters (1 mile equals 1,609 meters). Running on a track of known circumference makes estimating the distance easy. Divide the distance in meters by fifteen to find speed in meters per minute. Your maximum oxygen uptake is approximately:

$$MaxVO_2 = ([speed\ in\ meters\ per\ minute\ minus\ 133] \times 0.172) + 33.3$$

Minimally fit people score around forty. Champion endurance athletes score in the seventies and eighties.

Sports that guarantee a high, sustained heart rate are the best preparation for backpacking. Hiking, cycling, cross-country skiing, and running, particularly over hilly terrain, are all excellent because they train not only the heart and lungs, but also those muscles that will be taxed most heavily on the trail. Swimming, while great for the heart and lungs, should be supplemented by training that works the legs in ways similar to backpacking. Intermittently strenuous sports like tennis and racquetball are good only if played hard enough so that your heart rate goes up and stays up for the entire game.

will tell you the length of your route and how much elevation gain and loss it entails. You can annotate the map, name the route, then print out a customized map along with an elevation gain and loss profile. Computer-printed maps aren't a substitute for an original USGS topo because the map can only measure 8½ by 11 inches and the digitized data isn't sufficiently detailed to reproduce contour lines as crisply as on a USGS map, but they're still a handy reference. Computerized maps also let you create GPS waypoints, which you can link together into a route and then upload to your GPS receiver.

Most trails twist and turn much more than any mapmaker can show or you

Everyone has a "training threshold," the minimum intensity and duration of training that stimulates his or her body to adapt. The more slack your body, the lower your training threshold. The more taut your body, the higher the threshold. To keep making progress, increases in the intensity and duration of your training are essential. Brian J. Sharkey, author of *Physiology of Fitness,* gives this rule of thumb for estimating your training zone, the range of heart rates that will produce a training effect.

The lower limit is:

Heart rate = 55% (max heart rate − resting heart rate) + resting heart rate.

The upper limit is:

Heart rate = 70% (max heart rate − resting heart rate) + resting heart rate.

Your maximum heart rate is about 220 minus your age. To determine your exercise heart rate, take your pulse for ten seconds immediately after you stop exercising. Find your pulse with your fingertips at either your wrist or at the carotid artery in your neck, just below the point of your jaw. Then multiply by six to get beats per minute. For a twenty-five-year-old with a resting heart rate of 70, the training zone ranges from approximately 140 to 160 beats per minute.

If you are in poor condition now, a workout lasting only fifteen minutes may be enough to nudge your body over the training threshold. As you get more fit, extend the workouts until you can train comfortably for forty-five minutes to an hour or more. Working out every other day is the minimum for making significant progress. Using an intense burst of effort for about one twentieth of the workout (for example, by picking up the pace for the last quarter mile of a 5-mile run) gives your heart and lungs a useful added training stimulus. To keep track of your progress, record your workouts in a training log.

can measure. Regardless of the measuring method you use, adding a 25 percent fudge factor will probably get you closer to reality. Better to overestimate distance and be pleasantly surprised when you arrive sooner than you expected than to underestimate and arrive long after dark!

If you're not using a computer to plan your trip, the next task—the one we neglected on our hike up Mount Baldy—is to estimate the elevation gain and loss along your route. To do this, you need to track the trail carefully as it climbs up and down. Add up each increment of elevation gain and elevation loss to get a true picture of the amount of exertion required.

Most people carrying moderate loads walk about 2 miles an hour on a level trail. Each 1,000 feet of elevation gain adds an hour to that basic estimate; each 1,000 feet of loss adds about half an hour. Rest stops are in addition to these figures. Time can add up quickly, so if you're trying to pour on the miles, keep an eye on your watch. Cora and I find that 8 to 10 miles with 2,000 or 2,500 feet of elevation gain when carrying an overnight pack is a full but certainly not overwhelming day. Anything much longer than 12 miles starts to feel like the Bataan death march; anything less than 6 is a romp. Your own appetite for miles may vary tremendously from ours, depending on fitness, motivation, and whether you place greater value on comfort in camp or a light pack on the trail.

There's no need to train for three months before embarking on your first backpacking trip. It's not a marathon. Nonetheless, fitness—or, rather, operating within your level of fitness, whatever it is—will make your trip more enjoyable unless you relish the challenge of pushing yourself beyond your normal limits. One bad health habit—smoking—clearly inhibits your ability to enjoy backpacking, although backpackers also will walk a mile for a camel—if it will carry their load the rest of the way.

Once you have planned your trip, whether it's for a day or a week, write down your itinerary and leave it with someone responsible. Your itinerary should include what Cora and I call a "drop-dead" date. This is the day and time at which she should call search-and-rescue if I haven't returned. It's particularly important to leave a written itinerary with someone if you'll be going by yourself, which I do frequently. Going alone is a practice that is rightly discouraged by land managers and search-and-rescue groups. Solo wilderness travel, and particularly solo climbing, has its risks. Even a relatively minor mishap, such as a broken ankle or severely sprained knee, could turn a Sunday stroll into a survival epic if you happened to be far enough off the trail that no passersby could be expected. However, in the summer, if you stick to well-traveled trails, the added danger of going alone is slight. In the winter, or off-trail at any time of year, the extra danger is real. Cell phones cannot be counted upon in the backcountry. Just in the last few years, however, lightweight emergency locator beacons that can send an SOS via satellite almost anywhere in the world have become available. I'll have more to say about them when I discuss emergencies in chapter 13.

Packing Your Pack

Once you've selected an itinerary and heaped up everything you want to bring in the middle of your living room, you need to find a way to stuff all of it in your pack. For walking on decent trails, you generally want to put the heaviest gear high in your pack and as close to your spine as possible. That allows you to assume a more comfortable, upright posture because the weight is balanced over your hips. For off-trail scrambling, skiing, and snowshoeing, you still want the heaviest items close to your spine, but you probably want the weight a little lower, to make you less top-heavy. These are general guidelines; as a practical matter, I always pack my pack with the items I'm least likely to need during the day at the bottom, then continue to stow items in ascending order of daytime utility. That means my sleeping bag always goes in first, followed by my extra sweater, stove, fuel, main bag of food, etc. Lunch goes in the pack's top pocket. I stow my water bottle at the very top of the main compartment or in a side pocket. I lash my tent onto the front of the pack near the bottom; I strap my sleeping pad to the very top.

The only time I've noticed a significant deterioration in the way my pack rode was when I lashed something quite dense and heavy, like a big tripod or heavy tent, to the front or on one side of the pack. If you've got an internal-frame pack, try to place heavy items inside your pack near your spine. If the item won't fit inside, try to divide the item in two and lash half on each side. For example, you might lash the body of a big tent on one side of the pack, the poles and fly on the other. The worst place to lash something heavy is the front of your pack. If you've got an external frame, try lashing the heavy item horizontally across the top of the frame near your shoulders.

In rainy country every item in your pack should be stowed inside a stuff sack. That way, if it's raining when you unload your pack at camp, you can set things down on the ground without them becoming instantly soaked. Sleeping bags and clothing not needed while hiking are worth extra care. I often reinforce the water-resistance of the sleeping bag and clothing stuff sacks with a plastic bag or second, larger stuff sack. The waterproof pack covers sold by some companies are useful added insurance, but aren't a solution by themselves since you have to take them off to unload your pack, at which time you'll want everything in stuff sacks anyway.

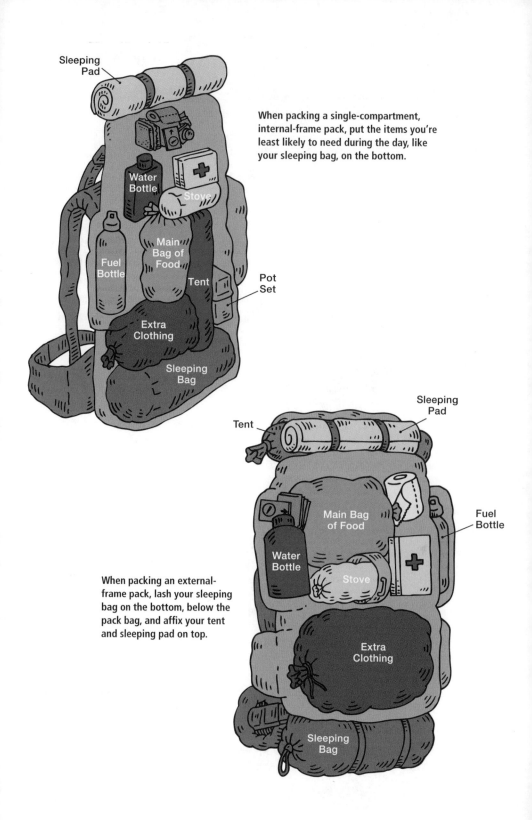

Sleeping Pad

When packing a single-compartment, internal-frame pack, put the items you're least likely to need during the day, like your sleeping bag, on the bottom.

Water Bottle

Stove

Fuel Bottle

Main Bag of Food

Tent

Pot Set

Extra Clothing

Sleeping Bag

Tent

Sleeping Pad

Main Bag of Food

Fuel Bottle

Water Bottle

Stove

When packing an external-frame pack, lash your sleeping bag on the bottom, below the pack bag, and affix your tent and sleeping pad on top.

Extra Clothing

Sleeping Bag

Also note that not all pack covers will fit over items lashed outside your pack.

The easiest way to get a heavy pack on your back is to set the pack on some solid support, like a rock, stump, or fallen log, that's about 3 feet high. Sit down beside the pack, slip your arms through the straps, and stand up. Lacking a friendly rock to help, you'll have to do it yourself. Face the back of the pack, the side with the straps. Loosen each shoulder strap slightly, then grab one shoulder strap with each hand and hoist the pack up onto your bent right knee. Steady the pack there with your left hand and slip your right arm and shoulder through the right-hand shoulder strap. The pack will now be on your back, supported by the right-hand shoulder strap. Slip your left arm through the left shoulder strap, snug down the shoulder straps, fasten and tighten the hip belt, moan and groan a few times to impress your trail companions, and you're set.

> ## Pack Liquids Safely
>
> The best way to pack small quantities of liquids you may want, like hand lotion or sunscreen, is in the little plastic bottles with screw-on lids that many hotels use to package shampoo for guests. You can also find "travel-size" bottles in well-equipped drugstores and supermarkets. Sunscreen often comes in squeeze bottles with flip-top lids that tend to pop open and create a problem that remains undiscovered until your entire pack or jacket pocket is coated with slime. I like to tape those flip-top lids shut, then unscrew the whole cap when I need access to the contents.

Well, almost set. Adjusting your pack is actually a continuous process that most people learn to do while they're walking. Hip belts sometimes loosen and need to be retightened. Shoulder-stabilizer straps get loose and need to be snugged down. Hips get sore, making it imperative to shift some weight to your shoulders by loosening the hip belt. Then your shoulders get sore, and it's time to cinch down the hip belt again and loosen the shoulder straps. One serious symptom to watch out for is numbness or tingling in your hands, caused by too much weight on your shoulders. If that happens, take the pack off for a few minutes until the tingling eases. When you put it back on, make sure the hip belt is tight enough to carry most of the weight.

When I'm carrying a heavy load, I try to take the pack off for at least a minute or two every hour or so. These "blood-flow breaks" let blood flow back into my hips and shoulders, easing the soreness that inevitably develops with even the best packs. I find I can carry the same weight farther, with greater comfort, if I adopt this procedure.

To pick up a heavy pack, start by facing the back of the pack, then grasp the shoulder straps and hoist the pack to your bent right knee.

Put your right arm through the right-hand shoulder strap, then insert your left arm through the left-hand shoulder strap, fasten the hip belt, and adjust all straps for a comfortable fit.

Route-Finding

If the trip you've planned goes through heavily traveled backcountry, such as that found in most national parks in the summer, then route-finding consists primarily of knowing the name of your destination, reading the trail signs, and staying on the trail. As the country gets wilder and more rugged, the trails more obscure or nonexistent, you need to become increasingly savvy about using a map and compass. In the winter in the high mountains, when snow obscures all trails and clouds frequently shroud the peaks, an accurate altimeter is another highly valuable tool.

The ultimate tool for really difficult route-finding is a Global Positioning System (GPS) receiver, which uses radio signals from a network of satellites to calculate your position to within 20 or 30 feet anywhere in the world. The least expensive receivers now cost less than a good pair of backpacking boots and weigh about as much as a cup of water. A GPS receiver is a dazzling navigational aid, but it does not stand on its own. It is essential that you bring a map and compass as well and know how to use them. What good is it to know you're at latitude 40° 39' 12' north, longitude 105° 42' 57' west if you can't take that information to a map and plot your position? It's true that better GPS receivers, such as the one I use, now do include detailed topographic maps. Just remember that the screen on even the best mapping GPS units only measures about 2 by 3½ inches.

All GPS receivers have a "go to" function. Let's say you record the position of your campsite, go exploring for a while, then take another position fix. By simply entering "go to camp" into the receiver, it can tell you the distance and direction to your campsite. That's highly useful information, but you need to take it to a map to see if following the compass bearing given by the receiver will lead you straight over a cliff or into an avalanche starting zone.

A full treatise on the art of backcountry navigation would fill an entire book of its own. If you'd like to pursue this subject in depth, you might want to read my book *Outward Bound Map and Compass Handbook*, third edition, published by FalconGuides / GPP. What follows is an introduction to the basics.

The best kind of compass for wilderness navigation is called a protractor compass or, more commonly, a baseplate compass. Its basic parts are shown in figure G. The baseplate is a rectangular piece of clear plastic. The round capsule mounted on the baseplate houses the compass needle, which can rotate freely within the capsule, coming to rest with its north end pointing to magnetic north. A viscous liquid damps the needle's swing. The capsule is marked with the 360 degrees that make a full circle. Zero (or 360) degrees equals north; 90 degrees equals east; 180 degrees equals south; 270 degrees equals west. The capsule can

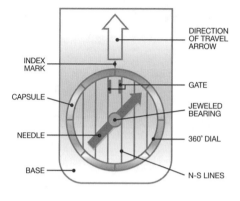

Figure G

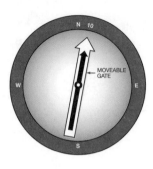

Figure H

be rotated in relation to the baseplate. The index mark on the baseplate aligns with the edge of the capsule to show you the bearing (the angle) you've set on the compass. The direction-of-travel arrow is essentially an extension of the index mark. The gate is a pair of lines (or sometimes a box) in which you position the north end of the compass needle when determining directions.

This combination of features allows you to do fancy tricks like taking the bearing of a landmark and measuring a course on the map. I won't get into measuring bearings and courses here, since you'll rarely need those skills if you stick to trails. What you do need to know is how to orient the map so that true north on the map corresponds to true north on the ground. To do that, you need to learn how to make the direction-of-travel arrow point to true north.

As most people know, true north and magnetic north do not lie in precisely the same direction. The difference is called the "declination." Compass needles point to magnetic north. Maps are drawn so that true north lies at the top of the map. Stated in another way, this means that the right and left edges of the map represent lines running true north and true south. Declination varies from place to place on the Earth. Sometimes magnetic north lies to the west of true north; sometimes it lies to the east.

I highly recommend spending a few extra dollars on a "set-and-forget" compass, one that takes care of complex declination calculations for you. With these compasses the gate can be moved in relation to zero on the capsule. This lets you set the declination once for your particular place on Earth. For example, let's say the declination is 10 degrees east, which means that magnetic north lies 10 degrees to the east of true north. The gate can be set so that it always aligns with the 10-degree mark on the capsule. Now when you align the compass needle in the gate and set the capsule so zero is opposite the index mark, the direction-of-travel arrow will point to true north rather than magnetic north, as shown in figure H (see page 104).

Orienting the map so that north on the map points in the same direction as north on the ground is simple if you've got a set-and-forget compass. Look on the margin of your topo map, where you'll find the declination for that region. Set the declination on your compass and you can forget about declination for the rest of your trip. Now set the capsule to zero and rotate the compass until the needle is within the gate. The direction-of-travel arrow now points to true north. Place the map so that the long edges of the baseplate are parallel to either the right or left edge of the map, and the map is oriented. North on the map equals north on the ground. This also means that a line from your position on the map to a landmark on the map should also point to the same landmark on the ground.

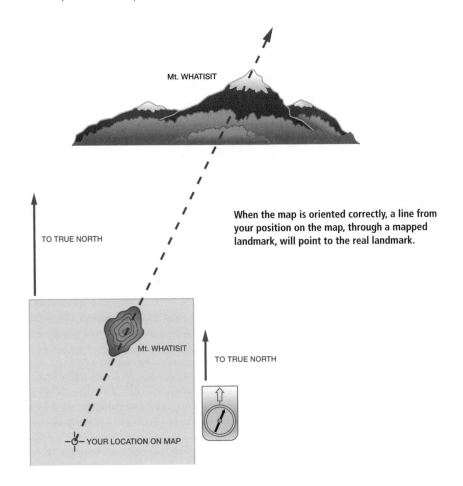

When the map is oriented correctly, a line from your position on the map, through a mapped landmark, will point to the real landmark.

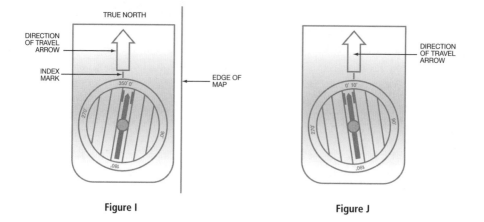

TRUE NORTH

DIRECTION
OF TRAVEL
ARROW

INDEX
MARK

EDGE OF
MAP

350° 0°

270°

90°

180°

DIRECTION
OF TRAVEL
ARROW

0° 10°

270°

90°

180°

Figure I

Figure J

Orienting your map if you don't have a set-and-forget compass is a tad more complicated. With these conventional compasses the gate is fixed so that it is always opposite the zero mark on the capsule. Let's say the declination diagram on your map shows that magnetic north lies 10 degrees to the east of true north. On the capsule, zero is the same as 360 degrees. Subtract 10 degrees from 360 to get 350. Set the capsule to 350. Orient the compass so the needle is in the gate. The direction-of-travel arrow will now point to true north, as shown in figure I . Place the map so that the long edges of the baseplate align with either the right or left edge of the map. The map is now oriented correctly. If the declination is 10 degrees west, you would set the capsule to 10 degrees and orient the compass so the needle is in the gate, as shown in figure J. Life gets even more complicated when you're trying to measure bearings and courses with a conventional compass, which is why I recommend set-and-forget compasses so strongly.

You should orient your map for the first time at the trailhead, before starting your hike. Study the oriented map, then relate the features marked there to the features in the terrain around you. For example, if there's a big mountain at the head of the valley you'll be hiking up, find that mountain on the map. Try to develop a general mental picture of the route you'll be following. For example, your route might head north up a river valley, then reach a trail junction just after the second large lake. At the junction you're supposed to turn west and climb the flanks of the valley to a high pass. If halfway through your hike you've already passed three large lakes and two 7-Elevens and still haven't found the trail junction, something is askew. As you travel, pause periodically to turn around and examine what the terrain will look like during your return trip. You'll find that terrain you've just traveled through can seem quite unfamiliar when you encounter it traveling in the opposite direction. On occasion during your hike, check the map and compass. Try to keep a general sense of the direction you're traveling. It can be surprisingly easy to get turned around, even for an experienced hiker.

One September about two years BC (Before Children), Cora and I embarked on a two-day backpacking trip in the Lost Creek Wilderness southwest of Denver. The wilderness derives its name from the astonishing way in which Lost Creek appears out of nowhere, then vanishes into caverns in solid rock walls, only to reappear a quarter mile farther downstream. The terrain is rugged and complex, full of granite domes, towers, and buttresses, and the trails corkscrew constantly.

A steady rain set in about noon on our first day, and by dusk we were tired, damp, and ready for camp. We knew that the place where we planned to camp was nearby when we pounded down a steep hill and rejoined Lost Creek just where it emerged from a cave in a cliff. Obviously the trail continued on the far side; just as obviously there was no bridge, a fact that should have raised our suspicions, since other stream crossings had been bridged. I remembered that the map showed that we wanted to follow the stream, however, so we gritted our teeth, waded across, and continued along the trail, which paralleled the stream.

Within a few hundred yards, the trail grew faint and overgrown, then vanished into a morass of swift water, dense brush, and giant, slippery boulders. I pulled out the map. As I remembered, the trail was marked as continuing along the stream. Still, something was wrong, and it was too late in the day to try to figure it out then. With our feet squishing in our frigid boots, we walked back to the stream crossing and pitched the tent. Once inside I pulled out the compass. What I had thought was north was actually south. We had followed the stream in exactly the wrong direction.

In the morning everything became clear. The trail we had followed down to the stream was simply a well-trampled spur trail leading to a popular campsite. The trail on the far side of the creek was probably made by horsemen trying to reach the excellent campsite where we eventually spent the night. After all, horsemen don't worry about crossing streams without bridges; it's not their feet that are getting wet. The trail we wanted had indeed continued along the stream, but in the opposite direction. We had lost it the night before where it made a hard right a hundred yards above the creek and sneaked up a narrow, boulder-strewn defile for 50 yards to avoid a cliff. The spur trail down to the well-worn campsite had been much more obvious, and we had simply followed our noses—an easy task on a horse trail. The whole experience recrystallized a lesson I thought I'd learned long ago: When the correct route is in doubt, the first thing to do is get out the map and the compass.

Another common error traps careless hikers who decide to drop their packs and dash up to some scenic overlook, then forget precisely where they left their gear. On a trip many years ago into Utah's Maze, I encountered a pair of hikers who'd dropped their packs to go in search of some petroglyphs. They'd set their packs right on the trail and continued up a narrow canyon, undoubtedly assuming that there was no possible way they could miss their packs upon their return. During their descent, however, they'd followed the dry river bottom rather than taking the parallel trail up on the stream bank that they'd followed on the way up. By the time I encountered them, they'd already walked a good half mile beyond their packs. Fortunately, I had noted their packs and was able to tell them where they were. If you do choose to leave your pack (or camp) for a short jaunt, make sure you note the landmarks nearby very carefully.

While it's important to keep track of your gear, it's even more important to keep track of your companions. Staying together prevents a lot of unnecessary confusion. Early in my climbing career, I set off to climb a peak in the Sierras with a much older and wiser companion. He stopped to adjust clothing, but I continued

Tracking Your Position in a Desert Canyon

Conventional techniques can be nearly useless when you're trying to track your location in one of the Southwest's steep-walled sandstone canyons. The vertical walls usually block your view of nearby landmarks, and the canyon itself may lack features that can be clearly identified on the map. GPS receivers may have trouble locking on to satellite signals. The secret is to start using your map and compass at the very beginning of the trip. The best clue to your location is the direction the canyon is heading. As you enter the canyon, orient your map. In this situation I like to carry the map and compass in my hand as I walk, referring to it every few hundred yards. Mark your position on the map with your thumbnail and continue along the canyon. Let's say the canyon starts out heading north, then bends to the east. If you keep your map oriented as you hike, you'll notice immediately when the canyon begins its bend and you begin traveling east. Move your thumbnail to your new position. Continue in this way, tracking each twist and turn of the canyon until you reach your destination. Such careful route-finding may be unnecessary if you are planning to do an out-and-back hike with no particular turnaround point in mind. If you're searching for a particular side canyon or petroglyph, however, or are attempting a loop that requires you to exit the canyon at a particular point, this method is invaluable.

on and turned up the wrong gully. He continued on to the right gully and spent the rest of the day wondering what had happened to me. I finally stopped and waited for him. Eventually I descended to our camp and spent the rest of the day waiting for him to return, which he did in late afternoon. My impatience had cost me the summit. If your companions are behind you and out of sight when you reach a trail junction or other fork in the route, be sure to wait so they know which way you went. If you must separate, be sure to agree very clearly on when and where you will meet up again. Staying together is almost always the safest course.

Tricks of the Trail

People who have never hiked with a substantial load often pace themselves poorly. They fall into the sprint-and-drop routine, rushing up the mountain for a few hundred yards, then collapsing in a heap, panting. When you're backpacking, particularly at the altitudes common in the Rockies and Sierras, slow and steady wins the race. After all, the backpacker's role model—the tortoise—has its home on its back too. One study of walking showed that the energy expended doubles with each mile-per-hour increase in speed. To reach your destination without exhausting yourself, slow down until you've adopted a pace you can sustain comfortably for an hour without resting. On really steep grades with heavy loads, particularly at high altitudes, you may want to try the rest step: After each step, let the trailing leg straighten completely and lock your knee for a second or two. This allows your skeleton to support most of your weight while the unweighted leading leg gets a brief rest.

When you do pause to rest, rest completely. Get your pack off and sit down. Try to pause at areas that won't suffer from the use. Rest stops are most effective when they're kept brief because of the way your body gets rid of lactic acid buildup, one cause of muscle fatigue. One researcher found that your body can get rid of about 30 percent of the lactic acid buildup in the first five to seven minutes of rest. In the next fifteen minutes, however, you get rid of only about 5 percent more. Prolonged rests also let the body cool down too much, making it even harder to get back on your feet and start humping that load again.

Nearly all stream crossings in popular wilderness areas are bridged these days, but it's still useful to know how to cross a stream that isn't. The first tactic is to look for a natural bridge: a fallen log. Depending on the ruggedness of the terrain and the difficulty of fording, it may be worth searching upstream and downstream for a quarter mile to try to find a suitable log. Don't feel compelled to emulate the Flying Wallendas by walking across the log if it's too narrow or too high for comfort. There's no shame in straddling the log and working your way across inch by inch.

If the search for a log proves futile, conquer the natural inclination to cross at the narrowest point in hopes of spending as little time as possible in the stream. Narrow means deep, and deep means a good chance you'll be swept off your feet if the current is strong and the water comes up over your knees. Instead, look for a wide spot in the stream where the water is as shallow as possible. Don't cross right above a waterfall or rapid. Loosen your shoulder straps, undo your sternum strap, and loosen or completely unhook your hip belt so you can shed your pack in a hurry if you do get swept off your feet. Focusing your eyes on the far bank rather than the rushing water will help you keep your balance. If the terrain permits, go diagonally downstream as you cross rather than crossing along a line directly perpendicular to the banks. You'll waste less strength fighting the current. Make sure each foot is firmly planted before moving the next. Sometimes it's best to shuffle your feet without crossing your legs. It can also be helpful for two people to link hands to help support each other. Trekking poles make fording a stream much easier. Unless the water is clear and the bottom is uniformly sandy, it may be best to wear your boots while fording to protect your feet. Wear your boots without your socks while crossing, then put your socks back on before you resume hiking. After the socks have absorbed some of the moisture from the boots, exchange them for dry ones and hang the damp ones off the front of your pack to air-dry. This procedure will help your boots dry as fast as possible and reduce the chance of blisters. If you, like me, hate the idea of soaking your boots, and you know you'll have a very difficult stream to cross on your trip, consider carrying a pair of water sandals like those worn by white-water rafters. Remember, it's easy for the inexperienced hiker to underestimate the difficulty of fording a stream. When in doubt, turn back.

Large, late-lingering snowfields that obscure portions of the trail are another possible hazard in spring and early summer in the West's higher regions. In the early morning such snowfields can be frozen hard and nearly as slippery as pure ice. Even mountaineers equipped with ice axes, which supposedly give them the ability to stop a slip while snow climbing, have often discovered at great cost how easy it is to slip, fail to catch themselves, and immediately accelerate out of control on steep snow. Usually snowfields that obscure trails will have a deep, rutted path pounded into them by hikers who cross after the snow softens in the midday sun. Carefully following the beaten path can be safe at any time. Danger arises, however, when unwary hikers venture off the path onto steep snow when the snow is frozen hard.

When the snow softens toward midday, a snowfield can present an additional hazard. Very often the edges of the snowfield, and even the center, can be undercut by melting, particularly if water is flowing underneath. It's easy to break through the thin remaining bridge of snow and drop abruptly a foot or more to the rocky ground underneath, endangering your knees and ankles. Tread lightly, particularly near the edge of the snowfield and in low-lying areas where you suspect a stream may be flowing underneath.

After the snow melts, steep mountain slopes present a different hazard: rockfall. In regions where the rock is naturally rotten, rockfall frequently occurs spontaneously, particularly during a hard rain or when the sun melts the frost holding shattered cliffs and gully walls together. A bigger threat, even in regions where the rock is basically sound, is hikers dislodging stones that then tumble onto hikers below them. In loose terrain, hikers should never travel with one person directly above another. If a gully is too narrow to permit side-by-side travel, one person should move at a time, with the others waiting in a safe place.

The slickrock canyons of the desert Southwest hold danger of a different sort. Sooner or later all novice hikers make the unpleasant discovery that it's much easier to climb up something than it is to climb down it. The deceptively easy-looking slabs, buttes, and spires that abound in the Southwest have tempted many an unwary hiker into an attempt to scale them. The rock seems so low-angled; beginners don't know that what really makes rock difficult to climb is not steepness, but lack of holds, a characteristic for which sandstone is notorious. If you're tempted to scramble up something, go up just 10 feet, then turn around and come back down. If descending is completely comfortable, then it may be reasonable to continue upward cautiously if the rock becomes no more difficult. Just remember that every step up will have to be reversed, and that a slip even 20 or 30 feet off the ground can easily be fatal.

Trail Etiquette

One beautiful July day when Cora and I were hiking in the Indian Peaks Wilderness, we came across a lush field of flowers sprawling across a steep hillside. The trail cut right across the hillside, directly through the flower patch, but it was obvious to me that the best vantage point for a photograph was about 30 feet below the trail. I examined the area carefully and finally selected a circuitous route to my vantage point that allowed me to avoid trampling any flowers. No sooner had I made my picture, returned to the trail, and continued onward, however, when I overheard a couple arguing behind me. "Stay on the trail!" the woman scolded her boyfriend, who was about to follow in my footsteps to make his own photograph. "But he did it!" the man replied, obviously referring to me.

Immediately I realized that I had made a mistake. The slope I had descended to reach my photo op was steep and unstable. Although I had watched my footing carefully, I had undoubtedly disturbed the soil and the low-lying plants as I edged my boot soles into the slope to avoid slipping. In addition to the damage I'd done, I'd set a very bad example—an example that had almost been followed immediately. Regardless of how careful subsequent photo maniacs were, the fragile vegetation holding the highly erodible soil in place would inevitably have been damaged. Once it died, erosion would have begun. Snowmelt and summer rains would have stripped away what little topsoil existed in that harsh, alpine environment, and within a summer or two that flower field, which had delighted thousands of visitors every summer for decades, would have been marred by an ugly scar.

The first rule of trail etiquette is simple: Stay on the trail. The more heavily used the wilderness and the more fragile the landscape, the greater the importance of this guideline. Some beauty spots, like that flower field, should be treated like works of art. Few people are so boorish that they would trample across a painting if it were laid out on the ground in front of them. Alpine meadows should be treated with equal respect.

Staying on the trail also means refraining from cutting switchbacks. Switchbacks are the places where a trail makes a hairpin turn and almost doubles back on itself. It's tempting to the ill-informed to leave the trail just before the turn and take a "shortcut," regaining the trail just after the turn. This too is an invitation to severe erosion, which, once started, is extremely difficult to stop. For the same reason, you should avoid walking side by side on a trail unless it was built to accommodate such traffic. Few trails are. Walking side by side will widen the trail and, if it crosses a steep slope, tend to break down the outside of the tread, the level portion of the trail where you walk, causing the trail itself to deteriorate. Whenever possible, avoid walking around mud holes that form in low spots on the trail. This practice turns narrow wilderness paths into highways as hikers' boots trample and kill the trailside vegetation. Instead, buy yourself a pair of waterproof boots and charge fearlessly ahead, straight through the puddle. You may find it gives you a perverse pleasure as it reminds you of your childhood when you went stomping through the puddles, throwing a glorious spray of water in all directions and greatly annoying your mother. In any case mud will fall off your boots faster than vegetation will grow back. Treat little snow patches on the trail the same as mud holes: Blast on through the snow rather than walking around and killing the vegetation to the side of the trail. During spring hikes, when snow patches are frequent, you'll probably want to wear gaiters to keep the snow out of your boots.

The meaning of "staying on the trail" can be quite difficult to decipher when you suddenly find yourself confronted by three trails, all running parallel to each other about a foot apart. Multiple trails frequently begin when fussy hikers with porous footwear walk alongside a muddy trail rather than directly on it. In other places multiple trails begin when the original trail has been built with too few water bars, the low wooden or stone barriers across a trail that divert flowing water off the tread. Without sufficient water bars the trail itself becomes a stream during the spring runoff. Soon the trail erodes into a foot-deep, narrow slit choked with boulders. Even when dry, such a mangled trail offers only difficult walking, and so thoughtless hikers begin a new trail paralleling the old. I've seen "trails" in rainy Scotland that could have accommodated a truck towing a double-wide trailer. A ranger once described to me a trail in Tuolumne Meadows, near Yosemite, that was six lanes wide. The best solution when you're confronted with multiple trails is to pick the one that seems most used and stay with it as much as possible. To be part of the long-term solution, consider volunteering on a trail maintenance crew. Many local conservation organizations organize such crews each summer. Federal land managers can often tell you which group is doing what.

There are a few exceptions to the stay-on-the-trail rule. The most common involves horses. Hikers should yield the right of way to horses by walking a few feet off the trail and standing quietly while the horses pass by. If the trail is crossing a slope, move to the downhill side of the trail. If the horse spooks, it will try to bolt uphill, which is much safer for both the horse and the rider than plunging downhill. Predators always seek the high ground. By stepping off the trail downhill, so you are lower than the horse, you look much less like a threat. Speak quietly to the horse and rider so the horse knows you are human. Hikers traveling downhill should also yield to hikers laboring uphill. After all, they're working harder than you are.

As you gain more experience, you may find situations where you want to leave the trail behind completely and take off cross-country. In many parts of the nation, the alpine tundra above timberline provides easy walking and breathtaking 360-degree views. Unfortunately, it's not always environmentally acceptable to succumb to the off-trail urge. In the White Mountains of New Hampshire, for example, rangers urge all hikers to stay on the trail at all times. There are simply too many people, and the land is too fragile. In Rocky Mountain National Park, short footpaths lead from heavily traveled Trail Ridge Road across the alpine tundra to scenic overlooks. Signs there urge visitors to stay on the paved footpaths rather than wander off across the easily damaged tundra. In another part of the park, however, off-trail tundra-walking is permitted, simply because the people pressure is far lower. In that part of the park, hikers have to follow a steep trail for a couple of miles to reach timberline. As always, the need to flex a little boot leather quickly discourages the masses of people. When in doubt about the environmental acceptability of a cross-country hike, ask a ranger.

If you're walking off-trail with friends in places where there's no sign of previous passage, your group should spread out to avoid walking in each other's tracks. This minimizes the possibility that your passage will create the beginnings of a herd trail, which other hikers are likely to find and follow. Try to walk through areas that can tolerate the traffic: sandy areas, slickrock and granite benches, talus and scree fields, lingering snowfields. On the alpine tundra in parts of Rocky Mountain National Park, for example, boulders stud broad areas of alpine grass dotted with tiny wildflowers no bigger than a thumbtack. Try to hop from rock to rock as much as possible to avoid trampling the vegetation. Avoid marshy areas where your boots will compact the porous, waterlogged soil. You should also avoid steep slopes where you will have to dig in your toes on the way up and heels on the way down. Your footsteps can start a slope on the path to erosion. Yosemite has a regulation limiting groups to fifteen people if they stay on the trail, but limiting groups to eight if they plan to travel more than a quarter mile off the trail. This sensible regulation should be adopted by large groups everywhere.

On occasion you will face a dilemma while hiking off-trail. You come across an incipient trail. Do you use it to confine your impact to already disturbed ground, or avoid it, hoping it will heal? If a durable route aside from the incipient trail exists (a granite bench or a sandy wash, for example), then take it. Otherwise, use your best judgment, balancing the fragility of the land around the trail with the degree of damage already done.

At times when you are hiking off-trail, you may be tempted to build a few cairns (small piles of rocks) to guide you on your return trip. In general you should refrain. Instead, learn to memorize landmarks both large and small. Make a careful mental note of that odd-shaped boulder that marks the correct gully for your descent off the ridge crest. Master a few additional map-and-compass skills so you can shoot a bearing to follow if a whiteout blows in. Turn around frequently and study the terrain as it will look during the trip home. Buy a GPS receiver and practice with it until its features become second nature, then create a waypoint rather than building a cairn. If you absolutely must build a few cairns for safety's sake, be sure to restore the area to its natural appearance by dismantling them during your return trip.

Trail etiquette includes a few other pointers, some of which are backed up by actual regulations. Pets are usually prohibited in the backcountry in national parks, as are weapons of any sort. Harassing wildlife is also prohibited. Enjoy animals from a distance. If you want to photograph them, buy a long lens (300mm or longer) or content yourself with composing a landscape photograph with the animal as part of the scenery. Feeding animals is prohibited too. Handing out tidbits corrupts the animals' normal eating habits and increases the population artificially, beyond what the land can support in the off-season when all the tourists are gone. In wilderness areas and national parks, every facet of the land is protected. That means that visitors shouldn't pick the flowers. It also means leaving antlers, bones, wind-sculpted driftwood, and all historic and prehistoric artifacts in place. This includes pot shards and arrowheads as well as other objects. Ralph Waldo Emerson expressed the leave-it-alone ethic well in 1846:

I wiped away the weeds and foam,

I fetched my sea-born treasures home;

But the poor, unsightly, noisome things

Had left their beauty on the shore,

With the sun and the sand and the wild uproar.

CLEAN CAMPING 101

> A man is rich in proportion to the number of things which he can afford to let alone.

> —*Henry David Thoreau, 1817–1862*

So now you've honed your map-and-compass skills and broken in your new hiking boots on several day hikes. You're ready for your first overnight trip. Can you just load up your pack and sally forth into the wild green yonder? Not quite.

First you have to get a permit. It's sad, it's frustrating, it's depressing, but it's a necessity, at least at many of the more popular destinations. There are just too many of us who love the wilderness. The backcountry is fragile, at least in comparison to the hordes of people who want to use it. Most national parks began requiring backcountry permits in the late 1960s or early 1970s, as the backpacking boom went ballistic and the damage caused by unregulated camping became apparent. Backpackers quite naturally picked the most beautiful spots to camp: the meadow with a view of the lake, the stream bank beside the joyous brook, the tundra just above timberline with an incredible view of snow-crowned peaks. And if only a few people per summer had camped in those locations, the damage might have been tolerable. But the number of backpackers grew exponentially.

In 1977, the peak year of the boom in many parks, backpackers spent at least 60,000 user-nights (one person for one night) in Shenandoah National Park and another 102,000 user-nights in Great Smoky Mountains National Park just to the south. Rocky Mountain National Park saw 62,700 user-nights. Yosemite peaked in 1975 with 219,000 user-nights. All told, the national parks recorded about 2.5 million backcountry user-nights in 1977. Waterproof tent floors smothered meadow grasses, streamside vegetation, and alpine tundra. The endless tramp of booted feet compacted the soil around these camps until the soil literally died. Air is vital to the billions of organisms that inhabit the soil. As the soil's porous structure collapsed, so did the soil's ability to support life. The only crop that thrived was fire rings, which sprouted everywhere. The heat of the fires sterilized the soil; the fire itself blackened the rocks with charcoal that would last for thousands of years. As downed wood became scarce, hikers broke, chopped, and sawed dead limbs off trees. When those were gone, they attacked live limbs, scarring the trees permanently. In a misguided effort to save a few ounces on the hike out, backpackers buried their trash or tried to burn it. Too often fire rings became trash pits as well. Toilet paper flowers flourished as hikers failed to adequately bury their waste. In the Indian Peaks Wilderness near Denver, camping pressure and destruction grew so great that the valleys leading away from the most popular trailheads were closed to all camping from May 1 to November 30. The only time you can camp there now is when a thick blanket of snow protects the fragile landscape. Similar problems forced managers to impose restrictions in many other areas.

The number of backpackers declined in the mid-1980s, then began climbing again in many areas as the 1990s began, reaching boom-year levels again in the mid-1990s. Although the people-pressure has declined somewhat since then, land managers in most areas feel, with good reason, that restrictions are still necessary. Some areas, like Rocky Mountain National Park, use a designated-site system for the most popular destinations. Backpackers are required to camp in a specified site marked by a stake in the ground. Sites can be reserved. Popular sites are booked up months in advance. In addition to the reserved sites, Rocky Mountain National Park also has twenty-three cross-country zones, all below timberline, which have no trails and no designated campsites. Hikers can camp anywhere they want within those zones, constrained only by the low-impact camping guidelines and a time limit of one or two nights per zone, no more than one night per camp.

In Yosemite, pressure on the backcountry is controlled by using a quota system limiting the number of backpackers who can start in from each trailhead in one day. About 60 percent of the available slots can be reserved; the others are available on a first-come, first-served basis. The quotas for the popular trailheads fill up quickly, sometimes as much as twenty-four weeks in advance. After obtaining a permit, backpackers can camp anywhere they choose (with a few exceptions), again within the constraints imposed by low-impact camping practices. The park strongly recommends that people camp in places where others have camped before on the theory that the damage has already been done. Why ruin a new site as well? This recommendation is now universal, even in well-watered regions with long growing seasons where vegetation can regenerate quickly, such as Shenandoah National Park.

Permits are free or cost a nominal amount. You can obtain a permit in person or, sometimes, by mail, but rarely by phone or online. Some parks let you fax in a reservation request. For popular parks like Rocky Mountain, Grand Canyon, and Yosemite, and particularly for popular destinations within those parks, plan as far ahead as you can—months ahead, if possible. Some areas limit how far ahead of time you can make a reservation. Permits are usually required year-round, but winter use in mountain areas is often low enough that regulations are relaxed.

Rules vary from place to place, but one principle is a constant: Abide by whatever regulations land managers have applied to the wilderness. For the most part these regulations have been developed by backcountry rangers who spend a lot more time in the backcountry—and see its problems more often—than you and I do. If a particular regulation seems onerous or unnecessary, write a letter to the backcountry office or park superintendent after you get home. Don't flout the regulations in the backcountry. I know, I know, I sound like your mother demanding that you eat your vegetables. Experience will soon teach you, however, that nearly all the regulations, as obnoxious as they may at first appear, actually enhance your enjoyment of the wilderness by helping keep it clean, untrammeled, and relatively uncrowded. One final note: Regulations do change, so check the park's website or call the rangers at the park or wilderness area you plan to visit before planning your trip.

Selecting a Campsite

Camping in a designated site is like pulling into slot 76 at the KOA: no thought required. If camping is not restricted to designated sites, then choosing a site requires a bit more thought. Consider the land before shrugging off your pack with a weary groan and pitching your tent on the first patch of semi-level ground that's not a minefield of anthills and horse manure. Most popular backpacking areas are pockmarked with sites that have already seen intensive use. If a previously used site in an environmentally sound location is available, use it again to confine your impact to as small an area as possible. However, meadows and areas that are wetlands in the spring, even if they are almost dry in late summer, are always off limits even if someone has camped there before. Catalog pictures and magazine ads that show tents in lush—meaning wet—meadows are trumpeting a lie and encouraging abusive practices that should never be tolerated. Let those sites recover. The same goes for stream and lake banks. Try to camp at least 200 feet from water, even if the regulations permit you to camp closer. By maintaining your distance you'll spare the vegetation along the bank and be sure that animals can come for a drink without intimidation. Desert bighorn, in particular, will shy away from waterholes if you camp nearby. Avoid camping in the beauty spots, the scenic overlooks and spots with climactic vistas across the lake or up the valley that will certainly draw other visitors. Relish the view from these spots for as long as you want, but don't camp there.

The alpine tundra above timberline is another highly fragile area. Plants there must endure severe cold, an extremely short growing season, powerful winter storms, and the desiccating effect of near-constant wind. Give those plants a chance. Wind and weather also besiege the highest timberline trees, the hardy survivors in the last outpost of the forest empire. Admire their tenacity, but don't stress it further by camping among them. Camping near timberline or above also puts you in danger from lightning storms, which are frequent in most mountainous areas from late spring to early fall.

In high desert areas, avoid camping or even walking on the dark, knobby crusts of cryptobiotic soil that carpet some regions. This crust, a symbiotic association of fungi, moss, and cyanobacteria, is literally the glue that holds the soil together, helping prevent erosion when rare but powerful thunderstorms pound the desert. The crust is extremely fragile and takes fifty to one hundred years to fully regenerate if it's crushed beneath a careless foot. According to some biologists, microbial crusts similar to cryptobiotic soil may well have been the first colonizers of land when life emerged from the sea as much as three billion years ago. Those microbes, in turn, may have accelerated the weathering of rock into soil, a process that removed carbon dioxide from the atmosphere. That may have reduced the strength of the greenhouse effect and lowered the Earth's temperature by as much as 54°F, making the land much more hospitable to the development of more complex forms of life—such as, eventually, you and me. So don't even think of walking on the cryptobiotic soil, much less camping on it.

The best sites in forested regions are usually deep in the woods, well away from lakes and streams and out of sight of trails and other campers. If you can't find an established site, look for areas where pine-needle duff or deciduous leaves—not grass—carpet the forest floor and where your tent will not crush any low-growing plants. Beware of standing dead trees or large dead limbs that could topple or break off in a storm and flatten your tent. In some areas the vegetation in dry meadows and grassy areas is resistant enough to tolerate one night (and one night only) of low-impact use. Unfortunately, such sites are highly visible to both wildlife and other campers, so they are best avoided in most situations.

The best site in the desert is often a level slickrock bench. Sand in your clothes, your hair, your food, and your camera is the bane of desert camping. Camping on slickrock gives you a place to lay down your gear, and yourself, where sand will not immediately infiltrate everything. Lacking a convenient slickrock campsite, grit your teeth (you'll soon be grinding them regardless) and look for regions that don't support vegetation—which means sites graced with sand or gravel. Camping in a sandy wash is tempting because such sites have very little impact, in part because there's no vegetation to harm and in part because the infrequent rainstorm big enough to cause water to flow in the wash will remove any sign of your camp. Of course, if you happen to be there when the flood descends, it might wash you away too. Even if it's clear overhead, a thunderstorm upstream can create a dangerous flash flood that wipes out your camp. Resist temptation. Don't camp in the bottom of a wash.

The best sites are found, not made. Save your engineering for winter when there's 4 feet of snow on the ground. Don't level sites or "improve" them by digging trenches around your tent to drain away rainwater. Trenches promote erosion, which eventually creates gullies. Refrain from building windbreaks or benches from stones or logs. The archaic practice of cutting pine-bough beds that some turn-of-the-twentieth-century woodcraft manuals recommended should be relegated to the history books. Try to remember that you're spending a night, not founding a settlement. The longer your stay, the more your campsite will begin to look like the beginnings of a city. If you've camped in a pristine spot, move on after one night.

If you're camped in a previously used site with an established path to water, use the path. If no such path exists, avoid making one. That's easier to do if you can avoid making multiple trips to your water source by bringing an extra water bottle or two, or perhaps a large collapsible water jug if you're traveling in a large group, then filling all your water containers in one trip to the stream or lake. Multiple trips over the same route soon create a visible herd path that encourages more people to walk the same route. If multiple trips are necessary, choose a different route each time to spread the impact out so thinly that no one will notice. Wherever your site, consider bringing a pair of lightweight sneakers or sandals to wear around camp to help reduce your impact on the vegetation. Think of it as evening out the odds in the confrontation between your massive waffle-stompers and the fragile vegetation. (Okay, in cactus country the odds are pretty even to begin with.) The goal should be to leave your camp so undisturbed that a visitor the next day would think no one had ever camped there. You do yourself a favor as well as the next visitor by leaving an immaculate camp. Backcountry rangers monitor the damage to the backcountry. If the land suffers, so do you, because quotas shrink.

Large groups must take extra care in their selection and use of sites because the potential for damage from such concentrated use is high. Many parks limit group size, so inquire in advance. In the Great Gulf Wilderness in New Hampshire's White Mountains, for example, the group limit is ten. In Yosemite it's fifteen—eight if you want to travel off-trail. In Mount Rainier National Park it's five unless you reserve a group site.

At times you'll face a dilemma in whether to use a slightly worn site or not. If you think there's a chance it will recover, based on your estimate of the amount of damage that's already occurred and the probability of other parties using it in the near future, then it's probably best to leave it alone and camp in a pristine site. If it's already over the edge and looks like vegetation won't be able to regrow in the compacted soil, then it's probably best to confine your impact to that one site.

The real gurus of low-impact camping use a sleeping setup that rivals, in its concern for Earthly life, the Jain practice of sweeping the ground ahead of them as they walk for fear of crushing an insect. Their solution? Sleeping in a hammock slung between two trees. Surely no lower-impact way of spending the night in the woods could be devised. A simple plastic or nylon tarp draped over a cord tied between those same trees and staked out at the four corners serves to deflect rain and provide a dry, sheltered nook for cooking in inclement weather. Alas, that tarp cannot serve to deflect mosquitoes, black flies, deer flies, no-see-ums, and other assorted nasties whose collective assault on sanity is the prime reason I rarely go camping without a tent. Although winter in the mountains is too harsh for hammock camping and deserts often lack suitable trees, in the right time and place a hammock and tarp might well be a lightweight way to practice the low-impact art.

Pitching a tarp over a hammock is the lowest-impact way to spend a night in the woods.

Campfires

Campfires and the outdoor life have been connected in a deep and visceral way ever since the days when there was no "outdoors" because there was no "indoors" with which to contrast it. Unfortunately, campfires are now like pine-bough beds, lakeside campsites, and four-wheeled brontosaurs that get 8 miles to the gallon: a luxury that we can no longer afford. First, fire rings are an ugly and extremely long-lived reminder that people have passed that way before. Blackened rocks remain discolored for hundreds, if not thousands, of years. That same soot will blacken your pots, which will, in turn, stain everything they touch. Often, and mistakenly, people believe their fire will burn almost anything, including food scraps and their trash with its plastic and aluminum foil components. When the fire fails to consume those items, they're often simply left behind, which converts the fire ring into a trash pit for rodents and birds to scavenge. Wood smoke will penetrate your clothes and give them a lingering odor, which may make you feel like Daniel Boone in the backcountry, but will make you smell like a Neanderthal in the city.

In addition, wood smoke is a health hazard. Evidence is growing that inhaling wood smoke leads to reductions in lung function and increased susceptibility to lower respiratory diseases. Other research has linked compounds in smoke to cancer, heart disease, and central nervous system disorders. One study in the late 1980s showed that 25 percent of Denver's infamous brown cloud was caused by wood smoke. Many mountain towns have enacted restrictions on wood burning to preserve air quality. Murphy's first law of fire building states that no matter where you sit in relation to your fire, the wind will always shift and blow the smoke in your face. Why expose yourself to the risk? Why contribute, in even a small way, to degrading the quality of wilderness air? Traveling to the wilderness, only to build a fire, reminds me of the billboard I saw outside Santiago, Chile, a city choking on filthy air caused by millions of automobiles. The billboard, erected by the local Chevy dealer alongside a major highway leading from Santiago to the Andes, showed two children in a car driven by their father. The sign read, "Thank you, Daddy, for taking us to breathe clean air."

Fire building causes other problems. Pyromaniacal backpackers camping night after night in the same popular spots soon scour the ground of all burnable dead and downed wood—which should, in any case, be left to decay, thereby enriching and renewing the soil. In a mindless quest for their nightly fire fix, many campers turn to living trees, first breaking off dead limbs, then chopping off live limbs, scarring what should have been a pristine forest. A fire's intense, concentrated heat sterilizes the soil beneath it and in its immediate vicinity. Even if the rocks of the fire ring are removed and the ashes scattered, the ground will remain lifeless for years, if not decades. Careless fire builders have also caused numerous forest fires. Too many people have broken camp and left behind a fire that they were sure was out—when it wasn't. Hours or days later the smoldering embers sprang to life and ignited an inferno. In most national parks, fires are simply banned in the backcountry. In all places where fires are permitted, only dead, downed wood may be burned. One of the lightweight backpacking stoves described in chapter 7 provides a far more convenient alternative for cooking than a wood fire: faster to light, easier to regulate, and useful in any weather. And you save yourself the weight of a hatchet, saw, and guilty conscience.

An argument is sometimes made that a fire on a beach that is well supplied with driftwood, constructed below the high-tide mark where all evidence will soon wash away, is acceptable. Or that in really remote country, where very few people go, a small fire can be condoned if all traces are erased. Frankly, I don't buy it. I remember picking over the remnants of a fire on a Grand Canyon beach, striving to locate and pick up every ash for removal. It was impossible. Even after my best efforts, the sand was still peppered with charcoal flakes. What is today remote country, hardly ever visited, is likely to be heavily traveled all too soon. Even if it's not, what right do we have to remake every part of the world to our own fancy? Let's make it our goal to leave untouched, forever, that last, tiny, dwindling fragment of the Earth that has somehow miraculously escaped human encroachment until now.

Litter

It should go without saying, but I guess it has to be said, because I still see litter along the trails: Pack out what you pack in. Then add a double handful or two of other people's trash. On popular trails (popular with litterers, at any rate) I sometimes hike with a small plastic bag in my hands to accommodate the trash I pick up. That keeps my pockets from bulging with stinky cigarette butts and allows me to refrain from imposing on my companions by stuffing trash in one of their outside pack pockets. Burying trash is not acceptable: In most cases it will soon be unearthed by rodents, birds, or erosion and scattered in the four directions.

Even trash that remains buried can still come back to haunt you. By one estimate, a steel ("tin") can takes 20 to 40 years to decompose in a wet climate, 100 years to vanish in a dry one. A thin polyethylene bag will mar the landscape for 10 to 20 years; thicker plastics can easily take 50 to 80 years. Aluminum cans will scream, "A slob was here!" for 80 to 100 years, perhaps as much as 500.

A glass bottle may last 1,000 years—some people say 1 million, or just a few months shy of the Second Coming. While hiking in Rocky Mountain National Park one day, I spotted a bit of foil emerging from ground that was gradually eroding under the drumbeat of many feet. A little scuffing with my boot revealed an entire trash cache, including an empty bottle of Duffy's Delicious Drinks. The trash must have been buried more than 20 years ago, but it was still perfectly intact.

Food scraps, including things like apple cores and orange peels, should also be packed out. Orange peels take anywhere from one week to six months to decompose beyond recognition. Don't feed the animals, either deliberately or inadvertently. (Actually there are three exceptions, but I don't imagine you'll want to take me up on this. You can, to your heart's content, feed the mosquitoes, ticks, and deer flies.) Feeding creatures that don't normally consume human flesh and blood disrupts their natural eating habits, makes them dependent on human food, and turns them into pests that will eat holes in your pack in search of goodies. Bears that learn to associate people and gear with food often become so aggressive that rangers feel compelled to destroy them. When you get out of the woods, recycle what you can—your trash won't decompose any faster in the landfill than it will in the backcountry. Recycling saves energy as well as reducing the need for new landfills. For example, making aluminum cans from recycled aluminum uses 95 percent less energy than making them from scratch. The energy saved from making one aluminum can from recycled aluminum will operate an old-fashioned, CRT-style TV set for three hours.

Sanitation

Until recently you'd have been thought rather peculiar not to leave three things behind in the wilderness: urine, feces, and toilet paper. Leaving behind the first is still always acceptable. Urine is relatively innocuous, since it rarely contains significant quantities of bacteria. In well-watered climates, simply get out of sight of the trail and at least 200 feet from any lakes or streams. Some animals, such as mountain goats, are tremendously attracted to the salts and minerals found in human urine. They are so attracted to urine that they will fight each other to lick at the places where backpackers have peed. They will also dig up the turf in an effort to get at the urine. To protect the meadows and tundra, backpackers should seek out rocky areas to relieve themselves.

Heavily used desert regions like the river corridor through the Grand Canyon require a different approach. Beaches there are used so intensively by river-runners that if everyone urinated on the sand, the beach would soon stink of uric acid.

The only solution there is to urinate directly into the river, which is flowing by at a rate of tens of thousands of gallons per second.

Leaving behind the second item—feces—is still okay in most areas, but not in all. The goal in disposing of feces is to promote rapid decomposition and to prevent the spread of bacteria from the feces to the water supply or to insects that will then land on your food. First, locate a site at least 200 feet from flowing or standing water or a marshy area. Avoid dry watercourses that may become streams in the rainy season. Try to find a place where you can easily dig a hole 4 to 6 inches deep. Don't dig deeper than that; the organic soil in many alpine areas is only that deep. If you dig deeper, you may go below the zone that supports the active bacteria that hasten decomposition. Avoid pure sand for the same reason. In many regions, digging an adequate hole requires carrying a small plastic or metal trowel. For years I resisted carrying the extra weight, thinking, "Aw, shucks, I can just dig a hole with my boot heel." It doesn't work, at least in a lot of places. Carry a trowel. Do your job thoroughly. Backpacking trowels weigh between three and five ounces (the trowels sold at garden-supply shops will be heavier). When you're done, refill the hole and try to disguise your handiwork. If you're digging a hole in a grassy region, try to remove the sod in one piece, then replace it carefully. I often look for a cantaloupe-size rock that I can roll out of the way to create a ready-made hole. When I'm done, I roll the rock back into place, and no one is the wiser.

In the winter in snow country, digging a hole into the ground will be difficult to impossible, depending on snow depth and how hard the ground is frozen. The best solution now, given the relatively low number of people who go into the backcountry in winter, is to deposit your waste a long ways—like 100 yards—from watercourses, lakes, and any place where a summer hiker is likely to go, literally or figuratively. In Rocky Mountain National Park, winter backpackers are forbidden to camp within 100 feet of a designated summer site for precisely this reason. If possible, locate a tree well (an area surrounding a tree where the snowpack is shallow) so there's at least a chance of feces getting down to ground level and beginning to decompose quickly come spring. In most areas, so far, this approach is working. If use goes up, or if winter campers are careless about sanitation, this approach may present a problem. On Mount McKinley, for example, traffic on the popular West Buttress route is so heavy in peak season that snow contamination is a real threat to climbers' health, since snow is the only source of water and no one wants to go too far from camp for fear of crevasses. When I guided a team on that route in 1982, we camped at 17,200 feet, in a harsh, windswept basin where climbers congregate in preparation for the summit push. I still remember seeing clots of brown turds and toilet paper dotting the landscape. Climbers are now required to defecate into a plastic garbage bag, then throw the bag into the nearest large crevasse. All trash, however, must be carried off the mountain. No trash disposal into crevasses is allowed. If human waste becomes a problem in the mountains of the Lower 48, land managers may start requiring backpackers to pack out everything. River-runners in the Grand Canyon have been required to carry out all feces and toilet paper since 1979. As distasteful as this may at first appear, it is absolutely essential given that the narrow river corridor, with its limited number of campsites, receives over 160,000 user-nights every year, mostly in a five-month period.

In times past it was considered acceptable to bury toilet paper alongside feces. Too often, however, people failed to dig a deep enough hole to adequately bury everything. "Toilet paper flowers" have become one of the most common forms of visible trash. I've seen scraps of toilet paper protruding from the sand smack in the middle of the trail alongside Utah's Paria River and in less obvious but equally unsightly places in Grand Canyon and Canyonlands National Parks. While heading up before dawn one morning to do a spring ski descent of Grays Peak, a 14,000-foot mountain near Georgetown, Colorado, I realized I needed to take a dump. The trail was lined with dense willows, but eventually I found an opening and headed away from the trail, quite convinced that no one had ever gone that way before. Almost immediately, however, my headlamp picked out the telltale white of toilet paper matted down and clinging to the base of the shrubs. Near timberline on Twin Sisters Peak, in Rocky Mountain National Park, I came across an incredibly twisted and ancient limber pine, a stalwart survivor of hundreds of years of winter storms. Entranced, I grabbed my camera and began circling the tree, searching for the most evocative angle. In my preoccupation I nearly stepped into several piles of feces, complete with toilet paper, that more than one utterly irresponsible hiker had deposited on the ground at the base of this marvelous monument to nature's perseverance. Setting up my tripod with care to keep the tripod legs away from the sewage, I composed a photograph that excluded the mess at my feet—only to discover that some idiotic backpacker had taken a saw to one of the magnificent tree's gnarled limbs. To me that whole scene represented vandalism far more offensive than the repugnant scrawls found on city bathroom walls.

The solution to these disgusting scenes is simple: Pack out your toilet paper. Canyonlands and Grand Canyon National Parks already require backpackers to do just that. Some parks still allow backpackers to burn or bury their toilet paper, but the practice leaves much to be desired. If it's raining, the paper won't burn.

In any weather it often doesn't burn completely. Or a gust of wind picks it up when you least expect it and wafts it off to who knows where. An outdoor education instructor in Canyonlands once set off a minor grass fire trying to burn his toilet paper. He spent several hours busily trying to erase the evidence of his good intentions gone awry. Attempts to burn toilet paper have caused several significant fires in the Grand Canyon, and in 1989 a federal judge in Washington found a hiker liable for $132,700 in firefighting costs after his attempt to burn his toilet paper ignited a 450-acre forest fire. I carry used toilet paper in a tough Ziploc bag that rides inside the clean toilet paper bag.

When you're done, if possible, wash your hands using a small amount of biodegradable soap. Don't wash your hands in a lake or stream. Instead, have a companion pour water from a water bottle or pot over your hands while you scrub and rinse 200 feet from any water source. A good alternative to soap-and-water handwashing is to apply a small amount of antibacterial gel.

Noise and Visual Pollution

Two more subtle forms of pollution deserve a mention: noise pollution and visual pollution. We all know that we're rarely the only people out there enjoying the woods on any given day, but why emphasize that fact by making excessive noise? Shouting, banging pots and pans (except when a bear is threatening to steal your M&Ms), or, heaven forbid, bringing a radio or music player into the woods destroys the illusion of solitude and disturbs wildlife. Noise carries a long ways over a mountain lake or in a stone-walled canyon. Keep the racket to a minimum. Large groups should exercise particular care in this regard.

Visual pollution is a tougher issue. Bright color combinations are popular these days for clothing, packs, and, to a lesser extent, tents. Brightly colored gear stands out boldly against the greens, browns, and whites of the summer and winter wilderness. Some people argue that using flashy gear diminishes the feeling of solitude a wilderness should offer because other hikers and their camps stand out like searchlight beacons half a mile away. Others argue that bright clothing and tents could help rescuers trying to locate victims in an emergency, or, more selfishly, that vibrant colors make photographs look better. Personally I find the most garish equipment distasteful and offensive, not so much because it represents visual pollution, as because it seems ostentatious and affected. To learn the lessons that a wilderness sojourn can offer, to preserve the fragile portions of the wilderness, and to stay alive in the face of forces vastly greater than ourselves, we need to enter the wilderness in a spirit of humility, almost reverence. Donning some puce, chartreuse, and aquamarine garment seems antithetical to that spirit. With that said, I must admit that I like cheerful colors, and I do not always avoid reds and yellows. Movement catches my eye as much as color when I glance across a lake or meadow and spot some other hiker. It's always courteous to camp out of sight of your neighbors, and in some places it's required. Tent color makes no difference if you can't see the neighboring tent. A blue tent can be a rather dark and gloomy place during a long winter storm, but it does blend in better in the summer than a yellow one. Perhaps the best advice I can offer is to think about the effect of your color choices on your own consciousness as well as your fellow hikers when choosing your gear.

Pitching Camp without Pitching a Fit

Enough lecturing on the do's and don'ts. Let's say you've reached the designated site that you reserved, or selected a previously used but environmentally sound site, or, if it's the most appropriate, located a completely untouched site that you plan to leave that way. What's the first order of business?

If the afternoon is waning or a thunderstorm is threatening, erecting the tent takes top priority. Most tents have an uncoated canopy with a waterproof fly. If you pitch your tent during a real downpour, the canopy, and hence the tent interior, will get damp if not soaked before you can attach the waterproof fly. Many thunderstorms are brief; if you arrive at camp in the rain, it may be best to wait until the storm passes before setting up the tent. If the storm looks unrelenting, your only recourse is to pitch the tent as fast as you can. Avoid the temptation to bring your soaking wet pack and sopping rain gear into the tent with you. You'll bring in so much moisture that condensation on the tent roof will be almost inevitable. Instead, unload the contents of your pack into the tent as quickly as possible. The contents should be drier than the pack itself if you packed everything in stuff sacks and plastic bags, like you should. Then shed your rain gear, stuff it into your pack, and jump inside the tent. Carrying a sponge will help you mop up whatever moisture does creep inside as well as soak up condensation on the walls or a cup of tea that gets spilled. In rainy country a tent with a vestibule or rain fly that overhangs the door prevents rain from falling into the tent when the door is open, making it easier to unload gear and keep it and the tent dry.

Select the most level site you can. What seems to be a small tilt when looking down from an erect position will undergo a surprising magnification once you lie down. Even a slight tilt is usually sufficient to promote a caterpillar-like creep toward the lower end of your sleeping pad as you toss and turn during the night. Lying down is the most certain way to determine an acceptable degree of tilt and to determine which end of the tent is higher. In general your head should occupy the high ground.

It's important to remove small stones and sticks from your site before erecting the tent to protect both you and the tent floor, but be sure to replace them if you're camping someplace no one has ever camped before. Don't camp in low spots, where puddles will form if it rains. Your tent may have a "waterproof" floor with "sealed" seams, but it isn't a boat. Don't assume it's as seaworthy as Noah's Ark.

So many varieties of tents exist today that it's impossible to give specific advice on pitching each type, but a few general hints may be helpful. Most important, be sure to master a new tent's idiosyncrasies by pitching it at home in your front yard or living room a couple of times before heading into the woods. That way you won't be inserting the right pole in the wrong pole sleeve on some pitch-black, frigid night with the rain pelting down.

In high winds, with most tents, stake out the corners first, before inserting the poles. With a few tents, staking the corners first can inhibit or prevent inserting the poles. Treat your poles with care. Nicking fiberglass poles or denting aluminum ones will weaken them significantly. When assembling the poles, make sure each pole segment's end is inserted fully into the neighboring segment's socket. The quickest way to break a pole, besides fending off grizzlies with it, is to flex a pole joint when the mating halves have not been fully inserted. The second quickest way is to bend a pole into a tighter curve than it assumes when the tent is pitched. Don't let the ends of the pole segments snap together, which can nick the pole ends and abrade the shock cord. Keep the poles clean; don't let grit and dirt enter the pole joints, which can then jam shut.

Many tents today are freestanding, meaning they don't need to be staked to stand upright. They must be staked, however, to prevent them from blowing away like expensive, high-tech tumbleweeds. I was standing with some hapless rock climbers once at the base of a crag when they happened to glance down into the meadow half a mile away and saw, to their horror, their tent rolling and bouncing across the field, driven by the downdraft from a looming thunderstorm, looking for all the world like the monstrous white ball that always overtook and swallowed the fleeing star of the old TV series *The Prisoner*. The tent continued its lumbering, ungainly journey for fully a quarter mile across the meadow until finally coming to rest, torn and battered, against the edge of the forest. Moral: Always stake your tent! In sand, on very hard ground, and on slickrock, where stakes work poorly or not at all, rocks weighing at least twenty pounds apiece form good anchors. If smaller rocks are the only ones available, tie a stout cord coming from the tent around one, then pile more rocks on top to anchor the bottom stone. Stuff sacks full of sand or small rocks also make good anchors. To keep grit out of your stuff sacks, turn them inside out before filling them. Don't rely on a couple of sleeping bags and foam pads tossed inside the tent to weight it down. The tent will take off like a nylon clothes dryer with the sleeping bags tossing about inside.

As a general rule, rocks and logs form better tent anchors in summer than many stakes do. Wire stakes, the kind that come with some tents, have little holding power; plastic ones frequently break. Good stakes made of hardened aluminum or titanium are available, but usually must be purchased separately. If you do uproot rocks to anchor your tent, please replace them where you found them when you leave.

Comfort in Camp

For me the first night or two in a sleeping bag is always a bit restless. Hard ground and the confinement of a sleeping bag are a big change from the luxury of a queen-size bed and flannel sheets. That minor discomfort, and many others, vanish after a few days, and I quickly begin to feel much more at home in the wilderness. I don't know of any shortcuts to sleeping bag adaptation—unless you want to bivy in your backyard for a night or two before the trip.

Sleeping cold, on the other hand, is a preventable problem even on the first night. The first line of defense, of course, is an adequate sleeping bag and, equally important but sometimes neglected, adequate insulation beneath you in the form of your sleeping pad. Although some people have a philosophical objection to sleeping in their clothes, you should not ignore how much warmth those clothes can give. I like to sleep in enough clothes that I can slip out of the bag at night or in the early morning without immediately feeling uncomfortable. In the winter, on truly bitter nights, I sometimes even wear my shell gear.

In addition to wearing adequate clothes, make sure you go to bed warm and well fed. A nightcap of hot chocolate or tea is a great way to start a cozy night's slumber (although unfortunates with small bladders may prefer different methods). If you go to bed cold, it can take a long time to warm up even in the best sleeping bag. Be sure you use your bag to its fullest extent. It's easy to slide into the sack on a cool but not cold evening and fall asleep without cinching down the hood, then awaken at 2 a.m. uncomfortably chilled and spend the rest of the night clutching the bag around your shoulders, trying to warm up. Many people in that situation fail to realize how much heat they lose through the mouth of the bag. Take the time to carefully fasten the sleeping bag collar (if it has one) around your neck, then cinch down the hood, leaving just your nose, mouth, and eyes exposed. Try not to breathe inside the bag. You'll cause condensation that will soak your insulation.

Close confinement inside a tent during a prolonged storm can erode even the warmest of friendships. Minor quirks and innocuous habits that are easily overlooked in the city can mushroom into major irritants in the backcountry. David Roberts, in his book about an attempt to climb Alaska's Mount Deborah with Don Jensen, wrote how he "learned to loathe the way Jensen ate his soup." I've felt the same irritation, utterly irrational but real, during long, demanding expeditions in the Alaska Range when my partner chose to snack on an item he'd saved after I'd already eaten my rations for the day. Ask for your tentmate's okay before you start chomping on another stick of bubble gum. Look into her glowering eyes before humming the twenty-fifth repetition of "Having My Baby." A little extra empathy will defuse most problems before the spark hits the dynamite.

When the sun finally does begin to shine again, the first priority is often to dry out the gear that inevitably became soggy during the storm. Condensation can soak the inside of a tent fly even if no precipitation fell during the night. If you plan to move on that day, remove the tent fly as soon as you get up, and spread it upside down on a rock or branch to dry. You'll save yourself carrying the extra weight of a soaking-wet tent, and you'll help preserve the coatings on the tent fabrics. You can usually pick up a freestanding tent by the poles (after dismantling the anchors) and shake loose dirt out the door before striking the tent. Be sure to pick up the inevitable twist-tie or candy wrapper that emerges from hiding when you do so.

Before leaving your site, scour the ground of all bits of trash, big or small, yours or the previous party's. If the site has never been used before (or looks that way), be sure to leave it just the way you found it. Restore natural litter to the tent site, and replace any rocks you may have moved. Give others the same pleasure you enjoyed when you chanced upon such a pristine, perfect site.

Some novices worry about thieves stealing gear left behind at a backcountry camp while the owners go for a day hike. Or they worry about being assaulted. Fortunately, such incidents, while not unheard of, are very rare. In Rocky Mountain National Park, for example, no backcountry thefts or assaults were reported in 1998, although the park recorded 46,555 backcountry user-nights. Other national parks report similar statistics. Backcountry crime is nothing to lose sleep over.

Car break-ins at trailhead parking lots are a bigger but still manageable problem. There's not much you can do about car-clouting except to avoid leaving valuables like your wallet or purse in your car. If you must leave something worth stealing, be sure it's out of sight when you leave. Thieves have been known to hang around and see who leaves what choice items in which trunk. Consider stopping some distance away from your final destination, stashing your valuables out of sight in your trunk, then driving to the trailhead and hitting the trail. Not all thieves are human: Bears have also been caught clouting cars, although they're usually more interested in the bread in your cooler than the bread in your wallet. Avoid storing odorous food anywhere in your car, and avoid storing food or items resembling food anywhere in plain sight. With any luck your car will be fine when you return.

One reason is never given openly, rather is disguised and hidden and never even allowed in suggestion, and I venture to think it is because it is really the inmost moving impulse in all true mountain-lovers, a feeling so deep and so pure and so personal as to be almost sacred, too intimate for ordinary mention. That is, the ideal joy that only mountains give—the unreasoned, uncovetous, unworldly love of them we know not why, we care not why, only because they are what they are; because they move us in some way which nothing else does . . . and we feel that a world that can give us such rapture must be a good world, a life capable of such feeling must be worth the living.

—*F. W. Bourdillon, 1852–1921*

My friend Steve Glenn and I were experienced rock climbers but novice backpackers when we ventured unwittingly into one of the most notoriously bear-infested backcountry regions in the nation: Little Yosemite Valley. We did know, however—because the rangers had told us—that we were supposed to hang our food from a tree to keep the bears from getting it.

So when we arrived in camp, we picked the nearest tree, tossed a flimsy bit of twine over a spindly branch about 8 feet off the ground, tied our food bag to the end of the twine, and hauled it up as far as it could go.

It was almost dark when we glimpsed a large, furry, and very intimidating shape moving toward us through the trees, followed by two smaller shapes. A mother black bear and her two cubs were starting their nightly rounds. Soon the entire family was prowling the outskirts of our camp. We realized immediately that we'd hung our precious provisions at precisely the right height for a bear punching bag. I began having nightmares of ascending Half Dome the next day as my empty stomach and calorie-starved muscles traded insults. In a last, desperate attempt to save our food, we mobilized our only weapon—our vocal cords—punctuating our shouts with the cacophony of pots and pans smashed together. The bears yawned. They'd heard all this before. Sure of their ultimate victory, they retreated briefly, and we seized the opportunity to grab our food and hustle over to the "bear-proof" food-hanging cable the rangers had installed. One end of the cable was anchored to a tree about 20 feet off the ground. The cable then ran horizontally to a pulley at the same height on an adjacent tree, then down through the pulley to a stout, spring-loaded clip attached to an eyebolt firmly embedded in the tree's base. The cable continued below the eyebolt, providing the slack necessary to lower the cable and attach the food. We unhooked the clip, lowered the cable, tied our food to the middle of the cable between the two trees and hoisted it back up, leaving the food 20 feet off the ground exactly in the middle between the two trees. With the bears advancing upon us once more, we retreated, smugly satisfied that we would indeed have something edible to fuel our climb the next day.

The mother bear, who had watched all this commotion from a slight distance, now strolled up and deftly climbed the tree supporting the pulley end of the cable. The food bag was hanging at least 10 feet out from the tree trunk, far beyond her reach as she clung to the tree, and we were certain she wouldn't even come close to stealing our food. We soon learned that we had underestimated her intelligence. Once at the height of the cable, she reached out and gave the cable a mighty downward jerk, causing our food bag to swing toward her like a pendulum. As the bag neared the apex of its arc, the bear took a swing at it with a massive paw. Even a glancing contact would have shredded the bag and dropped its contents to the hungry cubs waiting below, but she missed by inches. By sheer luck we had tied the bag to the cable with a short enough string to keep the bag from swinging within the bear's reach.

When her repeated jerk-and-slash technique proved futile, she descended the tree, grabbed the free end of the cable in her teeth and began yanking, evidently hoping to break the eyebolt or the clip anchoring the lower end of the cable. Still she was defeated, and our hopes rose that she would soon abandon her efforts. Then she turned her attention to the clip itself. Less than a minute later, she found a way to unlatch it, and our food plummeted to the ground. The cubs pounced on the defenseless bag, and all our hopes of breakfast vanished into their hungry gullets. Steve and I climbed Half Dome the next day with the hypoglycemic blues, then ran back down to the floor of Yosemite Valley, where I came as close as I've ever come to literally eating myself sick.

Protecting Your Food

Before you hurl this book into a bonfire and vow never to set foot off pavement again, let me hasten to add that this was not only the first but also the last time I have ever lost food to bears in forty years of backpacking. I've never even seen a bear in Rocky Mountain National Park, where I've done much of my backpacking, much less had to battle one for my breakfast. In fact, in nearly forty years of living in Colorado, I've only seen four black bears. I saw one in my backyard (we live near the foothills); I came across another in the Boulder Mountain Parks just outside the city limits; and I spotted the last two while driving rural roads in the San Juan Mountains. Except in a few places where black bears have learned that backpackers mean packs full of food, your chances of seeing a bear in the wilderness are actually slight. Full-blown attacks are extremely rare. No bear attack has ever been recorded in Mount Rainier National Park, for example. Although rare attacks have occurred in Yosemite National Park, no one has been killed by a bear. According to Yellowstone National Park, home to grizzlies as well as black bears, your chance of being injured by a bear during your visit is less than one in a million. If you, like me, drive about 15,000 miles per year, which is close to the national average, your chances of dying on the highway in any one year are about 1 in 6,000. You might say bear attacks are a "bearly" perceptible risk.

All Yosemite bears, and most bears in other parts of the Lower 48, are black bears, which are persistent and intelligent but basically timid. Yellowstone and Glacier National Parks and many parks in Alaska are also home to grizzly bears, which are far more dangerous than black bears. Aggressively defending your food, which will work with black bears, is not recommended for use with grizzlies.

Once a bear learns to associate humans with food, it will return again and again to drive-up campgrounds and backcountry campsites alike. Rangers respond by capturing the bear and transporting it to remote and rarely traveled regions, but all too often the bear finds its way back and becomes such a nuisance that it must eventually be destroyed.

For the sake of the bears as well as the backpackers, rangers in Yosemite, Denali, and Rocky Mountain National Parks, among other places, eventually abandoned the notion that backpackers could reliably safeguard their food by hanging it from a tree. Today backpackers in those parks are required to carry their food in a bear canister, a stout plastic container about the size of a small keg of beer. The canisters are too tough for a bear to break and too rounded to be picked up and carried off. Bear canisters work well, but have several big disadvantages from the backpacker's perspective. For one, the canisters are heavy, averaging nearly three pounds empty. They're also bulky, and their bulk doesn't diminish as the trip progresses, unlike a stuff sack full of food. And finally, their capacity is relatively small, which puts a huge premium on packing foods that are not only lightweight but also compact. On any trip longer than an overnight, you can forget about bringing lightweight but bulky luxuries like a box of crackers. While I applaud the goal of protecting both bears and backpackers and understand the necessity of bear canisters in parks like Yosemite that still allow backpackers to choose their own backcountry campsites, I think there are better solutions in parks that have gone to a system of designated sites.

In Canyonlands National Park, for example, which is sometimes visited by bears who live in the nearby La Sal Mountains, rangers have installed army-surplus rocket boxes at every campsite. Backpackers store their food in these ultra-tough steel trunks. Rocket boxes also protect backpackers' food from ravens, which are a bigger threat than you might expect. Once while backpacking in the Needles District with my wife and two daughters before rocket boxes were installed, we decided to go for a day hike on our last day before we humped the big loads back out to the trailhead. We struck camp to make way for the next occupants of our designated site, stashed our gear in garbage bags, then hiked up to Druid Arch. When we returned from our day hike, we found that ravens had completely shredded the plastic bags and torn holes in the stuff sacks inside. Fortunately, we had left our food hanging in a juniper tree. It was unscathed. I've never seen ravens attack a hanging food bag in the Lower 48, but one incident in the Escalante region of Utah raised my suspicions. Cora and I had hung our food from a tree and were leaving camp for a day hike when two ravens flew into our campsite. I'd seen ravens on Mount McKinley wreak havoc with unprotected food caches as high as 16,000 feet, so I knew that a raven's powerful beak could shred our tough nylon food sacks in seconds. With two days to go on our trip and no desire to seek visions through a forty-eight-hour fast, I retrieved the food bag and carried it with us throughout the day hike. Paranoid? Perhaps. Hungry? No way.

Rocket boxes are very convenient for backpackers *if* everyone is responsible enough to pack out all their trash *and* extra food. Don't succumb to the superficially generous but actually lazy notion that "the next group will eat my extra food." In almost all cases your extra food will become trash. Leave the rocket box clean and empty.

In Mount Rainier National Park, which requires backpackers to camp in designated sites along the ultra-popular Wonderland Trail, the rangers have installed "bear poles," tall steel shafts like flagpoles that are anchored in the ground and have crossbars at the top. Backpackers stash their food in stuff sacks, as usual, then use the lightweight pole that the park also provides to hoist their food up and hang it from one of the crossbars. Bears can't climb the bear poles, which are much too hard for their claws to penetrate, and they don't seem to have figured out how to pick up the lightweight pole and unhook the food that dangles so temptingly just out of reach.

In contrast to many national parks, most Forest Service–managed wilderness areas still allow backpackers to hang food. The most bear-resistant method of hanging food is called the counterweight method. It will work well with either black bears or grizzly bears. All provisions should be stored with this method at all

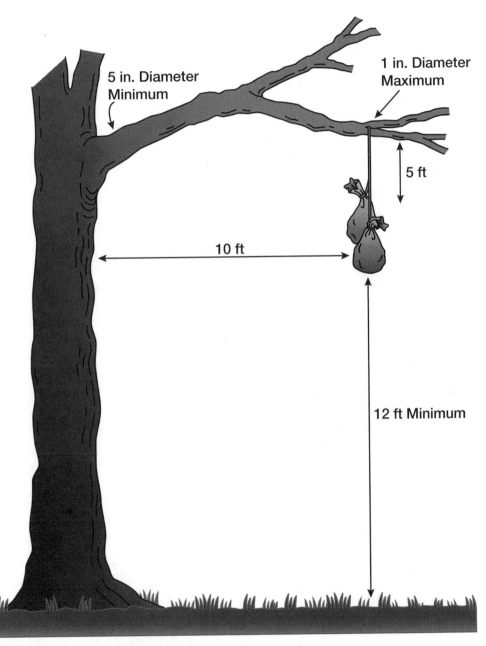

5 in. Diameter
Minimum

1 in. Diameter
Maximum

5 ft

10 ft

12 ft Minimum

The Fort Knox method of hanging food in bear country.

times except when you're actually preparing a meal. Never store food in your tent or pack. That's a sure way to lose both your food and your equipment—and maybe your life. Make sure you stash odoriferous nonfood items in your food bag as well. Potential bear attractants include garbage, toothpaste, sunscreen, perfume, sanitary napkins, tampons, etc.

Now find a suitable tree. You're looking for one with a live branch 17 or more feet off the ground that's still 1 inch in diameter 10 feet from the trunk. Basically the idea is to find a branch that's strong enough to support your food's weight, but not so strong that a cub could crawl out on it and swipe your food. The tree must lack strong branches beneath the food-hanging branch that could serve as a platform for a bear. Although such trees may seem as common as unicorns, persist and you will be rewarded. Tie a rock to the end of a stout cord that's 40 or 50 feet long, and toss the rock over the branch. Separate your food into two bags of roughly equal weight, and tie the first bag to the cord. Haul the first bag up to the branch, and tie the second bag to the cord as high as you can reach. Leave a loop of cord hanging out, and put the remainder of the cord inside the bag. Push the second bag up with a long stick until the two bags hang side by side. To retrieve the food, snag the loop of cord with the stick, tug the free end of the cord loose from the food bag, and gently pull the bag down.

If it's absolutely impossible to find a suitable tree, try this approach. Locate two trees about 20 feet apart. Tie a rock to the end of a 75-foot cord and toss the rock over a branch about 10 or 15 feet off the ground. Untie the rock and tie that end of the cord to the tree. Now tie the rock to the other end of the cord and toss the rock over the highest possible branch on the second tree. Tie your food bag to the middle of the cord between the two trees, then pull on the free end of the cord until the cord is tight and your food is suspended as high as possible. Tie the loose end of the cord to a branch. This method will put your food out of reach of any bear standing on the ground. Obviously it will not protect your food against human-habituated bears who've learned to attack the nylon cord where it is tied to the tree trunk. So far, in the areas where I backpack, I haven't had a problem, but if backpackers become careless about protecting their food, wilderness managers may start requiring bear canisters everywhere.

What to Do If You See a Bear

If you see a black bear in the distance, back off quietly and leave it alone. Approaching the bear may help it lose its fear of humans, which can eventually be lethal for the bear. If the bear approaches you, immediately make as much noise as possible, throw rocks, and chase the bear vigorously. The more people who chase the bear, and the longer and farther they chase it, the better. The idea is not to harm the bear but to restore its natural fear of humans. Don't get carried away, however. You should never corner a bear, nor come between a mother bear and her cubs. If a bear does manage to steal some of your food, leave the bear alone until it abandons it. Bears are like two-year-olds: They haven't learned to clean up after themselves, so you'll have to do it for them. Pack out everything the bear doesn't eat. Don't leave it as litter to entice other bears or ruin the next visitor's enjoyment of the wilderness.

If you're backpacking in grizzly country, you must take additional pre-cautions. In Denali National Park, rangers recommend that backpackers refrain from cooking in a tent even if it's perfectly well ventilated. The cooking odors can permeate the nylon and attract bears even if you stash your food elsewhere. While cooking, be prepared to store your food quickly in your bear canister. Keep your other gear packed so you can leave immediately, leaving nothing behind, if a bear suddenly intrudes. The goal is to prevent an aggressive grizzly from receiving a reward for its intrusion. After cooking dinner, move on a mile or two before making camp.

To avoid startling a grizzly who may be invisible in deep brush, make noise as you walk. Some people tie a bell to their pack or rattle pebbles in a can. Others sing, talk, or chant high-school fight songs. Pay attention to your surroundings so you know when bears might be nearby. A bear's five-toed paw print is as long as a human's but twice as wide. The claw marks extend well beyond the paw print itself. A grizzly's droppings are massive, often resembling a cow's. After the berries ripen, droppings may consist of a pile of partially digested berries.

If you encounter a grizzly, refrain from approaching it. Grizzlies can start to feel threatened even if you're a hundred yards away. Bears will defend their cubs, their territory, their food, and themselves. If you spot a feeding grizzly that's unaware of your presence, retreat slowly while the bear's attention is absorbed by its food. If the bear becomes aware of you and approaches, remain calm or, if that's impossible, at least try to look calm. Hold up your arms, speak firmly and confidently to the bear, and slowly back away. The idea is to let the bear know that you're not a threat. Don't turn and run—you can't outrun a grizzly. If there's a suitable tree nearby, climb it, but remember that a grizzly standing on its hind legs can reach 10 feet. If the grizzly stands up and waves its nose in the air, it's trying to identify you. Talking to the bear and waving your arms helps it do so. If the bear makes a series of woofs and grunts, it's challenging you to either fight or leave. If it stands sideways, it's displaying its size in an attempt to intimidate you (probably not a difficult task).

Take the hint: Retreat slowly. If the bear charges you, stand your ground. In most cases charges are bluffs. If the bear calls your bluff and is about to strike, fall to the ground, keeping your pack on, and play dead. Do not abandon your pack except as a last resort. Don't inadvertently teach the grizzly that charging hikers is an easy way to get a meal. In a very real sense, grizzly country belongs to the bears. They are the dominant predators, not humans. Tread with caution.

One other potential wildlife threat deserves mention before we move on: mountain lions. These solitary and secretive ambush hunters are found in many backpacking areas from the Rockies to California, but you're quite unlikely to see one, much less be attacked by one. In forty years of knocking around in the mountains and deserts of the western United States, I've never seen one. I may have heard one, once. Unlike bears, mountain lions aren't attracted by human food. Young children are the most vulnerable to attack. Don't let them run ahead or lag behind on the trail. Rangers at Yosemite National Park offer these additional tips on what to if you do see a mountain lion:

- Do not run.

- Pick up small children.

- Shout in a low voice and wave your arms or hold your coat open to look large and threatening.

- Maintain eye contact and do not crouch down.

- Throw sticks or rocks.

- If an attack occurs, fight back.

Squirrels and Rabbits and Marmots, Oh My!

The biggest threats to your food and gear are so small, cute, and cuddly that it's hard to believe the amount of damage they can cause. I'm talking about chipmunks, squirrels, rabbits, and the worst offender of all, marmots. I've returned to my pack after leaving it alone for just five minutes and discovered a human-habituated marmot stealing my peanut butter and jelly sandwich from an open pack pocket. To add insult to injury, two hikers were standing nearby enjoying the fat rascal's bold performance and doing nothing to intervene. On several occasions I've had witless rodents chew their way into a pack pocket even though there was no food inside.

I used to leave my pack on the ground at night, covered with a large plastic garbage bag to keep it dry in the event of rain. Recently, however, I've had so many problems with marmots and other varmints chewing on my pack that I've taken to hanging it from a tree. Occasionally you'll get lucky and find a tree with a stubby branch that slopes upward and forms a convenient hook for hanging your pack. More often, however, I find it necessary to tie a short piece of cord around a tree and hang my pack from that using a small, lightweight, toy carabiner. To protect the contents from rain, I place any extra gear in a plastic bag before putting it in the pack.

Marmots don't climb trees, so it's easy to protect your pack and food by hanging them up. Unfortunately, you can't hang your tent (unless you're using a hammock). Marmots are attracted not only to food, but to anything with a chemical odor, even if it smells like an oil refinery to a human. I've seen them chew on sweat-stained pack hip belts, on my companion's bandana left outside the tent to dry, on the wrist straps of hiking poles, and on boots placed just inches from my head. A few years ago I backpacked in to Ruby Basin, a remote valley in the Needle Mountains of southwest Colorado, to shoot large-format landscape photographs. On the second day of the trip, I left some of my extra film in the tent while I went off to shoot. Sheets of 4 × 5 film have a strong chemical odor. When I returned, I found that a marmot had ripped right through the wall of my single-wall tent, leaving it wide open to the approaching thunderstorm, then, oddly enough, torn through the floor before leaving the way he came.

The most outrageous incident, however, occurred just a year ago in Navaho Basin, near Telluride, Colorado. On the third day of my trip, I climbed 14,017-foot Wilson Peak. After enjoying the view from the summit for an hour, I descended to my camp just below timberline and got a shock. My credit cards were strewn across the ground outside my tent. Had some thieving backpacker ransacked my belongings? I unzipped the tent door and saw what had happened. An inquisitive marmot had ripped a hole through the body of the tent, clambered inside, and started chewing. The cash I'd stashed in the tent was scattered about. Fortunately, this marmot apparently preferred laser-printer toner to the scent of greenbacks. He'd taken a single bite from a one-dollar bill, ignoring all the twenties, and moved on to the letter-size pages I'd printed from an online guidebook. Five full pages had disappeared. Even worse, he'd done some serious chewing on the antenna of my brand-new, state-of-the-art GPS unit, apparently attracted by the odor of the rubbery cladding. He'd then dragged my credit cards outside and abandoned them. Fortunately, the gaping hole in the tent body was under the fly, so no rain could get in.

I looked around for the culprit, but he was gone. Toward evening, as I was settling down to sleep, I heard a rustling just outside the tent. I looked up to see a marmot—undoubtedly the culprit—poking his nose through the hole in the tent wall. Perhaps he wanted to sample my Therm-a-Rest this time around.

"Get out of here!" I shouted, and landed a solid punch on his nose with my fist. The marmot fled instantly and did not return. When I got home several days later, I spent four hours replacing the mosquito-netting panel in the tent wall that the marmot had shredded.

That experience taught me not to leave anything with a new or chemical odor inside a tent. A new tent, all by itself, may also have enough chemical odor to smell like marmot candy. A backpacker I met recently told me how a marmot had ripped up his new tent during his first trip with it. If you've got a brand-new tent, it may be best to pitch it in a sunny place for a day or so to bake some of the new odor out of the fabric and its coatings.

Stove Safety

A friend once lost half his tent—and half his hair—when his stove overheated and the pressure-relief valve burst open and spewed a 2-foot arc of flame. Two experienced Swiss mountaineers died on Mount McKinley in 1986 from carbon monoxide poisoning caused by operating a stove in an unventilated tent. If mishandled, every type of stove and every kind of stove fuel can cause an accident that destroys expensive equipment and inflicts severe burns. All stoves produce carbon monoxide, a deadly, odorless gas. To operate a stove safely, you must know and follow these simple rules.

Never fill a liquid-fueled stove or change the cartridge on a canister stove near a source of heat or sparks. If you're using a liquid-fueled stove, be sure to use a funnel when filling it to reduce the chance of a spill that could accidentally ignite. Never refill a liquid-fueled stove while it's hot. To avoid temptation when you're hungry and impatient for dinner, make sure the stove is full before you start cooking. That way you won't run out of fuel in the middle of preparing your salmon soufflé. Most stoves should be filled only three-quarters full to allow room for an air space. Pumps actually compress air, not fuel. The compressed air then drives the fuel out of the tank and up to the burner.

All reputable backpacking stoves come with explicit lighting directions, but a few general pointers may be helpful. First, never lean over any stove while lighting it: It could flare up and singe your eyebrows or worse. Never light or operate a stove inside a tent. You risk both burning down your wilderness house and asphyxiating yourself with carbon monoxide. Use the minimum amount of priming fuel possible. Excessive priming is a leading cause of accidents. Make sure that your fuel tank doesn't become overheated, as it might, for example, if you confine it too tightly within some kind of homemade windscreen system. Liquid-fueled stove tanks will normally be warm but not hot when the stove is running; the cartridge on a canister stove should be cool to the touch. Be sure to carry your liquid-fueled stove and extra fuel separate from your food and pots. Gasoline fumes can permeate food with surprising ease. Finally, if your stove is liquid-fueled, you should expect it to malfunction periodically. Carry a repair kit containing all the little washers and gaskets that are likely to crack or begin to leak. Most backpacking shops carry repair kits for specific brands of stoves. I've never seen a canister stove break down, but I'm sure it has happened. Most of those stoves cannot be readily repaired in the field, so your only option in situations where a stove breakdown would be very serious is to carry a backup stove. I've carried a backup on lengthy Alaskan expeditions, but never while backpacking in the Lower 48.

The amount of fuel you need depends on the efficiency of your stove, the kind of food you're cooking, the wind speed, the altitude, and the temperature. Rather than trying to plug all those variables into some formula, try this approach. Most stove instruction manuals give run time on one tank of fuel. Add up the amount of cooking time you anticipate, taking into account the fact that food easily takes 20 percent longer to cook above 10,000 feet than it does at sea level, then give yourself a 25 percent safety margin. Don't forget to add in the time it takes water to come to a boil as well as the actual cooking time. You'll probably come home with a lot of extra fuel, but that's better than the alternative. Stretching food is easy. Stretching fuel is not, and many backpacking foods are completely indigestible unless they're cooked. In the summer I generally allow one ounce of canister fuel per person per day, enough to make a hot drink morning and night, sometimes a freeze-dried package of scrambled eggs for lunch, and a freeze-dried dinner every evening. A two-person team using a liquid-fueled stove in summer might go through two or three ounces of fuel each day.

Fuel consumption with either kind of stove will be much higher if you have to melt snow for water. On McKinley a two-person team using a liquid-fuel stove will burn a minimum of eight ounces of fuel per day. During winter trips in Colorado using a canister stove, I figure that one eight-ounce cartridge will last me two days. By eight-ounce cartridge I mean one with eight ounces of fuel. The total weight of a full cartridge, including the cartridge itself, is about thirteen ounces. These figures assume the use of freeze-dried food that doesn't require cooking. You'll need more if you're boiling non-instant rice or macaroni. Bring plenty of fuel on your first few trips with a new stove and log the amount you actually burn. You can determine how much fuel is left in a fuel cartridge by weighing it on a postage scale and subtracting the weight of the canister itself. You'll soon learn how much you need for your style of backpacking.

Kitchen Chores

You may go backpacking to "get away from it all," but there's one thing you never really get away from: washing dishes. As a first step toward simplifying the process, try to cook only as much as you can eat, so you don't have any leftovers. If some food does remain, put it in your garbage bag and pack it out. You may need to double-bag the leftovers to prevent the garbage bag from leaking inside your pack. Burying leftovers will only encourage rodents, camp-robbing blue jays, and bears to come calling.

Cora and I have tried bringing various scrubbing pads to clean our pot, but found that they trapped food particles, which quickly rotted and stank. If you're in sandy or snowy country, scrape the pot as clean as possible with a spoon, then scrub it with a handful of sand or a snowball. If your local soils turn uncooperatively to mud, persist with the spoon, aided by the application of warm water. On short trips we carry a few squares of paper towel, which we use sparingly to polish off the last spots of grease. We also sterilize the pot every day by boiling clean water in it. You can use the hot water to make a cup of tea or as the first step in boiling pasta or rice. While the water is boiling, dip your utensils in to sterilize them as well. One advantage of most freeze-dried foods is that your dinner rehydrates in its own foil pouch, so the pot never gets dirty. Dishwashing soap is generally unnecessary in the backcountry. Even biodegradable soap pollutes streams, and it's hard to rinse away soap completely. Any residue that remains becomes an unpleasantly effective laxative. Refrain from washing or rinsing pots or dishes in any stream or lake. Instead, carry your dishwater and rinse-water at least 100 feet away from streams or lakes and scatter it on the ground. By the time the water filters back to its source, it will be clean again.

> It is life near the bone where it is sweetest.
> —*Henry David Thoreau, 1817–1862*

You should read this chapter like a newspaper. Sure, there are many things that can go wrong on a backpacking trip. If you dwell on those possibilities like a newspaper dwells on wars, disasters, and atrocities, you'll probably never want to go hiking again. You need to remember, however, that newspapers never print headlines that read, "The vast majority of the world's people had an okay day today." In the same way, nearly all backpacking trips go off without a hitch. The following discussion of potential backcountry problems will start with the commonplace but annoying and lead up to the life-threatening but exceedingly rare. In the space available I can only provide a brief overview of what backpackers should know about wilderness medicine.

Mosquitoes

Unfortunately for backpackers, mosquitoes agree with Thoreau that life is sweetest when it's closest to the bone. These voracious pests have probably ruined more trips for poorly prepared backpackers than all the thunderstorms and rainy days put together. When you add in the threat of chiggers, ticks, deer flies, and black flies, it's no wonder that consumers spend some $200 million on insect repellent every year.

Nearly all commercial repellents contain DEET, so named because it sounds like the maddening hum of a mosquito about to pounce on your ear just when your hands are fully occupied with draining boiling water off your wilderness pasta. (Actually, it's a contraction for N, N-diethyl-meta-toluamide, which sounds so hideously toxic that you should probably forget you ever knew the real explanation.) Mosquitoes are attracted by the carbon dioxide that people give off. Repellents generally work by masking that odor. When used as directed—the standard caveat—DEET doesn't give most people any problems. A few people suffer minor skin irritations, and my friends tell me that if you get the stuff too close to your lips, it will make them tingle. To reduce the possibility of any problems, use repellent sparingly, keep it away from your face, don't put clothing over repellent-coated skin, and wash the repellent off once you come inside. If you do experience problems and want to continue using a repellent, try a product with a lower concentration of DEET or one with a time-release formulation. The incidence of allergic reactions goes up with the concentration. The "natural" repellents that I've tried were all significantly less effective than DEET.

Even under the best of circumstances, repellents provide imperfect protection. A better solution when mosquitoes are swarming may be to bring pants and a loose-fitting, long-sleeve shirt made of a tightly woven material through which mosquitoes cannot bite. Today several companies make pants and shirts impregnated with insect-repelling permethrin to further discourage the voracious hordes. Cap off your pants and shirt with a brimmed hat with a skirt that drapes down past your collar, and you'll have put a solid physical barrier between those rapacious mosquitoes and your precious hide. Many companies now make baseball-style hats with removable skirts. If you don't want to buy something new, attach an old handkerchief to a hat you already have with a few safety pins. You'll be contributing personally to a reduction in the mosquito population, since female mosquitoes need a meal of mammalian blood to reproduce. Under really grim conditions, pull a mosquito headnet over the skirted hat. A mosquito headnet is just a bag made of mosquito netting that you pull over a hat with a broad brim. The bag comes down to your collar. Ignore all snide jokes about veiled women and enjoy the insect-free peace. You may also want to wear a pair of light gloves to keep mosquitoes off your hands.

You might object that all this extra clothing must lead to a nuclear meltdown when you're pumping out the miles with a full pack. In practice, however, mosquitoes are rarely a problem when you're walking steadily. It seems to take them a minute or two to find you as you pass through their vicinity. By that time you've moved out of their territory. I normally wear shorts if I know I'll be walking without interruption. If you sit down for lunch or start to make camp, however, mosquitoes will soon come swarming like ants to spilt honey. Once you've stopped moving, however, extra clothing is much more tolerable.

Mosquitoes operate within a limited range of temperatures. In the high mountains they usually go to bed at sunset. In the warm lowlands they may be scarce during the day and active all night. Knowing the local mosquitoes' habits can help you avoid them. All mosquitoes like wet, marshy areas and dislike wind. If you have the choice, make your lunch stops on the ridge crests and passes and place your camp on a dry, breezy knoll well away from lush meadows.

Stopping Sunburn and Blisters

Pants, long-sleeve shirts, and skirted hats also provide protection against another backcountry assailant: the sun. Sun-blocking lotions work well too, if applied liberally and regularly. Many flatlanders underestimate the intensity of sunlight at high altitudes, particularly if snowfields are adding their reflection to the glare. When I was embarking on an expedition to McKinley in 1982, my assistant, who was quite pale after the long, dark, Alaskan winter, told me she hoped to come back with a gorgeous tan. I told her, "If you do the absolute best you can to protect yourself, you'll come back with a tan. If you do any less, you'll come back peeling like weathered paint."

Blisters rank with mosquitoes and sunburn as the miseries that beset backpackers most often. The first defense, of course, is properly fitting boots. The second is to avoid boots that are stiffer than you really need. If you need stout boots because you'll be packing a heavy load, be sure to break them in thoroughly by wearing them around town, then on progressively longer day hikes.

If a hot spot does start to develop, stop and deal with it immediately, before it erupts into a full-fledged blister. Sometimes the problem can be fixed simply by straightening out a wrinkled sock. On long, steady descents it can help to lace your boots extra tight to prevent your feet from sliding forward at each step, thereby blistering the soles and toes. Wearing a thin pair of socks under a thicker pair can also help. If these tactics fail, I employ moleskin, an adhesive-backed felt-like material found in nearly all drugstores. I usually slap a piece of moleskin directly over the hot spot and leave it there for the duration of the trip. If a pair of boots frequently gives me trouble in the same spot, I'll counterpunch by applying moleskin before starting the hike. Don't forget to bring a knife, preferably one with scissors, to cut the sheets of moleskin to the right size; you can't tear it easily as you can adhesive tape.

If a blister does develop, cover it with something that won't stick to the blister itself, like an adhesive bandage or a piece of moleskin reversed so that the sticky side faces away from your skin. Once you've protected the blister, cover the area with moleskin or tape to keep the protective layer in place.

Purifying Water

When I started backpacking, most people drank directly from streams and lakes in alpine regions without bothering to purify the water. After all, mountain streams were literally as pure as the driven snow, right? That was in the 1970s, before the word *giardia* began appearing in backpackers' vocabularies and an occasional backpacker's gullet. *Giardia lamblia* is a protozoan parasite that can cause a disease called giardiasis, characterized by explosive diarrhea, cramps, bloating, and vomiting. Carriers of the disease excrete the parasite in the form of cysts, which can survive for months in water as cold as 32°F. Some thirty species of animals, including humans, have been identified as carriers. Treatment is with drugs that produce their own unpleasant side effects; fortunately, many people seem to recover spontaneously without medical intervention. Studies have shown that over 90 percent of the surface water in the United States is contaminated with giardia and another, equally common, protozoan parasite called cryptosporidium, which can also cause nasty bouts of diarrhea, nausea, and vomiting. Disease-causing bacteria and viruses can also be a threat, particularly in Third World countries or in regions of North America with human habitation upstream. That includes almost any river big enough to float a raft and some desert regions.

More recent research has shown that high-country water is probably much more pure than we thought in the 1980s. The cause of at least one of the early and most well-publicized cases of giardiasis afflicting a large group of backpackers turned out to be poor hand-washing practices, which allowed the disease to spread from person to person, not contaminated drinking water as originally thought. Some experts now recommend parsing the risk of drinking wilderness water by assessing how heavily the area is used by people or by whether or not domestic livestock may be grazing upstream.

Those experts may be right, but here's the problem: It's impossible to assess the risk based on a visual inspection of the water, and there is no simple field test to detect microorganisms that can make you sick. The risk is almost certainly smaller at high elevations than we thought fifteen years ago, but it still seems sensible to me to purify my water before drinking it. Recent research has also pointed out that hand-washing remains just as important in the backcountry as it is in the city. Don't wash your hands in a stream or lake; instead, use an iodine- or alcohol-based hand sanitizer every time after going to the bathroom and before preparing food.

Boiling your drinking water will kill giardia and every other waterborne pathogen that might be lurking in the murk. The time recommended varies widely, but a vigorous rolling boil for one minute should easily be sufficient to make the water drinkable by healthy people. The disadvantage of boiling is that it consumes a great deal of time, fuel, and patience. More convenient methods are available.

In the past Cora and I used water-purification tablets containing the compound tetraglycine hydroperiodide, which releases iodine when dissolved in water. These tablets are widely available under the name Potable Aqua. Iodine readily kills bacteria and viruses. The manufacturer used to recommend using one tablet for one quart of water and waiting ten minutes, but now recommends two tablets per quart and waiting thirty minutes. Using two tablets produces such a disagreeable iodine taste that the water is almost undrinkable, in my opinion, and waiting thirty minutes to slake your thirst is frustrating. A further disadvantage is that iodine does not kill cryptosporidium. A newer product containing chlorine dioxide can, but it can take up to four hours to do its work. Tablets are very light compared to a water filter, but the unpalatable taste, wait time, and questionable effectiveness under some circumstances makes me shy away.

A much better solution is a water filter made specifically for backpacking. These devices use a microporous filter with a pore size below one micron to screen out bacteria and larger organisms such as giardia and cryptosporidium. In addition, some contain an activated charcoal component that removes many organic compounds such as pesticides. Microporous filters do not claim to strain out viruses, which are far smaller than bacteria. Manufacturers of filters that work solely on a microporous

One model of water filter, the MSR MiniWorks.

principle, without the chemical disinfection necessary to kill viruses, assert that viruses simply aren't an issue in mountainous wilderness areas in North America. Expert opinion concurs. You should be concerned about viruses, however, if the water you're eyeing suspiciously may be contaminated with sewage from people living upstream. The easiest solution in that situation is to use a water purifier (as opposed to filter), which contains both a microporous filter and some means of killing viruses. One approach is to use a mass of iodinated resin beads. As the water flows past the beads, enough iodine is released to kill viruses so long as the concentration of viruses is moderate. In other words, don't rely on a water purifier to decontaminate water directly downstream from a Third World village or a North American sewage treatment plant. If you're really worried about the water, boil it.

The best water filters weigh less than a pint of water. On a long hike you may need to drink two, three, or even four quarts to stay hydrated. Carrying all the water you need for the whole day means starting out with two to four quarts (four to eight pounds) in your pack. If your route passes streams and lakes regularly, however, you can save a lot of weight by starting out with just one quart of water plus a water filter. That combo weighs less than three pounds.

All good water filters eventually clog. I say "good ones" because a filter that never clogs isn't doing its job of removing bacteria and protozoa. Filter manufacturers state the filtering capacity of their filters, but you should treat these numbers with skepticism. In poor-quality water the actual capacity may be only one-tenth of the rated capacity. Even apparently clear water can clog a filter after a few quarts if the water is full of invisible microorganisms. Most filters can be cleaned a limited number of times in the field. After that you need to replace the filter cartridge. On long trips, be sure to carry at least one spare cartridge. If your filter is supplied with a pre-filter for the coarser particles, use it religiously and carry spare pre-filters as well. If possible, filter from a lake rather than a swiftly flowing stream. Sediment, as well as giardia and cryptosporidium cysts, tend to sink to the bottom of calm water, so you'll have fewer nasty little critters to get rid of, and your filter will need cleaning less often.

Hypothermia

I regard it as a point of professional pride that I never get cold in the mountains, even in the dead of winter. Of course, that's not to say my pride has never been wounded, sometimes quite uncomfortably so. Nonetheless, I've never actually been hypothermic, the condition in which the body's core temperature drops low enough to impair normal muscular and mental function. If you carry the clothing described in chapter 2 and use it wisely, you'll never get in serious trouble from hypothermia. Your companion may not be as well prepared or as conscientious about body maintenance as you, however, so you should know the symptoms of hypothermia.

Hypothermia begins with a sensation of chilliness, numb skin, shivering, and loss of coordination and strength in the hands. It progresses to more severe shivering and loss of overall muscular coordination. Victims begin to stumble and fall frequently. Hands become numb, useless claws. Thought and speech slow to a crawl. Severely hypothermic victims lose the ability to walk and become incoherent and irrational. If cooling continues, death occurs because of heart failure.

Treatment for moderately hypothermic victims is simple: rewarming, starting with the trunk. Simply adding more clothing does not help, because hypothermia victims have lost the ability to rewarm themselves. Adding more clothing only serves to reduce the rate of heat loss; it does nothing to actually rewarm the body. To do that, external heat must be applied. The easiest way to accomplish this in the field is to zip two sleeping bags together and have a warm rescuer climb inside with the victim. A conscious victim should drink warm liquids; however, you should never try to force an unconscious victim to drink. They're likely to choke. Severely hypothermic victims require hospital care.

The key to preventing hypothermia is staying dry. Good shell clothing will ward off rain and snow. Preventing sweat from soaking your clothing is more difficult. If you let yourself sweat while working hard in the cold, you'll get chilled when you stop. Despite the obvious threat of discomfort, however, sweating seems almost impossible to avoid. Why?

Perhaps because, in some primeval way, we like it. Researchers at Kansas State University's Institute for Environmental Research found that people exercising in a test chamber considered themselves more comfortable when they were sweating than when they weren't. The harder they worked, the more sweat they were producing when they declared themselves most comfortable, even though they had the option of cooling the test chamber until they stopped sweating completely.

We also sweat in the cold because the evaporation of sweat inside clothing rarely provides more than half the cooling of sweat evaporating off bare skin. The reason? Some sweat vapor inside a jacket condenses and gives up its heat before it can escape to the outside air. If you're sweating but not cooling, your body responds by producing more sweat in an accelerating cycle that can only be stopped by removing insulation.

In cold weather you must consciously fight your natural tendency to sweat. That means dressing in layers that can be removed to prevent sweating when you're working hard and added to hold in heat when you stop moving. The human body generates about five times as much heat when hiking with a load as it does when at rest. Savvy backpackers adjust clothing as often as needed to remain comfortable.

Hypothermia cases are by no means limited to the winter months. In fact, hypothermia is actually quite common in the summer, when inexperienced and poorly prepared hikers get caught above timberline by a 40°F rainstorm and 20-mile-per-hour winds—a potentially lethal combination.

Finding Water in the Desert

In the desert, water is life, and your pack is likely to be quite heavy with it. Water weighs eight pounds per gallon. Since you'll need at least a gallon a day in the warm months, more at the height of summer, planning a backpacking trip in the desert revolves around the quantity of water that you can reasonably carry and the likelihood of finding additional sources along your route. Always carry enough water that if the spring or intermittent stream at your proposed campsite is dry, you can make it back out. Don't count on water being available just because the map shows a spring. You can probably trust people who have actually been there—so long as they were there yesterday, not the week or month before. Even in that case, bring along some extra water.

In an emergency your map, your eyes, and your trowel are your best bets for finding water. Examine the map not only for springs and streams, but also for man-made structures like wells, cattle tanks, and windmills. As you hike, look for bright green vegetation. There may be a seep or spring nearby. Keep an eye out for cottonwoods, sycamores, and seep willows growing in dry streambeds. They too may mean water is close at hand. If you find damp sand, dig down with your trowel. You may find water farther down, or you may be able to wait until the depression fills up. Search out places in canyons where flash-flood waters have scoured away the sand and gravel, exposing bedrock. Shallow depressions in the bedrock, called "tinajas," may have trapped pools of rainwater. If you're hiking the ridges in hilly terrain, examine the canyon floors below you for the bright flash of sunlight reflecting in a water-filled pothole. Lava and limestone are porous rocks that often contain springs. A cave in a limestone cliff or a place where lava abuts a sandstone cliff may contain a seep or a spring. Look for the dark stains and green moss that mark seeps in sandstone cliffs. In the high desert in the winter months, examine the shady north sides of cliffs where the sun never shines. Lingering snow patches may provide a source of water. Whatever the source, an easily cleaned water filter will not only remove whatever critters may exist but also the inevitable sand and silt.

Heat Exhaustion and Heat Stroke

Backpackers who venture into the desert in summer face a different set of problems. Heat exhaustion is an easy-to-remedy malady in which the victim feels faint, dizzy, and nauseated. Significantly, however, the victim's core temperature is not elevated above the normal 98.6°F. The solution is to rest in the coolest area available and to drink salty fluids. Most victims recover quickly.

Heat stroke is a far more serious malady in which sweating stops, the skin feels hot to the touch, and the body's core temperature soars to 105°F or higher. Heat stroke is a true medical emergency requiring rapid cooling of the victim. If possible, immerse the victim in tepid (not cold) water. If that's not possible, cover the victim with water-soaked clothes and fan the victim to promote evaporation. Massage the victim's limbs vigorously to prevent blood from pooling in the extremities. By increasing circulation you'll also help cool the overheated core. A heat-stroke victim's temperature can be quite unstable for several days afterward.

The key to preventing heat injuries is to drink. And drink. And drink—up to eight quarts of water per day in extreme conditions. Don't try to conserve water, thinking that you'll "teach your body to make do with less." Your body doesn't work that way. Don't rely on your sensation of thirst to tell you when to drink. You're likely to drink a pint when you need a half gallon. Your urine should be copious and clear. Dark yellow urine is a sign you're not drinking enough. Pound those fluids! Wear light-colored clothing and a well-ventilated sunhat with a broad brim or skirt that hangs down over your neck. Schedule your hiking for the early morning and late evening hours when temperatures are lower. Find some shade and hole up in the middle of the day. Only mad dogs and overeager backpackers go out in the midday sun when the temperature is in the triple digits.

Altitude Illness

Cora and I often find that we sleep restlessly on the first night of a mountain backpacking trip. The lack of a familiar bed undoubtedly plays a role, but equally important is the sudden change in altitude. Many campsites in the Colorado Rockies are at 10,000 or 11,000 feet. Cora and I live in Boulder at an elevation of about 5,000 feet. We usually drive to the trailhead and hike in on the first day. The abrupt change in altitude is sometimes sufficient to produce a mild version of the malady known as mountain sickness, which is characterized by fitful sleep, loss of appetite, and a persistent headache, particularly at night while lying down. Flatlanders coming up from sea level often experience the same symptoms with greater intensity. For me and Cora the second night is usually much better than the first, while the third is better still. Drinking plenty of fluids—enough to keep your urine clear—helps prevent mountain sickness. If you can, spend a night at an intermediate elevation, perhaps in a nearby mountain town, before beginning the hike. Most people can adjust well if they give themselves enough time. If you do start to develop uncomfortable symptoms, avoid overexertion but don't confine yourself to bed. You'll often find that mild exercise actually makes you feel better. If the symptoms persist, descend. Losing several thousand feet of elevation is an almost certain cure. Backpackers in the Himalayas and Andes, who may be camping at much higher elevations than backpackers in the continental United States, should pick up a wilderness-medicine manual that discusses mountain sickness and its dangerous cousins, pulmonary and cerebral edema. One good one is Buck Tilton's book *Wilderness First Responder: How to Recognize, Treat, and Prevent Emergencies in the Backcountry*, published by FalconGuides / GPP.

Poisonous Snakes

We've now gotten so far down on the list of possible wilderness hazards that those remaining are unlikely to affect most hikers during their entire career. Take snakebite, for example. Approximately 8,000 people are bitten by poisonous snakes in the United States every year. However, in about 25 percent of all bites, the snake injects no venom. Roughly twelve people die of fatal snake bites per year in the United States. Lightning is a bigger cause for worry, as are allergic reactions to bee stings. Only about 20 percent of the snake species found in the United States are poisonous.

Most snakes are afraid of humans and will slither away given half a chance. To avoid surprising one, watch where you walk. Snakes like rocky slopes that catch the morning sun, river bottoms, and any kind of cover: rock piles, brush piles, fallen logs. They congregate in their kitchen: any place where rodents, frogs, and lizards abound. Look first before stepping over a log. If you're scrambling in likely snake habitat, don't reach up blindly for a hold you can't see. Most of the high alpine areas in the United States are completely free of snakes, as is Alaska.

If you do get bitten, avoid panic. Even if the snake is poisonous, the chance of its bite killing a healthy adult is small. Toddlers and elderly people are at greater risk. Keep the victim quiet to help retard the spread of the venom, and send someone out to get help in evacuating the victim. Clean and bandage the wound. Do not apply ice to the bite or attach a tourniquet above the bite. The result can be a disastrous case of gangrene. Do not try to cut open the area surrounding the puncture marks and suck out the venom by mouth. The risk of serious infection is very high, and your incisions can easily damage nerves, tendons, and ligaments, particularly if the snake bit a hand or foot. Some stores still carry snakebite kits that contain a razor blade to make incisions and some kind of suction device for extracting venom. While these are better than the cut-and-suck-by-mouth method, the danger of infection and cutting vital structures is still high when these devices are used by inexperienced, panic-stricken hikers. One study of a popular snakebite kit found it only removed 1 or 2 percent of the venom. Given the low risk faced by a healthy adult, it seems best for victims to refrain from heroic measures in the field and simply get to a hospital as soon as possible.

Lightning

Every year lightning kills around forty people in the United States, according to National Weather Service data. Only a handful are backpackers; the rest are mountaineers, golfers, boaters, swimmers, and others.

The difference in electrical potential between the ends of a lightning stroke may reach hundreds of millions of volts. When lightning flashes, the temperature in the lightning channel can reach 50,000°F—five times as hot as the surface of the sun. The air around the lightning channel heats up instantly and expands explosively, causing thunder. Sound travels about 1 mile every five seconds, so the interval between a lightning flash and the sound of thunder tells you the distance to the storm. If lightning is frequent, keep track of the time between a lightning bolt and its thunderclap. If the time is decreasing, the storm is approaching you. Find shelter immediately.

Thunderstorms are characterized by violent updrafts within the storm itself that can reach 60 miles per hour. Rapid condensation created as the updraft cools is the cause of a thunderstorm's pounding rain. When the rising air reaches the top of the cloud, it cascades down the outside of the storm and spreads out along the ground, creating the sudden, cool breeze that heralds a thunderstorm's arrival. Severe thunderstorms can be distinguished from less violent ones by the size, shape, and position of the cloud. Cumulus clouds with low bases should be watched carefully. The low base indicates air with abundant moisture that needs to cool only a little to begin condensing. Anvil-shaped thunderstorms have updrafts powerful enough to reach the upper limit of the troposphere, which is several miles high. Overshooting thunderstorms, in which the normally flat top of the anvil bulges, are more dangerous still.

Prevention is obviously better than treatment when confronted with an immensely powerful force of nature like lightning. Lightning most often strikes tall, isolated objects—a peak, a rocky spire, a single tree in a meadow—or a person standing in an open area. If a thunderstorm threatens, get off the summits and ridges. If a dense forest with tall trees is nearby, plunge in and relax—you're safe. Stay away from isolated trees and clumps of trees, which can act as lightning rods. If you're caught in the open with nowhere to hide, set metal objects such as tent poles, ice axes, and tripods aside and move several hundred yards away. Kneel down and put your hands on your knees. The idea is to reduce your height to the greatest extent possible to avoid acting as a lightning rod, yet minimize your contact with the ground so that the ground current set up by a lightning strike has the smallest possible avenue to enter your body. If possible, crouch on an insulator such as a pack, sleeping pad, or climbing rope. Ground currents caused by lightning tend to flow along the paths taken by the rain as it runs off cliffs or hillsides. Shallow caves and overhanging rocks don't necessarily offer good protection from ground currents, which can flow along the cave walls or arc across the cave's mouth. A person hit by lightning frequently stops breathing. In addition, the victim's heart may stop beating. Be prepared to start cardiopulmonary resuscitation, a technique that requires specialized training in advance. Prompt CPR has saved the life of many lightning victims.

Emergencies

What should you do if someone is injured so seriously, or becomes so ill, that he cannot walk out on his own? The answer depends on the number of people in the group, what types of electronic communication devices you're carrying, if any, and which electronic devices will actually work at your location.

In the past a solo hiker could only attempt to perform basic first aid on himself, then shout and hope—or, better, blow an emergency whistle. A pair of hikers faced a difficult decision. After stabilizing the victim, should the uninjured member go for help, leaving behind a companion who may be unable to take care of himself? A group of three made the problem easier; one person could stay with the victim while the other went out. Four was even better because two people could head out together to get help, reducing the chance of another accident, while the third person stayed with the victim.

The advent of inexpensive cell phones and the increasingly widespread coverage offered by cell phone companies has made it easier, in some cases, to get help if you need it. Be forewarned, however: Carrying a cell phone is no substitute for common sense, good judgment, and experience. Cell phone coverage cannot be relied upon. If you manage to time your accidents and illnesses so they all occur high on a ridge within sight of a town in the valley below, yes, your cell phone will probably work. If you're down in a wilderness valley when the accident occurs, your cell phone is probably useless. I do carry a cell phone on solo trips because it does offer some additional safety (and I like calling Cora from the summit of Fourteeners!), but I continue to tread as cautiously as always. Handheld, portable satellite telephones are also available now that claim worldwide coverage, even in wilderness areas. However, at present the cost both for the phone and the airtime is prohibitive for most recreational users.

Recently a new option has become available: a personal locator beacon (PLB). In an emergency these devices can transmit an SOS signal, complete with your GPS coordinates, to search-and-rescue teams around the world via a network of satellites. Most can also send a message that all's well. The more sophisticated versions of these devices can communicate with a smart phone wirelessly, which allows you to type a short text message on your phone and transmit it via satellite, again complete with your GPS coordinates. The most sophisticated versions will let you receive text messages via satellite as well as send them.

PLBs will work when cell phones will not. Used responsibly, they can be a lifesaver that also saves the hardworking volunteers on the search-and-rescue team a tremendous amount of time and effort. They no longer have to mount exhausting searches involving dozens of rescuers. The SAR team knows exactly where the victim is located, which means it can accurately estimate where a helicopter can land and how far the victim will need to be carried, over what type of terrain. Speaking for myself, I know that if I ever needed a PLB, I would feel like an idiot. On the other hand, if I ever needed a PLB and didn't have one, I'd feel like an even bigger idiot. I do a lot of solo trips, almost always without incident. After spraining my knee severely on a simple overnight photo shoot, however, I finally bought a PLB that will pair up with my smart phone so I can send short text messages as well as call for help in an emergency.

It's important to emphasize that sending an SOS with a PLB doesn't guarantee you'll be rescued. Rescue, in fact, may be impossible due to weather, terrain, or any number of other variables. You should not let ownership of a PLB lure you into situations you would have avoided if you didn't have the apparent security of the PLB, and you should exhaust all possibility of rescuing yourself before you call out the cavalry.

Owning a PLB that offers the ability to send "all-okay" messages raises a dilemma: What should the policy be for its use? Should you check in with your ground-control person, who let's say is your wife, every day? If that's the policy, what should your wife do if she doesn't hear from you? Should your wife assume the worst and immediately call 911? Or should your wife assume you are perfectly fine but that your PLB malfunctioned, or its batteries are dead, or you're camped in dense timber that the satellite signal can't penetrate, or you dropped your PLB off a cliff or into a lake? If she assumes the latter, then clearly she should wait until you're actually overdue before calling 911.

Cora and I debated this for some time before deciding that our policy would be this: I would check in every day if possible, but she would not call 911 until I was actually overdue. I still leave a detailed, written itinerary with her, complete with a deadline for returning to civilization. We decided that the chance of the PLB not working for some reason was higher than the chance that I would become hurt but be unable to trigger the SOS function of the PLB. Rather than risking false alarms, we would take what we see as the very small chance that I would become immobilized by some injury but be unable to trigger the beacon, and so would have to wait longer for a rescue. This policy works for us, but you should carefully consider what your policy will be if you do purchase a PLB.

Novices also fret over this question: What should I do if I get lost? If you take the time to keep track of your position throughout the hike, you're very unlikely to get seriously off track. If the trail seems to peter out and vanish abruptly, stop and think. The usual cause of such an event is that you missed a turn in the trail a few hundred yards back. Retrace your steps and look for where you might have gone wrong. (You were looking over your shoulder periodically so you could easily retrace your steps, right?) You may need to hike all the way back to the last point you can positively identify on the map and start over again from there. If nothing seems familiar as you try to retrace your steps, get out the map and compass, orient the map, and try to identify some landmarks. From these you should be able to determine your location. If you have a GPS receiver and you can get a position fix (not always possible in dense woods or deep canyons), then getting lost is practically impossible.

If all else fails, sit down. Think about what could have gone wrong. Have a bite to eat. Food can have a very calming effect. Make noise. Perhaps someone will hear you. The odds are good that two parties didn't manage to get lost simultaneously in exactly the same spot. The other group can probably tell you where you are. Above all else, don't panic, pick a direction at random, and blunder ahead hoping to stumble across something familiar. You're all too likely to leave the area that searchers will concentrate on, making their task much more difficult. Instead, wait for rescuers to find you. If you can, make yourself visible to searchers on the ground and in the air. Spread out a brightly colored garment, sleeping bag, or tent in the middle of a meadow. Keep your group together to combine your strengths and to boost morale.

For most backpackers the question of what to do in a real emergency remains hypothetical throughout their career. In more than forty years of wilderness travel, I've never come close to feeling hopelessly lost. If you follow the precautions outlined in this book, you'll almost certainly build the same track record. I've also been fortunate to be a witness to only a few accidents, all of which involved rock climbing and mountaineering, not backpacking. Treat the wilderness with the respect it deserves, and you'll be able to travel safely in it for a lifetime.

> Most of the luxuries, and many of the so-called comforts of life, are not only not indispensable, but positive hindrances to the elevation of mankind.
>
> —*Henry David Thoreau, 1817–1862*

Joe Kaelin and I could hear the deep roar of the trucker's brakes on I-70 as we stepped into our ski bindings, shouldered our packs, and plunged into the winter wilderness of the Gore Range. Behind us, immediately adjacent to the four-lane highway, lay Vail, one of the nation's biggest and most popular alpine ski resorts. Ahead of us lay miles of untracked white and the jagged 13,000-foot peaks of the Eagles Nest Wilderness. We saw no people as we started up the trail. There were no other cars in the parking lot, although it was merely a quarter mile from the interstate; the lot's minuscule size indicated that very few cars were ever expected. Half an hour after we began, the old ski tracks we were following vanished and we were on our own, with no sign of human presence. Four days later, as we emerged on the far side of the range, we finally encountered another person—a rancher inspecting his herd.

That adventure more than thirty years ago ignited my love of the winter wilderness, a love that endures today. The wilderness in summer seems to become more crowded every year, but the winter wilderness is still only lightly traveled. Not long ago I did a solo winter ascent of 14,309-foot Uncompahgre Peak and didn't see a soul for three days. When I was standing on the summit at sunrise watching the full moon set over Wetterhorn Peak, I felt like I had the entire San Juan Mountains to myself.

Not all Colorado ranges are quite that empty. Still, by comparison to summer, winter is the season of silence in the high country, so long as you seek out the places where snowmobiles are banned. For example, backcountry use in Rocky Mountain National Park from October 1 to May 1—over half of the year—is less than 10 percent of the year's total. The lack of people pressure and the protection provided to the land by the carpet of snow allows rangers to relax the restrictions on where you can camp. In Rocky Mountain National Park, for example, you can pitch a tent almost anywhere you want if there's at least 4 inches of snow on the ground. If you want to get away from people, go to the high mountains when they're blanketed with snow.

Even in the lowlands, below the snow line, winter is usually the off-season. By Thanksgiving, if not sooner, the crowds have thinned considerably from the lemming-like hordes of summer. Snow-phobic backpackers will find that the cold months are a fine time to explore the southern tier of states and the Pacific and Atlantic coasts. Winter can be a wonderful time to hike in the desert Southwest, although I remember one New Year's trip to Utah's Arches National Park when the temperature dipped to 0°F every night and the daytime highs were only in the 20s. Backpacking below the snow line in winter is only a little different from summer backpacking. A few extra layers of clothing and perhaps a warmer sleeping bag are all that is really needed. To fully savor the season, however, backpackers should venture into the high mountains of New England and the West, where winter truly reigns supreme. Winter backcountry travelers there must be prepared to deal with snow.

Traveling in Snow Country

Early in the fall, when the first snows are sifting down, it's usually still possible, if occasionally laborious, to travel without the aid of snowshoes or skis. You'll need warm, waterproof boots, plus gaiters to keep snow out of your boot tops. Snow that is but a few inches deep will slow your pace only slightly as your feet grope for a solid purchase under the white velvet blanket. Trekking or ski poles can help steady your stride. As the snow deepens, you'll find yourself postholing, the

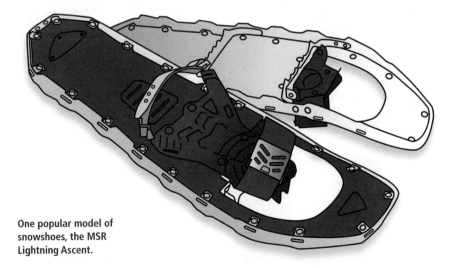

One popular model of snowshoes, the MSR Lightning Ascent.

hiker's nickname for plunging in to your knees with every step. Deep postholing can exhaust the strongest hiker in short order. By the time the snow, on average, is deeper than mid-calf, it's time to learn to walk on water—frozen, fluffy water, that is.

Snowshoes are much easier to use than cross-country skis. Most people master the duck-like waddle required within a few minutes. Although some people disdain them, I find ski poles reduce the number of times I trip over my newly acquired webbed feet. Snowshoes are also much less expensive than the kind of cross-country ski equipment you need to carry a substantial pack in the backcountry.

For snowshoeing footwear you can use insulated hiking boots or a pair of inexpensive pac boots, which have a molded rubber bottom, stitched leather or nylon top, and some kind of felt liner. Both types of boots are fine for day trips, but as I discussed in chapter 3, leather will eventually soak up water and freeze hard as iron if you're out overnight. The best solution I've found, an admittedly expensive one, is to use the same kind of plastic double boots used by winter mountaineers.

The smallest models of snowshoes work well, even with an overnight-size pack, if you'll be traveling on routes where skiers or other snowshoers have broken trail. By small I mean 8 by 22 inches or thereabouts. If you're trying to break trail yourself, however, small snowshoes will sometimes let you plunge in to your waist. You can either take that as a sign that you've lost favor with the Almighty or that you've encountered the rotten sugar-snow conditions common during some seasons in the Rockies and elsewhere. Supplication and medium-to-large snowshoes are essential under those circumstances. The pair I use for really big loads measures 9 by 30 inches, but most often I compromise with an 8 by 25-inch pair. Manufacturers offer suggestions on the right size of snowshoe depending on the total weight of you and your pack.

Snowshoeing is surging in popularity right now, and manufacturers have responded by designing better and better snowshoes. Newer models have substantial claws underfoot that offer improved traction in steep, crusty snow and better bindings that give you more control over your snowshoes when traversing a steep hillside.

Skis are a much more glamorous method of snow country travel than snowshoes. Unfortunately, skiing with a big pack in fickle backcountry snow while using supple cross-country boots attached to the ski only at the toe is vastly different from filmmakers' video fantasies. If your skiing experience is limited to schussing down beautifully manicured slopes at a posh resort while wearing combat equipment—stiff, high-backed boots locked down to wide, stable alpine skis—then your first venture into the backcountry may be, quite literally, a frigid plunge. In fact, there was many a time when I was learning to ski with a pack when I swore through clenched teeth that I could walk down the blasted slope faster than I could ski it. Even experienced skiers can be defeated by heavy loads, steep slopes, and tight slots through dense trees. One winter many years ago, Janet Gelman and I made an unsuccessful attempt on the Grand Teton. I was on snowshoes to avoid reinjuring a sprained knee. Janet, an excellent skier, was on skis. During the retreat I was able to march straight down through the narrow lanes between the trees while Janet struggled to make turns in the bottomless powder while carrying a huge pack. Inevitably the snow snakes would seize her by the ankles and she would fall. Extricating herself from the resulting craters required Herculean effort. In that situation snowshoes proved to be more efficient than skis.

From the vantage point of fifty-plus years, I regard skis as toys for having fun on day trips; snowshoes are tools for hauling overnight loads. Much of my time in the mountains for the last eighteen years has been spent making landscape photographs. When I'm by myself, in the dark as I approach a sunrise shoot, with a big pack on my back, tired and with inconsistent, unpredictable snow underfoot, I want to be on snowshoes. Skiing would be too dangerous to my knees. But when my pack is light because the camera gear is at home and I'm taking the day off from photography, I much prefer to be on skis.

When buying your first set of cross-country ski gear, avoid the mistake I made. I chose the flimsiest possible low-cut boots and lightweight skis without metal edges. They were more suitable for touring on a snow-covered golf course than tackling the Colorado high country. The result was that I floundered for years until two friends who owned a ski shop gently suggested that I might actually learn to ski some day if I invested in some decent equipment. As a minimum, buy yourself solidly built boots that are high enough to cover your anklebones and skis with metal edges so you have a fighting chance when the trails get scraped off and icy. You should also pick up a pair of skins to attach to the bottom of your skis for steep uphill sections. Skins are made of a furry synthetic material that allows your skis to slide forward but prevents them from sliding back. They save a tremendous amount of energy on long climbs when compared to using waxes to provide your skis with grip. Some people leave their skins on during difficult descents to slow themselves down. However, I find that wearing skins when skiing downhill causes a jerky gait in which the skis grab one moment, then slide forward the next. In my opinion that's worse than having a predictable, if fast, surface on the bottom of my skis.

I have a secret to share with those who love backcountry skiing so much that ski gear is a higher priority than next week's groceries. Backcountry skiers don't need to resign themselves to being Nordic nerdics performing telemark turns with one cross-country ski pushed well ahead of the other. They need not endure the shouted insults of alpine skiers ("Stand up and ski like a man! What are you doing, curtseying to the Queen?") when they're practicing with their cross-country skis on a lift-served hill. Backcountry skiers can now bring the control of alpine skis and the flexibility of touring skis into the backcountry with hybrid boots, bindings, and skis, collectively called alpine-touring equipment. Alpine-touring boots are high-backed and stiff, just like alpine boots, but they have a lever above the heel that lets you adjust the amount of forward lean. With the lever in the "ski" position, the boots force your lower leg forward, just like alpine boots do. With the lever in the "walk" position, the boots allow an upright stance suitable for walking and touring. The bindings are similarly Janus-like: In the locked-down configuration, they let you clamp your heel to the ski for maximum control on the downhill run just like alpine bindings do. In the touring configuration the bindings allow your heel to rise and fall while you walk just like standard three-pin or bar system cross-country bindings. Like alpine skis, alpine-touring skis are shorter and wider than cross-country skis. Unlike alpine skis, however, alpine-touring skis are relatively light, so they feel less like lead ankle weights when you're climbing a hill.

For me the purchase of alpine-touring equipment opened up a whole new world. Suddenly it became possible to actually ski instead of merely survive in crusty, windblown backcountry snow. For the first time I could contemplate skiing off the summits of high peaks (with due consideration being given to avalanche danger). True, alpine-touring gear has its limitations. It's heavier than ordinary cross-country equipment, significantly more expensive, and cumbersome to use in rolling terrain where you might feel the need to switch frequently from locked-down to touring mode. On flat ground, using alpine-touring gear is a slog. In most parts of Yellowstone, for example, alpine-touring equipment would be an expensive encumbrance. In much of the Colorado Rockies, however, where you're usually either climbing steadily or making a long continuous run back down, it's perfect. If you're a good alpine skier and want to be able to use your existing technique in rugged backcountry terrain rather than trying to master the telemark turn, alpine-touring gear may be the way to go.

Winter Shelters

The summer tent you have been using may be adequate for a winter excursion if you take care to pitch it below timberline in dense forest so it's not battered by high winds. You'll also need to shovel snow off the roof after a heavy snowfall to prevent the roof from sagging and possibly breaking a pole. If your winter adventures get

Winter: The Cool Adventure

more serious, you'll want to invest in a winter tent that will stand up to high winds and heavy snow loads. The discussion on tents in chapter 5 gives more details on desirable features.

Start preparing a winter tent site by stamping out a level platform with boots, skis, or snowshoes. Give the platform a few minutes to harden after you're done stamping to help prevent your knees and elbows from punching big depressions in the tent platform when you crawl inside your tent. You don't want to feel like you're sleeping in a bathtub or, worse yet, atop a series of irregularly spaced buckets. Sometimes tent pole segments can't be connected in exceptionally cold weather because the shock cord running through the segments freezes in elongated form. The excess cord protruding from the ends of the pole segments prevents the segments from being joined. If you encounter this problem, pull on the shock cord rapidly and repeatedly. Usually this will warm the cord just enough that it will regain its elasticity and allow the pole segments to be connected. Conventional tent pegs don't work in the snow, of course, so you'll need to find substitute anchors. Skis, ski poles, and snowshoes all work fine if you're going to be taking down the tent before you need that equipment again. If you plan to set up a base camp and leave the tent erect while you take day trips, try anchoring your tent to stuff sacks filled with snow and buried. I start by digging a hole a foot or more deep using one of the lightweight snow shovels made for winter backpacking and ski mountaineering. Then I fill the stuff sacks with snow, bury them (making sure the drawstring emerges from the snow), and pack the snow down on top of each sack. These anchors are usually bombproof after the snow has had a chance to set. In fact, it can require some serious digging to extricate the buried stuff sacks.

Some people prefer to leave the tent at home and dig snow caves instead. In severe weather snow caves offer several advantages: They're impervious to wind, and they're also warmer at night and quieter than a tent because the snow acts as an insulator. Most caves will warm up to near freezing after they've been occupied for a while. Despite these appealing aspects, snow caves also leave a lot to be desired. Digging a snow cave is a hard, wet job that can easily consume two or three hours. Finding a suitable site can be difficult, since the snow must be both deep and sufficiently consolidated. I've dug snow caves in near-emergency situations in Alaska when high winds threatened our tents. In those situations I blessed the security the caves provided. In general, however, I prefer to carry the weight of a tent, which in good weather admits more light and is much warmer than a snow cave. A light-colored tent can act as a greenhouse on a sunny day. The warmth boosts morale and helps dry sodden gear, which will actually dry faster

165

inside the tent than it will draped over the roof outside. When the sun is shining, crawling into a snow cave is like entering a walk-in refrigerator.

Backcountry skiers who want to continue making multiday excursions in the winter but who can't stand the idea of sleeping in the cold should investigate the possibility of staying in a backcountry hut or yurt. Over the past twenty years, several immensely popular chains of huts have blossomed in the Colorado backcountry. One of the most heavily used systems is the group of huts operated by the Tenth Mountain Division Trail Association in the triangle between Leadville, Aspen, and Vail. (See the appendix for the address and phone number.) Demand is so heavy that most hut space is allotted by lottery. These huts are equipped with wood heating stoves, propane cooking stoves, mattresses, and a photovoltaic system that powers energy-efficient electric lights. Skiers bring their own food and lightweight sleeping bags. Call your local outdoor shop or fire up your favorite search engine to find out what huts exist in your area.

Camping in Winter

Probably the biggest worry of newcomers to the winter backcountry is that they'll get cold. In reaction to this apparently logical fear, they often get out of the car, bundle up in six layers of clothing, and head up the trail. Within fifteen minutes sweat is dripping from their earlobes. When they stop moving, evaporation from their sweat-soaked clothes immediately chills them right down to their cotton underwear. In their attempt to avoid getting cold, they've actually made the problem worse.

Even more than in the summer, the key to remaining comfortable is to take the time to adjust clothing as soon as your temperature starts to feel out of balance. Pause to shed clothing before you're dripping. Add a layer before you start to shiver. Carry synthetic clothing that dries fast and doesn't absorb sweat. Select clothing that can be ventilated easily. I prefer jackets with full zippers rather than pullovers for this reason. I also like pile pants and shell pants with full side zippers that allow me to ventilate even while I'm moving. It's even better if the zippers separate completely into two halves when they're unzipped. Picture someone trying to pull on a pair of blue jeans while wearing skis, and you'll understand the value of full separating side zippers, which allow you to put on your pants without taking off your skis or snowshoes.

If you get serious about winter camping, you'll probably want to buy a full-on winter sleeping bag. See chapter 6 for details on what to look for.

In the wintertime every minute you spend thinking about the details before the trip is one less minute you'll spend cursing the details once you're out in the cold. For example, the slider on every zipper on your pack, outer clothing, and tent should be equipped with a short loop of stout cord so you can operate the zipper without removing your gloves. Avoid buttons on winter clothing—you'll need bare hands to manipulate them. Trying to button your shirt while wearing gloves is like trying to eat beef broth with chopsticks. Snaps are a little better, but zippers are best once they're equipped with zipper pulls. Velcro-closed pockets are often annoying because the Velcro either grabs your gloves (if you're wearing them) or scratches your bare hands, which are usually already sensitized by the cold. One other tip: Try storing your water bottle upside down in your pack so that any ice that forms won't cause the cap to freeze shut. The prerequisite for this trick, of course, is finding a water bottle that absolutely does not leak.

Once you've got the tent pitched, start the stove immediately. You'll probably have to melt snow to obtain water, and that takes a long time. To keep your hot stove from sinking into the snow and tipping over, bring a small square of thin plywood and set your stove atop it. Cover the plywood with a thin piece of sheet metal. Some stoves run so hot they can ignite the plywood if it's left unprotected. Take care in handling white gas in cold weather. It remains liquid at very low temperatures and can easily cause frostbite if spilled on unprotected skin.

Avalanches

Avalanches are probably the most fearsome hazard in the winter backcountry because they are both lethal and hard to predict. Everyone who travels in the high country in winter should take an avalanche seminar. Local mountaineering and search-and-rescue groups often offer such seminars; check with your local outdoor shop to see who offers one in your area. What follows are merely the basics.

Avalanches are most common on slopes ranging from 30 to 45 degrees in steepness, but they can occur even on more gentle slopes when conditions are very unstable. They occur most frequently on slopes that are heavily loaded with snow by the wind. Wind-scoured, west-facing slopes are generally safer than east-facing slopes where that wind-scoured snow is subsequently deposited. Cornices—overhanging, wave-like formations—frequently form at the top of dangerous, wind-loaded slopes. Avalanches can be triggered by the collapse of a cornice, by the addition of snow to a slope by wind or a snowstorm, or by the weight of a skier or snowshoer. Many avalanches run during and immediately after large storms. Gullies and broad concave bowls accumulate snow and are therefore more dangerous than ridges, where the snowpack is usually more shallow. However, travelers on ridges should take care not to walk on top of cornices, which can collapse under their weight. Not all steep slopes will avalanche if you ski them, but predicting which ones will slide and which won't is difficult even for experts. A trained observer can gain some clues by digging a snow pit and examining the layers in the snowpack, but digging a pit and then deciding to ski a slope because you think it's safe is like betting your life on a fortuneteller's reading of tea leaves.

To avoid avalanches, stay off open slopes between 30 and 45 degrees. Widely scattered trees will not necessarily protect you. To be safe from avalanches, a forest must have trees that are too closely spaced to provide enjoyable skiing. Give avalanche runout zones a wide berth. Avalanches that have fallen a considerable distance build up enough momentum to travel for long distances on flat ground. Finally, listen for warning signs. An unstable snowpack, even on level ground, will frequently settle with an ominous whompf! under the weight of your skis. The sound is caused by the collapse of weak layers in the snowpack. If you hear the snowpack settle, exercise even greater caution than normal. Many people have been hit by avalanches even though they themselves were on nearly level ground. The snowpack settled beneath their skis, and the fracture propagated uphill into the avalanche starting zone. The avalanche broke loose high above them, then swept down and engulfed them. Give avalanche runout zones an even wider berth than normal when you hear the snowpack settling beneath your feet.

Everyone traveling in avalanche terrain should be equipped with an avalanche beacon, a device that transmits a signal that other avalanche beacons can hear. If one member of a party is buried by an avalanche, the other members can set their beacons to receive the buried beacon's signal and so locate the victim. The newest models can provide the distance and direction to the buried beacon; older models simply beep ever more loudly as the rescuer comes closer to the victim. In addition to a beacon, every member of the party should carry a stout, aluminum-bladed shovel to quickly extricate a buried victim. Avalanche debris sets up like concrete, and time is critical. Only half of avalanche victims survive the first thirty minutes of burial.

Winter Weather

In the continental United States in winter, bad weather is usually produced by major low-pressure systems tracking west to east. If your trip will last only a couple of days, you should be able to get a decent weather forecast before you start. The National Weather Service, with its far-flung network of observing stations, will always be able to do a much better job of predicting the weather than you will by observing conditions in your immediate vicinity. However, a knowledge of the typical pattern of clouds generated by an approaching low-pressure system can be helpful, particularly if you're out for several days and the forecast you got at the beginning of the trip has become outdated.

About twenty-four to forty-eight hours before a storm hits, high cirrus clouds usually begin to cover the sky. These feathery or fibrous clouds are composed of ice crystals and found above 23,000 feet. As the storm draws closer, the cirrus thicken to cirrostratus, a more continuous, sheet-like cloud that often causes a halo around the sun or moon. Stratus means "stratified" or "layered." This sequence of cirrus followed by cirrostratus is important, for cirrus alone is not necessarily a sign of bad weather. As the storm gets closer, the cirrostratus lower and thicken further to altostratus, layered mid-level clouds between 6,500 and 23,000 feet. When the storm is imminent, the altostratus thickens and descends to form nimbostratus, a continuous blanket of low-level (below 6,500 feet) clouds, and snow begins to fall. Low-pressure systems less than 300 miles across usually die out within thirty-six hours. Bigger ones, from 350 to 1,800 miles across, often last three or four days. This idealized portrait of a low-pressure system doesn't correspond perfectly to every storm you'll encounter, but at least it gives you some clues on what to look for.

Springtime

Springtime may be my favorite time in the high mountains. The scenery still says winter, but the weather says spring. The avalanche danger has both diminished and become far more predictable. As the snowpack consolidates and stabilizes under the influence of the warm spring sun, the breakable crust of midwinter gives way to delightful corn snow, the world's easiest snow to ski. Very few people come to the mountains then, because there is a bit of a catch: You have to be willing to get up early.

Warm days and still-cold nights mean the snowpack goes through a strong daily cycle. At dawn the snowpack is usually frozen hard enough to bear a skier's weight, so travel is fast and easy. By midmorning the surface has softened to a depth of an inch or so, and downhill runs are silken perfection. By noon the snow has softened still further, and skiing has become more difficult as skiers must force their skis to turn in deep slush. The avalanche danger begins to climb. By midafternoon liquid water is percolating through the snowpack, loosening the bonds that hold the snowpack's layers together, and the avalanche danger is climbing to unacceptable levels. Even on the flats, travel can be difficult as skis plunge into the rotten snowpack. After sunset the snowpack begins to refreeze, and at dawn the cycle repeats itself. The key to enjoying springtime travel and avoiding avalanches, therefore, is to adopt this variation of Ben Franklin's motto: Early to bed, early to rise, makes a man healthy, wealthy, and alive.

The information contained here is only a primer on what you need to know to travel safely and comfortably in the high mountains in the snowy months. What's said of life in general is particularly true of winter camping: Good judgment comes from experience, and experience comes from bad judgment. Winter places far greater demands on fitness, route-finding skills, camping techniques, and the ability to take care of yourself in foul weather than summer does. Even with the best gear, the discomfort quotient is undeniably higher. At times fingers grow numb even if protected by the best gloves available. Loads are heavy with extra clothing, a heavy-duty tent, a winter-weight sleeping bag and extra-thick foam pad, a snow shovel, and on and on. In the winter, even more than in the summer, the wilderness demands respect. Despite the many challenges, however, winter travel in the high mountains is an experience that I find far more rewarding than cruising up some summertime wilderness highway masquerading as a trail and pulling into a designated backcountry campsite. In its solitary character and confrontation with nature in the raw, it is an experience far closer to what most people imagine wilderness travel should be like. Winter is a season that should not be missed.

When you lose the power of wonderment, you become old, no matter how old you are. If you have the power of wonderment, you are forever young. The whole world is pristine and new and exciting.

—Sigurd F. Olson, 1899–1982

Hiking with children is far different from exploring the backcountry with other adults. Children, to their credit, are rarely as obsessed with goals as their parents. They cannot fathom the notion of hiking nonstop for hours with eyes fixated on Dad's boot heels in order to reach some scenic vista. Instead, kids are interested in the little things right in front of them. They love to inspect the bugs, beetles, lizards, and leaves that line the trail. While backpacking in Rocky Mountain National Park with our neighbors Gregg and Amy Thayer, their daughters Maggie and Jessie became fascinated with renaming the flowers they encountered. The game occupied them for an entire mile—a long time for two young children. Kids don't comprehend why Daddy and Mommy, with their massive packs, are eager to cover the miles as quickly as possible so that they can drop their loads for the last time, and they don't grasp why adults don't share their fascination with the minute wonders that spring into view at every step. As the Little Prince put it in Antoine de Saint-Exupéry's novel of the same name, "Grownups never understand anything for themselves, and it is tiresome for children to be always and forever explaining things to them."

Before taking your kids into the wilderness, make sure that you yourself feel comfortable there. Don't try to learn how to pitch your tent and fire up your stove when you've got cold, hungry, tired kids in tow. Even experts should never go into the woods as the only adult with young children. If something should happen to the adult, the whole group could be in serious trouble. Two adults are a minimum. Ideally the ratio of adults to children under seven should be one to one. At worst there should be one adult for every two children.

The Stages of a Wilderness Childhood

In some ways infants are easier to take into the woods, at least for a day hike, than children of any other age. By comparison to older kids, infants are very portable and require minimal additional equipment. Up until the age of eight months or a year, infants ride comfortably in a soft chest pack. When infants outgrow the chest pack, they often enjoy riding on a parent's back in a child pack with a soft nylon seat and a rigid aluminum frame. Lou Dawson, the first person to ski all fifty-four of Colorado's 14,000-foot peaks, used to take his one-year-old son Louie with him in a child pack when he trained by skiing up, then down, the slopes of Ski Sunlight, an alpine resort near his home in Carbondale, Colorado. Needless to say, Lou was extremely confident that he would not fall. Louie never complained, and in fact seemed to enjoy it. In either kind of pack, infants need to be bundled up more warmly than you, since they aren't active. They also need protection from the sun and from mosquitoes and other biting insects. Don't apply sunscreen or insect repellent to areas that an infant might suck. Some child packs offer as an accessory an awning that attaches to the pack frame and shades the occupant. With the addition of a little mosquito netting, the awning can serve to keep bugs off as well. Child packs that hold children high let them see better, which may keep them happier. They also position children where they can easily yank on a parent's hair and where their screams have the maximum effect on a parent's tattered nerves. One study showed that a baby screaming in a parent's arms actually sounded louder to the parent than a jackhammer at 10 feet. Fortunately, babies in child packs often sleep soundly for much of the ride, so, with luck, you won't be able to confirm the results of the study.

Life grows more complicated when a child begins to crawl, then walk. Many parents feel that the ages between two and four are the most difficult for taking children into the wilderness. No longer are kids content to ride for hours in a child pack. They want to get down and walk, but they really can't—or won't—walk very far. The same child who will scamper about a playground for hours, displaying enough energy to power New York City in a blackout, will walk a hundred yards on a trail and begin asking, "When are we going to get there?" The difference is that the playground provides an exciting series of immediate diversions, while the designated campsite seems impossibly far away. The key to motivating a child on the trail, therefore, is to provide a tantalizing series of nearby goals: counting the pinecones under the big ponderosa a hundred yards up the trail, then examining the stream you can hear around the bend for tadpoles and trout. My mom and dad used M&Ms, doled out in small handfuls every twenty or thirty minutes, to entice me and my sister Amy up the trail. When my two girls were three and five, they loved to throw pebbles into any available body of water to watch the splash.

Some kids are easier to motivate than others. Cora and I took a 3-mile hike once with two nephews. Micah was two and Izaac was four. Micah, a sturdy little chap, strode along happily for most of the way, while his older brother hung back complaining and finally insisted on being carried in an ordinary day pack even though the cramped foot area put his legs to sleep. I felt like I was carrying a sack of squirming potatoes, but Izaac was happy and the rest of the hike went smoothly.

By the age of four or five, many kids will want to carry their own little day pack containing, at most, a sweater and a favorite snack. Even this minuscule load will often end up on Mommy's or Daddy's back before the day—or hour—is out. Outings should be short, a few miles at the most, and parents should remember that the fun limit is usually much less than the actual physical limit. One mistake my parents made was doing too much the first day. They recall one time in particular when I was five. The first day we walked to the top of Sequoia's Moro Rock, which provided a fine view of the Kaweah River valley. The 3-mile hike so wore me out, however, that I collapsed into bed immediately after breakfast the next day and refused to move until noon. Be prepared to provide entertainment during the frequent stops you will make. Snacks and juice have entertainment as well as nutritional value. Make up games as you go along, sing songs, or tell stories.

By the time children reach eight or nine, they're probably ready for a child-size internal-frame pack. In the past, finding such a pack was difficult to impossible. Fortunately, there are enough outdoorsy parents these days that several companies have found it profitable to produce decent kids' packs. When selecting one, look for the maximum possible amount of adjustability in the torso length—the distance between the waist belt and the point where the shoulder straps attach to the pack bag. As with all children's equipment and clothing, you want gear that can be adjusted to fit a growing body for as long as possible.

A child's load on a backpacking trip should be less than one-fourth of his or her body weight. With a bit of luck and a lot of cajoling, you should be able to get your kids to carry their own pint-size sleeping bag and most of their clothes.

Before the age of eight or nine, most kids can get by on dry trails with sneakers. Once they start carrying a pack with significant weight, however, you should consider buying them a pair of children's hiking boots if you do enough hiking and backpacking to justify the cost. Child-size hiking footwear is now available in both over-the-ankle and under-the-ankle models. Kids don't seem to mind wet feet as much as adults, but if you do much hiking in the spring and early summer when trails are muddy and may still have remnant snow patches, you may want to consider a waterproof pair. Parents should check their kid's feet periodically for hot spots. If you find reddened skin, cover it with moleskin immediately to prevent a blister from forming. Kids usually don't complain about their feet until a full-grown blister has erupted, so it's up to you to forestall trouble.

Up to the age of eight months or a year, most infants ride comfortably in a chest pack (left). For a year or two after outgrowing the chest pack, children often enjoy riding in a child pack carried on the parent's back (right).

At some point in the teenage years, your children's strength and stamina, which is on the rise, will surpass yours, which is on the decline. At that longed-for point you may actually be able to ask them to shoulder more than half the load. By that time, unfortunately, they'll probably prefer going off with friends their own age.

Camping with Kids

At any age, day-hiking with children is easier than backpacking with them. On a day hike, if the weather turns sour or a child suddenly gets sick, the car is usually just a short distance away. If a similar situation develops on a backpacking trip, the time required to get out is much greater. Backpacking is also more difficult than day-hiking because of the dramatic increase in the parents' load. Parents' packs are heavy with an oversize tent, extra food, all the group gear, and, often, most of the kid's clothing and gear. Dawdling along at a child's inchworm pace can be torture when you've got a monster pack on your back. Cora and I usually tried to plan trips so we had a relatively short hike to our campsite, which we would occupy for two nights. That gave us one day in the middle of the trip when we woke up in the wilderness, went to sleep in the wilderness, and had a full day to explore with a light load on our backs. We also tried to plan trips so we had a fun, not-too-distant destination for the day hike on our second day.

If the child is too young to walk, then one parent must carry the babe in a child pack while the other totes the remaining gear. If you're not careful, the sheer bulk of the necessary equipment will overwhelm the largest pack on the market, which means that two trips become necessary for the parent acting as educated alpine mule. That's feasible only if the campsite is just a mile or so from the trailhead.

Confining your backpacking with small kids to desert regions in the warm months is another possible solution. One couple I know took their two young boys on several desert backpacking trips without ferrying loads. Both boys were young enough they had to be carried most of the way. The couple managed it by stripping down the gear to an absolute minimum: one two-person tent for the family of four, one sleeping bag that, when unzipped, could cover both adults, and warm sleepers in lieu of sleeping bags for the kids. Each parent carried a child, plus half the gear.

An alternative to ferrying loads or doing hot-weather trips is to hire a teenager to act as a porter. Once the party reaches camp, the teenager can help babysit.

In some parts of the country, you can rent llamas to help carry the load. Llamas are generally docile, sociable animals who feel right at home in the woods. Most llama ranches require you to take a half-day course in llama wrangling before you embark on your trip. Once you're trained, they'll meet you at the trailhead with the llamas, so you don't need to worry about stuffing two llamas into the trunk of your Prius. Llamas also cause much less impact on the land than horses, which are still another way to carry the weight. Renting some kind of pack animal is really the only feasible way to do a weeklong backpacking trip with young children.

If backpacking with young children sounds like lot of work, you're right. Nonetheless, it can be done. My neighbors Gregg and Amy, who are both ex–wilderness guides, started backpacking with their two daughters when the youngest was still in diapers. Still, you don't see many couples on the trail with children who are not yet potty trained. At least in theory, cloth diapers can be washed out and reused if the weather is warm enough to permit air-drying and you bring along a separate diaper-washing pot. Wash water should always be dumped well away from any water source. If you bring disposables (a more realistic option), you'll have to pack them out inside several layers of plastic bags.

Children like the familiar, and the wilderness can seem like a strange and intimidating place to a young child. Initially at least, a tent doesn't seem like home, and children may find it difficult to go to sleep. To help alleviate those night fears, pitch your tent in your backyard and spend a night or two there before you go on a real backpacking trip. Children who like to sleep with a night light may find that a tent pitched in the wilderness seems awfully dark. To help relieve those fears, sit down with your children in the backyard and explain all the night noises they hear so they realize there's nothing to fear. Do the same once you're actually camping in the woods. Sometimes it helps to bring along a few favorite nighttime toys. Letting the kids help set up the tent familiarizes them with it and may make them less apprehensive about sleeping inside it.

As a general rule, letting your child sleep with you inside your sleeping bag is an invitation to trouble. The child may sleep well, but you probably won't because the child's squirming will keep you awake. Each child should have his own sleeping bag, which shouldn't be more than about 4 inches longer than his height. A bag that is too big is hard to warm up, and the child is likely to sleep cold. Adequate child-size sleeping bags are available now. Look for a model with a hood that can be closed down snugly just like an adult's. All children's sleeping bags have synthetic insulation, which in a kid's bag has the advantage over down that it can more easily be machine washed and dried.

If you have a choice of where to camp, try to select a site well away from other campers so the inevitable childish racket doesn't echo through the woods and disturb your neighbors. Check the site for nearby hazards: a waterfall, a cliff, a patch of poison ivy or poison oak. Equally important, try to find a site with child appeal. Water, whether in the form of a pond or a stream, is always enticing. One of my best memories of backpacking with my daughter Audrey was a Labor Day trip into the Never Summer Range. We camped near a stream that was about 20 feet wide but only 4 inches deep. It was studded with flat granite rocks like stepping stones. Audrey and I spent several enjoyable hours carving miniature "boats" from flat bits of bark. We even outfitted some with "sails," short twigs inserted into holes I drilled in the soft bark with the awl on my Swiss Army knife. When our boats were complete, we turned them loose to float down the stream, making guesses about which way they would go around each new obstacle and wondering when and where they would get stuck.

My daughters also took endless delight in rock-hopping along the shores of lakes and across boulder-strewn streams. Just be sure the stream is shallow enough and the flow is slow enough that the inevitable tumble into the water won't have any serious consequences. Carrying a spare set of dry clothes for your kids adds to your load, but keeps your kids comfortable.

Equally appealing for kids is a late-lingering snow patch, which provides endless ammunition for snowball fights and building material for snowmen and snow forts. Beware of snowfields that slope steeply and end abruptly in a boulder field or lake. A child can easily start sliding out of control and crash into the obstacles at the snowfield's foot. Although most kids love scrambling up small rocky outcrops, they often discover too late that it's much harder to climb down than to climb up. Be sure to supervise your budding mountaineers carefully as they test their developing skills.

Whether on the trail or in camp, parents should establish an absolute, unbendable rule that children will always stay within sight of an adult. The cooking area and the tent should be ruled off-limits to play. Little fingers can too easily be burned on a hot stove or hot pots, and little feet can easily trip over tent pegs and guy ropes. Consider giving children a whistle and then making another rule: The whistle will only be blown in the case of a real emergency. An adult should accompany children when they need to go to the toileting area, which, as with adults, should be well away from any water source. Adult supervision ensures that children don't wander off and that they bury their waste properly. Be sure your pack contains a well-stocked repair kit. Kids are hard on gear, both their own and community items like tents.

When it comes time to break camp, encourage your kids to help you police the site for any litter you may accidentally have dropped or that may have been left behind by previous campers. If need be, make it a game. Pretend you're trappers or Indians seeking to leave no trace of your passage so your enemies can't track you down. By teaching children at an early age about no-trace camping, you can be confident you'll be raising another responsible citizen of the wilderness.

Human subtlety . . . will never devise an invention more beautiful, more simple, or more direct than does nature, because in her inventions nothing is lacking, and nothing is superfluous.

—*Leonardo da Vinci, 1452–1519*

The scheme was so outrageous that I couldn't believe anyone had seriously suggested it—yet someone had. A gravel company had proposed a tenfold expansion of a small but already troublesome quarry on Eldorado Mountain, near Boulder, Colorado. The operation would have devoured the entire northeastern flank of the mountain and left a scar 2,000 feet high—as big as the northwest face of Half Dome in Yosemite National Park. Granted, we all use gravel every day, whether we see it or not—it's a necessity for roads, runways, and concrete structures of every kind. Still, the company had chosen the most offensive possible site for a quarry of that magnitude. Eldorado Mountain rises in the center of a broad complex of recreational land visited by half a million people every year. To the north lies Eldorado Canyon, a spectacular state park that is also one of the nation's finest rock climbing areas. The wide swath of land to the east is part of Boulder's Mountain Parks. Eldorado Mountain is also a prominent part of the western skyline for tens of thousands of nearby residents. Boulder, the closest city, began buying and protecting its mountain backdrop in 1898. Now that far-sighted program faced its most serious threat ever.

The gravel company was operating its existing quarry on land leased from the State Land Board. The board's mandate to earn money from its land to support public schools gave the company a strong public-relations lever. The state organization responsible for approving the company's application was notoriously friendly toward mining companies. Even in environmentally savvy Boulder County, defeating the proposal would not be easy.

For ten years I had enjoyed the steep climbs that abound on Eldorado Canyon's walls. Eldorado Mountain graced the southwestern skyline every time I went running in Boulder's Mountain Parks. I immediately joined the newborn organization fighting the expansion. Together we wrote flyers and raised the money to print and mail them. We assembled a slide show and spoke to civic organizations large and small. We took our message to planning boards, city councils, and county commissioners. In the end we won a unanimous verdict of opposition to the expanded quarry from every government body with jurisdiction. After months of negotiations Boulder bought the company's lease. The quarry shut down, and Eldorado Mountain seemed safe.

Safe, that is, until some California company unearthed an obscure federal law and began an attempt to build a waterpower project on Eldorado Mountain's southern flanks. The city immediately mobilized to fight this ill-conceived project, which would consume more energy than it produced and only make money because the power generated could be sold during daylight hours, when electricity rates are at their peak. Fortunately, the company cancelled the project when the strength of the opposition became apparent.

Organized, aroused citizens can make a difference. Our efforts helped preserve wildlife habitat, a healthy watershed, and recreational opportunities that will grow more valuable with each passing year. Sadly enough, however, most environmental victories require constant vigilance to remain secure. Conservationists need more than powerful lungs. They need stamina too.

Depending on exactly how you do the measurement, the United States is either the third- or fourth-largest country on Earth. Its boundaries encompass 3.79 million square miles, an area almost as big as Europe. Today less than 5 percent—171,114 square miles—has been protected as wilderness under the terms of the 1964 Wilderness Act. Even that number is deceptive, since just over half of America's wilderness is concentrated in Alaska. In the Lower 48 only 2.7 percent of the land has been preserved in its pristine form. Six states have no wilderness whatsoever. The vast majority of America has already been plowed and paved and put to human use in a thousand ways. Surely we owe it to the other creatures great and small who inhabit this land with us to leave a little undisturbed for their benefit. Surely we owe it to ourselves to save some scraps of land where we can escape the din of machinery and the oppressive crush of the crowd. As environmentalist and author Wallace Stegner put it, "Something will have gone out of us as a people if we ever let the remaining wilderness be destroyed; if we permit the last virgin forests to be turned into comic books and plastic cigarette cases; if we drive the few remaining members of the wild species into zoos or to extinction; if we pollute the last clear air and dirty the last clean streams and push our paved roads through the last of the silence, so that never again will Americans be free in their own country from the noise, the exhausts, the stinks of human and automotive waste."

Proof of how much people value wilderness can be found in the long lead times required to reserve a wilderness campsite in many of our national parks. Although the number of visitors to national parks and Forest Service and Bureau of Land Management recreation areas has leveled off of late, ongoing population growth will surely lead to an increasing number of visitors in the future. America's ongoing love affair with the wilderness is also one of the chief threats to wilderness. This book has spent much time detailing these internal threats and what you can do to reduce the impact of your presence. Equally important, however, are the external threats. All national parks and wilderness areas will suffer if intensive development is allowed just outside the wilderness boundaries. Few parks and wilderness areas preserve complete ecosystems. Their biological health depends on a buffer zone of undeveloped or lightly developed land around them. Logging, mining, oil and gas production, off-road vehicles, excessive grazing, and urban sprawl all threaten these buffer zones.

It's time to draw boundaries around civilization instead of around wilderness. The number of human beings that the planet can sustain at our present levels of consumption is limited. We must find a way to construct a sustainable economy based on the resources we have already diverted to human use. In the long run, pillaging what little wilderness remains will do nothing to help.

If you love the wilderness and the opportunities it provides to hike and camp, if you value its role as a reservoir of biological diversity, if the thought of its silent beauty cheers you even when you're a thousand miles away, speak up. Start by becoming informed. Scan the Internet or your local newspaper for items on environmental controversies. Join one or more of the major conservation organizations and read their magazines and newsletters. Environmentalists will never have the clout of major corporations unless they band together. Seek out the small, local organizations that often do the most to solve local problems, or found an organization of your own. Write letters to your local newspaper and your local, state, and federal representatives. E-mail newsletters from conservation organizations will tell you which issues are hot and which officials should feel public pressure. It's easy to be complacent, to think that the present wilderness system is secure and sufficient for all time. In fact, the battle to preserve wilderness in the United States is not over. Add your voice to those who are demanding that more land be preserved. Your duties to the land do not end when you pick up a last bit of litter as you stride back into the parking lot. In fact, they have just begun.

APPENDIX A: EQUIPMENT CHECKLISTS

This is the checklist Cora and I use for summer backpacking trips in the Rockies. It's an idiosyncratic list that I'm sure you will modify as you gain experience.

Personal Equipment

- ☐ two pairs of socks (one thick, one thin)
- ☐ boots
- ☐ convertible pants
- ☐ synthetic woven short-sleeve shirt
- ☐ woven long-sleeve shirt
- ☐ synthetic fleece sweater with hood
- ☐ ultralight down sweater
- ☐ fleece ski hat
- ☐ sun hat
- ☐ light gloves
- ☐ rain pants
- ☐ rain jacket
- ☐ sunglasses
- ☐ MP3 player with audio books
- ☐ headlamp with extra batteries
- ☐ bowl
- ☐ spoon
- ☐ mug
- ☐ Swiss Army knife
- ☐ sleeping bag
- ☐ Therm-a-Rest air mattress
- ☐ Therm-a-Rest chair

- ❏ pack
- ❏ lip balm
- ❏ two or more water bottles
- ❏ two large garbage bags
- ❏ a few small plastic bags
- ❏ toothbrush, toothpaste, floss
- ❏ watch
- ❏ trekking poles

Group Equipment

- ❏ tent
- ❏ stove
- ❏ 1¼-quart pot with pot grips
- ❏ lighters
- ❏ matches
- ❏ extra fuel
- ❏ food
- ❏ map(s)
- ❏ compass
- ❏ altimeter
- ❏ wilderness permit, Park Service sketch map showing location of campsite, parking permit (for vehicle dash)
- ❏ first-aid kit: moleskin, cloth tape, Band-Aids, 4 × 4 gauze pads, ibuprofen, Ace bandage, etc.
- ❏ mosquito repellent
- ❏ repair kit: pole patch, ripstop tape, stove parts, water filter parts, etc.
- ❏ water filter
- ❏ toilet paper
- ❏ trowel

- ❑ skin sunscreen
- ❑ 75 feet of cord
- ❑ cell phone
- ❑ personal locator beacon

For winter trips where we'll be traveling and camping on snow, we drop the short-sleeve shirt, rain pants, 75 feet of cord, water filter, trowel, ultralight down sweater, and mosquito repellent and add:

Additional Personal Winter Items

- ❑ additional pair of liner socks
- ❑ fleece pants or bibs
- ❑ second fleece sweater
- ❑ shell pants designed for skiing with full side zips
- ❑ shovel
- ❑ gaiters
- ❑ ski goggles
- ❑ heavy mittens
- ❑ heavy gloves
- ❑ second pair of light gloves
- ❑ vapor-barrier socks
- ❑ vapor-barrier sleeping bag liner
- ❑ heavy down jacket
- ❑ snowshoes or skis
- ❑ winter boots
- ❑ climbing skins for skis (if bringing skis)
- ❑ ski poles
- ❑ avalanche beacon

Additional Group Winter Items

- ❑ four stuff sacks for anchoring tent
- ❑ wax kit: waxes for different temperature snow, scrapers, cork (if bringing skis)
- ❑ ski repair kit: spare cables and tools to install them, wire and pliers with wire cutters (if bringing skis)
- ❑ GPS unit

For hut-to-hut cross-country ski trips, we know we'll be staying in a hut that's equipped with mattresses (but not bedding) and a complete kitchen. That means we can leave behind the Therm-a-Rest, Therm-a-Rest chair, stove, pot, fuel, bowl, spoon, cord, tent, tent-anchoring stuff sacks, and large plastic garbage bags.

If you're having trouble locating the gear you need locally, try shopping online at one of the following companies.

Campmor
(800) 525-4784
campmor.com

Eastern Mountain Sports
(888) 463-6367
ems.com

REI
(800) 426-4840
rei.com

APPENDIX B: RESOURCES

Backpacker magazine is the single most useful periodical for backpackers who want advice on where to go, what to buy, and what prized wilderness areas are currently under assault by loggers, miners, dam builders, and developers. Pick up a copy on the newsstand, or visit its website at backpacker.com.

REI has an extensive collection of up-to-date, well-researched, and unbiased articles on backpacking equipment and technique at rei.com/expertadvice.

USGS maps are available from the United States Geological Survey and many private map dealers. You can mail-order maps directly from the USGS using the contact information below.

USGS Information Services

Box 25286

Denver, CO 80225

(888) ASK-USGS or (303) 202-4700

Fax: (303) 202-4693

Website: ask.usgs.gov

Order Canadian maps from the Centre for Topographic Information, a division of Natural Resources Canada, using the contact information below.

Centre for Topographic Information

Natural Resources Canada

Customer Support Group

2144 King St. W., Ste. 010

Sherbrooke, Quebec J1J 2E8, Canada

(800) 661-2638 (Canada and United States) or (819) 564-4857

Fax: (819) 564-5698

E-mail: topo.maps@NRCan.gc.ca

Website: maps.NRCan.gc.ca

Trails Illustrated, a division of National Geographic, offers maps for popular recreation areas in thirty-five states. These tough, waterproof maps, which are printed on plastic, are based on USGS topos. They're very convenient because they usually cover the entire area you'll traverse in a typical trip with one map. On a trip in Colorado's Indian Peaks Wilderness, for example, you can carry just one Trails Illustrated map instead of four or more 7.5 minute USGS quads. The drawback is that the scale is smaller than on a USGS 7.5 minute quad, so the maps show less detail, which makes precision route-finding more difficult. Trails Illustrated maps are available from even more private map dealers and outdoor shops than USGS 7.5 minute topos.

Trails Illustrated

National Geographic Maps

212 Beaver Brook Canyon Rd.

Evergreen, CO 80439

(800) 962-1643 (United States and Canada) or (303) 670-3457 (elsewhere)

Fax: (800) 626-8676 (United States and Canada) or (303) 670-3644 (elsewhere)

Website: natgeomaps.com/trailsillustrated.html

National Geographic also publishes electronic maps through its Topo! division, some of which combine Trails Illustrated maps with the Topo! software. If you can't find them at a local retailer, check out shop.nationalgeographic.com/ngs/category/maps/mapping-software. If you don't like typing in huge URLs, just search for "National Geographic topo maps" at nationalgeographic.com, or call (800) 437-5521.

One of the most extensive backcountry hut systems in the country is run by the Tenth Mountain Division Trail Association. Contact them at:

Tenth Mountain Division Trail Association

1280 Ute Ave., Ste. 21

Aspen, CO 81611

(303) 925-5775

Website: huts.org

INDEX